Robert Pearce

THE STONER'S GUIDE TO THE PORTS AND HARBOURS OF THE NORTHERN MEDITERRANEAN

CW01498904

AUSTIN MACAULEY PUBLISHERS®

LONDON · CAMBRIDGE · NEW YORK · SHARJAH

A CIP catalogue record for this title is available from the British Library.

ISBN 9781035876471 (Paperback)
ISBN 9781035876488 (ePub e-book)

www.austinmacauley.com

First Published 2025
Austin Macauley Publishers Ltd®
1 Canada Square
Canary Wharf
London
E14 5AA

Robert Pearce was born in Torbay Hospital in 1977. He was blessed to grow up amongst a warm and loving family in a fantastic part of the UK. As a boy, he was fascinated by nature and the ocean in particular. He went on to pursue a career as a professional sailor for the better part of two decades. In later life, he suffered badly from mental health issues and had to retire from yachting. He now works as an artist and author.

I want to dedicate the book to my dad, Richard Pearce, without whom it would have never been written.

Anna Reidy, my niece and editor.

Hazel Burns, my neighbour and close friend.

Table of Contents

Introduction   11

1. Adrift Mid-Atlantic   14

2. The Absinthe Bar   24

3. Scampi in Dubrovnik   31

4. The Domino Shack   39

5. The Sniffer Dog and the Cake   46

6. The Good News Is, He Does Have a Brain   51

7. Top Three Close Calls   60

8. Chased by a Barracuda   70

9. The Beach Party   81

10. Top Three Close Calls   93

11. Brown Sky in Santa Margherita   106

12. Top Three Close Calls   121

13. Party with the Madman in St Tropez   130

14. Monte Grosso/Brown Girl in the Ring, with the Dude   141

15. The Mountain Adventure with Mush   157

16. X-Mas Eve Busted on the Beach   167

17. Lost in Deepest Darkest France   177

18. A Tight Spot in Antibes   193

19. A Pair of Double Whammies   207

Part 1. La Ballon   *207*

Part 2. A Short Stop in Puerto Rico   *215*

20. Shipwrecked in Switzerland   **226**

Epilogue: How I Quit Alcohol   **243**

Introduction

It all began long before I left the shores of the UK. In fact, I've come to understand that it's been there my whole life. The curious thing is that when I started writing this book, I didn't even have a name for it. For what, Bobby? What the bloody hell are you talking about, man? Well, now don't worry, I'm gonna get to that and you are going to have to get used to me talking in tangents.

I do this a lot, you see. I start talking about one thing and then to explain that thing better, I must start talking about another thing and then what usually happens is that I forget what I was talking about in the first place.

Well, the good news is that the written word is my friend in this respect but I'm just warning you that you may find that I can be somewhat indirect in my approach to storytelling. But don't worry. I always get to the point, and I think you'll find it was usually worth the ride.

So, the thing I started off talking about is what I've come to refer to as my "vortex of chaos". You're going to become just as familiar with its presence as I have throughout my life. Just in a more condensed format. I realise this may not be too clear exactly but let me tell you it is still not to me either. Perhaps let's have a think about the word chaos and what we interpret it to mean.

In some instances, chaos can be a good thing, like at a party. All the best parties must have some element of chaos in there wouldn't you say? Yet chaos on the road when you are late for work is many people's idea of hell. Unfortunately for me, my vortex of chaos doesn't seem inclined to pick and choose its moments. It's just there. Period.

And if you are someone who has had the pleasure of getting to know me at some point then you will be perfectly familiar with what I'm talking about. The conclusion I've reached is that it brings equal amounts of good and bad things to my life. But then that's all just a question of interpretation and believe me we'll be coming back to that and much more.

So, what's this book about then? Apart from chaos that is. I'm sure many of you will be familiar with the TV reality show "Below Decks". Well, if you've ever wondered what an X-rated version might be like then look no further. For those unfamiliar with said show let me explain that I spent the better part of two decades as a professional in the superyacht industry.

I sailed them, I raced them, I cleaned them, I lived on them, I partied on them, and I built them. If I were to tell you that at one point, my "breakfast of champions" consisted of a cannabis joint, a rum and coke and a line of cocaine then perhaps we might be starting to paint a picture.

An undeniable truth of the universe is "that which goes up must come down" and believe me I came down. With a resounding thump. And you are going to hear all about it.

One of the first notable arrivals of my vortex of chaos was while I was being driven to the airport by my dad on Boxing Day 1998. I was 20 years old. Now this is a date which some of you might be familiar with. It was early morning and still dark being winter.

We were approaching Heathrow Airport on the M25, and I had BBC Radio 1 on the radio, as usual, but also because it would be the last time I would hear it for a long time. The internet may have been born already but it was a model railway next to the bullet train that it's become today.

One of the things I missed the most about being away from the UK was the radio. I got into DJing when I was 18 and music had become a full-time passion for me by then. However, it was just one of many things I had to leave behind when I chose to pursue my dreams.

At that point in the car with Dad, we still had the UK radio and as the news came on, just as we were arriving at the airport, we started hearing about the unfolding Sydney-Hobart race disaster. It sounded bad. They knew for sure a bunch of lives had been lost and they were still searching for many more lost yachts.

I was on my way to start a new career on yachts and the thing I wanted to do more than anything was race across oceans. Talk about timing. It was the last thing I heard on UK radio before getting on a plane, setting off to pursue my dreams of being a professional ocean racing sailor. What's that I can hear?

It sounds like someone singing "There May Be Trouble Ahead". Well, trouble there most certainly was but the good news is that I, somehow, survived to tell the tale and it seems I have a good memory and a talent for storytelling, so, you guys are in for a real treat.

We start mid-Atlantic, then chill? in the Caribbean for a while before heading back to Blighty for a wicked beach party. Then we're off to the northern Mediterranean for a few laps of carnage before heading to the mountains of Chamonix for a little off-piste fun.

Then a quick trip to St Tropez for a spot of racing on a J-class before going rock-climbing the in Alpes Maritimes and then another lap around the Cote d'Azur for good measure. A quick little incident on a lake in Switzerland brings us hurtling back to the UK for a rather grim but ultimately victorious conclusion. Phew.

Just typing that has made me sweat and I missed half of it. I can also assure you I do a lot more than just sweat in the process of living it. Join me for a wild ride that might just change your life and if not, it's certainly going to give you a few things to think about. In the words of one of my all-time heroes, Pete Tong…We continue.

1

Adrift Mid-Atlantic

I think it would be fair to say that for most people who become involved in yachting their entry point was in their childhood and was through their parents or family. My parents had absolutely zero interest in things like yachts or any kind of sport at all. We were a church-going family and as such everything we did revolved around that.

However, I was a curious child, to say the least, and being the 80s, the media was just finding its feet and becoming mainstream. This meant that I had access to all sorts of literature like magazines and there was also TV which, despite only having four channels, showed a wide range of sports on a regular basis.

I was enchanted by it all but felt drawn to things that involved nature. Sports like rock-climbing, surfing, kayaking and skiing were just fascinating to me. I couldn't get enough and soaked it all up like a sponge.

Despite living in a seaside town, my only engagement with nature was through my family and involved simple walks and the beach. My mother had grown up as part of a beach-going family and so, it was just the done thing that we went to the beach when the weather allowed.

Despite being the UK, the weather in Torbay actually allowed us to go to the beach on a regular basis throughout the summer months. Once on the beach, I was left to myself and not in any way encouraged to pursue a sport.

We would play family games of rounders and cricket, but no one ever encouraged me to take up anything in particular. Nevertheless, I had a burning desire to find a way into these fascinating new emerging branches of sport.

I was lucky enough to be born in a town that has a wide variety of high-quality rock-climbing right within the town itself and in the 80s Torbay had an active community of local climbers. By 16, I had found my way into this and became immersed in the sport of rock-climbing. This would go on to be a lifelong passion. But growing up in a town like Torquay it was impossible for me not to be drawn to the ocean as well.

What I really wanted was to be a surfer, but I lived on the wrong coast for that and we very rarely got good surfing waves. What we did have instead was a prestigious yacht club with an active fleet of cruiser racers. Despite not having any kind of entry or gateway into this world, I found my own way. A technique that was to become something of a habit in later years.

But that's another story. For the purposes of this book, I'm going to tell you a few of my highlights and lowlights from the two decades I spent professionally involved with yachts. I'm going to have to leave one hell of a lot of good stuff out I'm afraid. But don't worry. Just consider this an extended trailer...If you like. So, let's get into it.

Somehow, I managed to move to France, get a job on a yacht and then get on another yacht to sail across the Atlantic to Antigua where I then spent a month before sailing back to France. What is truly amazing to me is that I somehow managed to get all the way to Antigua, spend a month there and leave again before my first really interesting event happened.

Believe me, plenty of interesting stuff happened before and, as I alluded to, I will get to it all later. As you are going to see, interesting events are a common feature in my life. I'm using the term interesting loosely here bear in mind. Another way of describing it would be a vortex of chaos.

Part of the reason for this is that I have a lot of ideas. Some of these ideas are very good and some of them are very bad. As a young man, I was not very good at telling this apart. It's quite possible that hasn't changed much but the good news is that it has made for one hell of a lot of interesting stories. So, without further ado, I'm going to try and get on with this one.

I say try because it's not as easy as just ABC you know. Before launching into the actual events of that day, it's necessary for me to first paint some context for you. For me as an artist who also paints, this feels very much like putting the first strokes down on paper or canvas.

Usually, these first strokes are long forgotten later as they are covered over by many more layers of paint. However, those early layers are the integral building blocks of the finished product. Without those early layers, the finish would not be that which it is. Even though the early work might not even be remotely perceivable. I'm finding that writing and painting are very much alike and so, allow me to put paint to canvas and let's see some shades of colour.

The year was 1999. Yes, that's right and contrary to what you might think, unless you were there, it was not one big, long continuous party. Not quite but I'm going to say that it was most certainly one of the best years of my life so far.

I sailed across the Atlantic three times that year. I also met and fell in love with Ariel. She was my first proper girlfriend and still to this day the only woman I've loved who was worthy of my affection. You are going to be hearing a lot more about her in the coming chapters.

Clearly, during this time my stars were aligned. I really can't wait to get into telling the whole thing but for now, we join me as deckhand upon the good ship Favonius, a Swan 651. I joined Favonius in Antibes, France, in March and the program was to cross to Antigua where we would pick the boss up and then compete in the Antigua race week event that was a big annual gathering for many similar yachts.

My first crossing was a massive adventure and there was really no shortage of interesting events but nothing which I feel qualifies for the purpose of this collection of short stories. Instead, we have to wait till after race week and I feel a good time to join the story would be on the dock in the Cat Club on Jolly Harbour Antigua.

It was the day before we were due to depart and sail back across the Atlantic and it's fair to say that tensions were running high. I should elaborate on the term we. The crew of Favonius at this point was as follows. Captain Bernard. Dutch, mid-30s, big stocky burly but in general good-natured and kind.

In general, that is but at the point of this story Bernard's wife (a wealthy American woman) was heavily pregnant with their first child and Bernard's stress levels were starting to peak. There was a rough plan for him to leave the Azores and fly back in time for the birth. So, there was some haste and pressure to get moving. Well, that would have been one way of putting it.

The first mate was AP, also mid-30s. A Dane whom we had met while in Antigua and who was looking for a passage back to Europe. The previous first mate had left when we arrived, as planned, and it had always been understood that we would have to find a replacement for the return leg.

AP's actual name was Anispenis. Or so that's what I was told. Anis penis. Seriously? By this stage, I'd learnt not to ask too many questions and I just took it that he was called AP. He was a decent enough bloke and stayed with us all the way to Antibes. In fact, he took over as skipper in the Azores when Bernard left. AP's deckhand from his previous yacht also came with us.

Jim was American, West Coast, and in his mid-20s so the closest to my age and we got on really well. He was a good crack and was very kind to me and taught me a load of useful stuff.

Next was Kiwi Dave. As you might have guessed Kiwi Dave is yes well, a Kiwi. Now ordinarily I'd try not to hold that against him. However, for a very long time, Dave and I really did not get on. Dave was in his early 30s and had recently been dumped by the love of his life.

He was not a happy chappy and although he was a very talented sailor and man in general, he was not in any way inclined to tolerate me and my antics. To be fair, most of the time we got on okay. But every now and then he would take it upon himself to act like the big man and lay down the law to me.

In fact, he had no right to do this as he was not captain or even mate and had no authority other than seniority. Now seniority is a big deal on yachts, but none take it as seriously as those who have no other form of authority. And I speak from both sides of the fence here.

Dave had a certain amount of right to give me shit but he often took it too far and Bernard had had to check him a couple of times. Bernard had also told me, in a very kind way, that I didn't have to take it from Dave and that if he continued to let him know.

Dave did continue. I had actually become bold enough by then to tell Dave to fuck off myself, but Dave was about twice the size of me and in some ways, this just exacerbated things.

Oh, hang on. I forgot someone. And how, oh how, could I forget Chicken? Everyone who knew Chicken called him Chicken. We all knew that his actual name was Paul but I had never once heard anyone actually call him that. Chicken was a native Antiguan and was already well into his 40s. He was one of the very few locals who found their way into the yachting world.

By this time, he had done more Atlantic crossings than all the rest of us put together. He lived in Antibes, France where he had a wife and kid and worked as a varnishing expert. He was the very best varnisher I ever knew. His reputation was everywhere in the yachting world. Both good and bad. Good for his work in the day and bad for his behaviour in the bars at night.

Chicken loved to drink, smoke and snort whatever he could get his hands on and was an absolute maniac the moment the sun went down. He was also a long-term, good friend of Bernard. In the end, he and I became good friends, and we had an enduring relationship for many years after. However, his part in the tale of Favonius is not an altogether glorious one.

One of the last jobs a yacht does before it leaves for a long passage is to fuel up. Rather than getting this done at the commercial dock like everyone else Bernard wanted to get a truck in and get it piped down the dock. The only advantage of this was that we wouldn't have to move the boat to get the fuel.

Bernard was not at all confident driving the boat as this was actually his first job as a skipper and his actual time driving boats like this was minimal. In fact, it wasn't totally unusual to get the truck in and we had seen other boats doing it while we were there.

Fuel was taken and everything else we needed for a crossing was also in hand so we were now ready to set off. The night before we left was not a pretty one. Chicken stayed on board for the first time since we had arrived in Antigua. We'd hardly seen him and it was generally assumed that he'd been high as a kite for the vast majority of the time we were there.

The interior of a yacht is a tiny place with six men who are all trying to get to sleep but for one reason or another, all are nervous and awake. Nobody slept well and the mood was grim the next morning as we cast our lines, stowed our fenders deep and made all fast for a long ocean voyage.

Our destination was the town of Horta on the island of Faial in the Azores archipelago. It was usually a two-week passage for a sailing yacht like us. At the midpoint, we would be over 1250 miles from the nearest land. That's pretty mind-blowing to a non-sailor but it's really not that remarkable when you do it all the time. In fact, once you lose sight of land it really doesn't matter if it's one mile or 1000 miles. It's just a big empty place.

Well not quite empty. There are birds, dolphins, whales, flying fish and even jellyfish that float on the surface and use a large fin on their back as a kind of sail to navigate the world's oceans. They are called Portuguese Men of War and are usually small enough to fit on one hand. Although they do get much bigger.

Out in the part of the Atlantic that I crossed there were massive…What's exactly? Can anyone tell me, without Google's help, what is the collective noun for jellyfish? Is there even one? Any suggestions? How about a flobble? There should be one because out in the Atlantic, these chaps like to hang out in big groups and drift around together.

Okay so to pick up where we left off. As was the standard practice on a yacht making a passage the crew was split into watches. Much to mine and Dave's horror there was no choice but for Bernard to put us together. In the end, it didn't work out too bad and what we found was that we had a fair amount in common.

The fact of the matter was there was a job to be done and we both took our profession seriously. So, by the time we'd been out a few days, things had actually settled down a little.

On many of the longer voyages, I've completed this is a nice stage. It's a time for the crew to settle into a new routine away from land and away from all the ties and chores that are normally associated with land. Unfortunately, the weather wasn't to play ball. The wind kept shifting around and we ended up with a nasty cross sea.

What this means is two swells coming from opposing directions. This makes it almost impossible for the yacht to find any kind of natural rhythm and one of the results of this is regular resounding slams as the bow would fall off a wave and then slam into the next one.

If that doesn't make any sense to you, then just imagine if your whole house was turned over to 45 degrees, then it started moving up and down at irregular intervals and then every minute or so it would be like the whole house was lifted about one meter in the air and then dropped. Every single thing in the house that is hard and can make a noise will make a noise. It's loud. Really loud. Believe me.

Yachts are designed to cope with this and all the things that are stored down below should be done so in a way meaning that this kind of motion will not damage them. Regardless of this, when it's happening every minute or so it becomes something of a chore.

We were attempting to sail as much as possible as the simple fact was that we did not carry enough fuel in the main tank to motor all the way to the Azores. We also carried four spare jerry cans but even with them, it was still not enough to motor all the way. Favonius was a performance cruiser racer and as such was designed more with sailing in mind.

The net result of this was that we had to sail whenever there was the chance. Especially in the early stages of the passage where we had no idea what might come later. Best to get the sailing done as early as possible and then the motor can be used if needs be.

It was about three days after leaving that the engine shit itself. We had to keep using it periodically as the wind kept failing and changing direction a lot. We were motoring along and I was actually manning the wheel when the engine abruptly stopped with a pathetic cough. Bernard immediately appeared with Dave as they had both been down below.

Dave spent a lot of his time down below at the chart table when he was meant to be on deck with me. As was his right by way of seniority. But he was taking too much advantage of this and had been spending more and more time down there and just leaving me on the wheel for most of the watch.

To be fair I was just a kid and needed whipping into shape and I had come to accept that by then so I wasn't complaining or anything. I actually just liked being left alone at the wheel of such an amazing yacht.

On this occasion, they both came scampering onto the deck shouting at me, 'What have you done?'

But they both knew I hadn't actually done anything, and the problem was actually something more serious. Investigations were made and it was discovered that we had dirty fuel filters. This was concerning considering they had been new for the passage.

The filters were changed and the engine duly stuttered back into life and off we set again but it didn't take more than 12 hours before the same thing happened. This time there were no more filters as there would never normally be a need to change them so many times in one trip. Therefore, we had a problem. A big problem.

Essentially we had no engine. Now at this point, the wind did something most unusual and was quite helpful. It picked up and settled down to a stable direction just aft of the beam. A lovely point of sail. We were able to make a nice spread of canvas and finally settle into a sort of ocean-going routine.

Everyone except Chicken that is. Chicken had basically been high as a kite on a cocktail of drugs for the whole month we had been in Antigua. He was now going full cold turkey and was not coping well. Actually, he was in the process of a full meltdown but we didn't realise this until much later. For now, he had just become the grumpiest man on earth.

On the first crossing, Chicken and I had got on really well and we had struck up a backgammon partnership. I never beat him, but we had a lot of fun playing together. In Antigua, he had taken me to his family house for dinner. Something he had hardly ever done for any other white person. Bernard had never been invited.

It was one of the most culturally diverse experiences of my life and one I cherish to this day. In later years, when people heard that Chicken had invited me to his family home, they were surprised and respected me on another level after.

However, right now Chicken would not speak to me or anyone else unless he had to for some reason. He acted like he hated us and we were none too fond of him. Even Bernard, who was on watch with him, was tired of his bullshit.

So, what with the Chicken situation and the now fair winds the problems with the engine were quickly forgotten and even became something of a taboo subject. We sailed through a pretty fierce storm and actually sustained some damage to the rig and deck in places, but no one was hurt and after 12 days at sea, we were within sight of the Azores.

Being active volcanoes, they stick up a long way and are easy to see from a great way off. They are also well known for what is called the *Azores high* which is an area of high pressure which has a habit of sitting over the whole archipelago. High pressure often has very little wind in it. Do you see where this is going?

At about the same time, we came within sight of the islands the wind died. With no engine, we had no choice but to just sit there. And look. Look at the island we had been at sea for 12 days to get to and that now we could see but not get to. Now as a young man so new to the ways of the world, I must admit I did a very good job of taking this on the chin. We all did really.

Well, everyone except Bernard who was losing his shit about the upcoming birth. Birth I said there. Not berth. At this stage of a passage, most captains would be worried about the berth they were going to be taking when they arrived at their destination. However, Bernard was more concerned about the birth of his first kid back in France.

Add to that the Chicken situation and you can see that things were not really that relaxed on board. I was though. I didn't worry as it didn't seem like me worrying would help. For someone born with abnormally high anxiety, this is quite remarkable and I believe is related to how certain people handle situations with serious consequences.

We sat out there for two days and really didn't move much more than a mile or so. The islands on the horizon looked just as far away the next morning as they had the day before. At one point, I was sort of hanging over the side, in the midday sun, bored out of my brain from days of doing nothing. I was staring at the water and into my view came one of the jellyfish that I mentioned earlier, a Portuguese man of war.

This brave little chap had managed to utilise the little sail on its back to collect enough fragments of a breeze to be able to just make progress through the water. It was slowly drifting down our hull and as I watched it passed the bow and I lost sight of it looking towards our destination. It occurred to me that we had just been overtaken by a jellyfish. Not an overwhelmingly positive experience I can assure you.

That night the breeze picked up and we were able to make our way to the mouth of the port of Horta where we got a tow onto the dock. As it happened, we had just arrived right at the start of the Easter festivities and being a Portuguese island and devoutly Catholic this meant that the whole island was going to be shutting down for the next two weeks. By the whole island, I mean anything connected to industry.

Of such, there was next to nothing anyway but there was a marine engineer's company who we needed to fix our broken engine and who now cheerfully informed us they would not be able to do so for about two weeks. We ended up staying in Horta for about three weeks. To put this into context most yachts passing through on their way home stayed for around three days.

Those three weeks could make a decent book all of its own. For me, it was a small insight into the chaos and carnage that goes down when yachties get loose. However, for the purposes of this collection, I have one particular event to tell you about.

If you know anything about absinthe and have actually consumed the real old-school version of absinthe (the kind that is illegal in most places), then you may have some idea what to expect because absinthe was legal in the Azores, and I certainly found out why it's illegal everywhere else.

2

The Absinthe Bar

We must have looked like a right motley crew being towed into Horta that morning. After 12 days of challenging sailing and two days of drifting, it's fair to say that our spirits were not all that they might have been.

Added to that was the birthing situation with Bernard and the Chicken situation which was rapidly escalating and about to assume full nosedive. By the time we had the boat tied up and washed down, the beers were already out, and a queue had formed for the shower.

Horta is the home of the world-famous Peter's Sports Bar and that's where we headed the moment we left the boat. Which, to be fair, we did together as a crew and that's a credit to the older guys for waiting for me. And that is a credit to Bernard who had himself risen through the ranks on the classics where the nippers cop it hard but turn out strong and capable sailors.

The classics are a fleet of traditional yachts that are spread all over the world, however, many of them come together for a series of regattas in the Mediterranean at the end of every summer. Actually, prior to being captain of Favonius, Bernard had been first mate on the highly prestigious schooner Mariette.

Mariette was one of those yachts that had such a powerful reputation that just uttering the name was like saying something religious. Anyone who was or had been involved with the yacht was a level above anyone else in the industry. Mariette wasn't unique in this sense.

There were a handful of other vessels, power and sail, modern and classic, that also held this status. I never made it to a full-time crew aboard any of these but I was certainly involved on many levels for many years.

After returning to France on Favonius, I remained on board for a few weeks while Bernard worked out what to do with me. At that time Mariette was berthed just down the dock and Kiwi Dave got invited over for a few *sundowner beers* as he knew many of the crew. He'd grown to quite like me by then and he dragged me along.

It was the only time I stepped foot on one of those elite yachts. I worked on many other highly prestigious yachts, but this was the only time I got close to the real top end.

The crew were all gathered mid-ships downing beers from the cooler. It seemed to work a little like rounds at a bar in that peeps took turns to go to the cooler and collect beers for everyone. You were not asked if you wanted one. You were just thrust one.

If you hadn't finished your previous one, you ended up double parked and being double parked is a bad look and a guaranteed way to attract negative attention from crew mates.

By this stage, it was starting to come clear to me that I was not much good at this kind of drinking. However, I was doing my best to keep up and at some point I ventured away from my perch by the forward mast.

As soon as I stepped out from the group and was alone on the deck the captain saw me and in a loud voice said, 'Hey, who the fuck are you?'

Silence descended in an instant. Everyone (about 20 hard ass sailors) stopped talking and stared at me.

I just froze and stood there and said, 'I'm um errrr ummmm a friend of Bernard's.'

Now at that point, I had no way of knowing that the current captain, Chris, and Bernard were not the best of friends and in fact, Chris was the reason why Bernard was no longer on Mariette. Accordingly, Chris was none too impressed by the answer but luckily Dave jumped in saying that he'd brought me and everyone's attention quickly returned to drinking beer, eating chips and talking shit. Standard yachty fare.

But let's get back to Horta and Peters sports bar. As we had been towed in we had arrived on the commercial part of the port and not at the actual marina where all the other yachts were. This was peak season for crossings back to the Mediterranean and at any given time there would be around 10 superyachts of varying sizes and types. What did not vary was the crew's desire to drink hard after a long ocean passage.

Let's remember that yacht crew tend to be quite hedonistic people even at the most uneventful points in time. Put them on an island in the middle of the

Atlantic after two weeks with no kind of anything and a hell of a lot of nothing and I can tell you that mayhem can and most certainly does ensue.

Peter's Sports Bar seemed to be open 24/7 while we were there. It might have closed from time to time but I never saw it closed. It never actually seemed to be that busy either. But at any given point you could be sure that there would be a group of hard drinkers going at it somewhere inside.

Let's do a quick recap of the crew. Bernard. By now, Bernard's wife was pretty much ready to drop and as such his stress levels were going through the roof. Plans were being made for Bernard to leave ASAP (with Chicken) but before that, he had some hard drinking to do. He also had to try and organise getting the engine fixed which wasn't proving easy as everything had already closed for Easter.

AP was a pretty easy-going guy and had only played a very subdued role in the events up till now. In fact, the whole time he was on board he only ever said or did anything noteworthy once. And that involved pinning me down on the ground one night and letting me know that if I gave him any more drunken verbal he would remind me how much larger he was than me in a very painful way. I got the message. Overall though AP and I got on very well.

Jim had really grown on me by now. About one week out from Horta he had started talking about the fun and games we would be getting up to there.

He did this funny Mexican accent and would go, 'Ehhhhhhh hoooooorta. We coming. Where are the wooooooomen at? Horta, we are coming.'

'Where are the women at,' had become something of a battle cry for us and I can still do the same accent and cry now.

So, Jim was a bloody good egg in my book. At this point and the whole time, he was with us.

Kiwi Dave. Despite completing two Atlantic crossings, racing in Antigua Classics Regatta and Antigua race week, Dave's spirits had not improved one little bit. He was still totally broken-hearted about his lost love. Every night in the bar he would find someone to give the whole sob story to.

By this stage, I was starting to strongly suspect that she had left him because he was such a miserable cunt. But despite that, he had earned a lot of respect in my book. Not just was he a very strong sailor but he had an amazing ability to fix just about anything. During the time I shared with him, I saw him pull apart all sorts of things that had stopped working.

Without fail, he fixed them every time. I couldn't believe it. Every time I was sure he had killed the thing but every time he would get it back together and it would work again.

This is actually a fundamental skill and an integral part of being a seaman. That is the ability to pull apart just about anything and make it work again with just a very simple tool kit. Out at sea, no one is going to come fix it for you. Fix it or lose it. This had a deep and long-lasting impression on me.

Firstly, it showed me that the inside of technical things is often not nearly as complex or mystical as one might imagine. Secondly, it showed me that almost anything is possible if you believe. These are two mindsets that I adopted over the next few years and went on to serve me well. Even bailing me out of some very tight spots in the future. Thanks for that Dave.

I never got the chance to thank him because, in that time and place, I couldn't possibly realise how useful this would later be. Having said all that, we still didn't really get on. Kiwis are big on shit-giving, piss-taking, taking the mic, throwing abuse, banter or whatever else you want to call it. They love to tease and abuse their mates and colleagues as often as they can.

It's just a way of life for them. Dave was clearly no exception and as the youngest on board that meant that I copped a lot of shit from him. I got used to it and it certainly helped give me a chin of some description.

Chicken. Oh Chicken. What can I say about Chicken at this stage? Well for a start he now had a massive afro. He had had his hair done in corn rows while he was in Antigua, but he had taken it out during the crossing and it had just gone into a massive black afro. It looked hilarious. Every time I looked at him I had to suppress a giggle. His meltdown was quite far progressed by now.

After that first night of drinking, he went downhill fast and fortunately for everyone involved, he left a couple of days later. But not before he pissed himself in the bunk below mine, really badly, several nights running and then shat all over the heads. He wasn't capable of cleaning any of this up and I had to do it all.

It takes days to get the piss out of mattresses. And cleaning his shit off the walls of the toilet cubicle was something I most certainly did not relish. It didn't do me any harm though and it taught me that sometimes in life things seem very unfair, but you just have to bite the bullet and get on with it.

And yes, well finally there was the ship's boy. Me. Robby from Torquay, innit. I'd just turned 22 back while we were in Antigua, and I was living the dream don't you know. Young, dumb and full of…a keen sense of adventure. Yes, yes.

The next few days were spent drinking, working a little in the morning to get the deck and interior shipshape again. Then more extended drinking. Bernard left with Chicken after a couple of days leaving AP as skipper. The pair of them couldn't wait to get out of there and by that stage, the idea of getting on a plane and being back in France a couple of hours later didn't seem terrible to me either.

One of the good things about our time there was that there was a constant stream of other yachts passing through and between us, we usually knew at least one of the crew on them. So, every time a new boat would come in (which was every other day) everyone would pile into the Peter Sports Bar and get right on the lash.

Everyone usually means the entire dock. By now, we had moved around to the main marina although we still didn't have a working engine. This marina was not designed or equipped to deal with a large number of superyachts. What this meant was a fair amount of chaos because a large number of superyachts needed to be catered for and where there are superyachts there is money.

Usually, a lot of money and anyone who lives in or around a place where superyachts spend time will know this and a lot of time, care and attention goes into extracting this money. Therefore, space was made and the reality of this was a short dock with big yachts rafted up three or four deep.

We eventually ended up buried in this mass raft and just sort of moved around inside it as other boats came and went. This made for a very communal atmosphere, and it was a lot of fun the majority of the time. However, after a week of hard drinking, we were tired. Tiring but not slowing and that's when things can get a little silly. As happened on a few occasions but on one occasion I decided to try this absinthe everyone was talking about in hushed tones.

Back in the year 1999, absinthe was banned in most civilised countries. I was informed that the reason for this was that it was so toxic that it made people go blind. However, the Azores were famous for allowing this concoction to be sold in bars. Not all bars. Peter's sports bar didn't serve it. Or at least not officially. It wasn't until well into our second week there that I got to try it.

One night I was drinking with a mate I had met in Antigua (shout out Archie) and somehow a decision was made to venture further back up into the town of Horta and get us a taste of this famous absinthe. This we achieved without too much trouble and that's as much as I can remember until the next day.

So, by now I'm hoping you will have reached the conclusion that I have a pretty good memory. So, if I have a considerable blank right in the middle of a very noteworthy part then that should tell you something.

I will next inform you of what I was informed the next day when I woke up and found the state of the galley aboard Favonius. Jim saw me first and just burst out laughing without saying anything. Now an unshakeable truth of the universe is that when someone does this it never bodes well for the future.

AP promptly poked his head down the hatch and said, 'You,' loudly.

Actually, none of them were at all angry with me. I'd really grown on them by now and although I was still the whipping boy they had some respect for me.

So, in due course, Jim informed me that he had been asleep in his bunk the previous night and had woken up to a boat full of smoke. He obviously jumped straight out of his bunk and into the galley where he discovered a saucepan with the gas (yes real liquid gas) on full blast sitting on the stovetop.

There was black smoke pouring out of the saucepan as it boiled dry but luckily all he had to do was switch the gas off as there was no actual fire as such. On the worktop, he found an empty packet of instant noodles and on the floor, he was to find me, in a deep drunken slumber.

Jim shouted at me and dragged me to my feet. Apparently, I snapped too, jabbered a load of something incomprehensible, then staggered to my bunk, got in and went fast back to sleep.

By now, most of the smoke had dispersed and as it happened no one else had even noticed. However, in the morning there were black marks from the smoke all around the hood over the stove and I had a long morning scrubbing with Brillo and elbow grease.

Considering how many yachts were anchored so closely together and how quickly plastic boats go up in flames I would say that was easily another one of my close calls with catastrophe. Although at that time I might have taken a load of other people and a fleet of superyachts with me. But then I've always maintained that all's well that ends well.

Eventually, we got the parts we needed to fix the engine and after what seemed like a lifetime, we left Horta and made our way back to Antibes France. Bernard was waiting on the dock with his little girl in his arms which was still one of the most touching things I've ever seen.

Unfortunately, there was no possibility for me to remain on Favonius as crew with Bernard simply because the boats program didn't call for an extra crew member. However, Bernard kept me on for a couple of weeks and then found me another job with a mate of his, Luigi, on the 72 ft ketch IKRA 2.

One small hitch was my sister's wedding, and I flew back to the UK before flying on to meet Luigi in Dubrovnik, Croatia for my first proper charter season. Now, the fun was really about to start.

3

Scampi in Dubrovnik

At the point of writing this, I have somehow made it to the age of 46. It's fair to say somehow because I seem to have the most ridiculous number of close calls or scrapes with death and yet somehow, for the large part, come away relatively unscathed.

For a good long while this puzzled me, I will confess. The subject would come up in discussion with friends and we'd find ourselves marvelling at all the times I'd cheated death. The reality of my life so far is that my two closest calls with death came much later and don't even feature in this book.

That's because they both happened within hours of each other and at a point in my life when we are going to need much more context to tell the story properly. Trust me, I'm going to come back to those two moments. In detail. But that's for another time.

I feel like I've come to know death quite well. I used to read Terry Pratchett's books and if you have as well then, you'll be familiar with his version of death. On Discworld death is like a character who actually appears, talks and follows people around before taking them away. I like Terry's view of this, and it's come to be my understanding of how death manifests in our reality.

I can say that I "feel" it or I should say I've "felt" it. Close at times. It's like a presence lurking nearby but never quite in sight. Always in another room or just behind the door but following wherever you are. Sitting behind you on the bus or train. Following a few paces behind while you walk in the park. Does this sound familiar? I hope not for your sake.

If it does, then it means you've felt the same kind of depression that I have felt, do feel and will feel again. Little by little I'm just coming to accept it as a part of me. It must be an integral part of what makes me because it's what creates contrast in my emotional path. I came up with a new quote recently which I'm quite fond of. I do that you see and you're going to have to humour me, I'm afraid.

Contrast is the essence of experience.

Experience seems to be something many of us are seeking. Yet at the same time trying to avoid. Contrast means change. Contrast means difference. Contrast means coming out of your comfort zone. If you want an experience, then simply do something different and if you want to be an interesting person then you need experience.

Listen to me harping on like Yoda again. I've become quite fond of assuming that croaky voice and talking backwards in riddles.

'Hmmmmmmmmm. If in three thousand years finish this book you do then wise beyond words shall you be yes yes hmmmmmmmmmm.'

To my mind, wisdom should at some point equate to success. And this is where I fall down because I really don't feel like I've been successful at anything noteworthy at this point in my life.

Now I say, at this point, because if you are reading this book then I must have had it published and in that case, I will have finally succeeded in something. But at this point, that's still a dream. But it doesn't feel much like a dream a lot of the time I can tell you.

I had an experience here at home yesterday that was closer to something from a nightmare. Still, it was an experience, and it will have fed into my work as all of it does. As everything does because whether we seek it or not, we are all experiencing, in the very literal sense of the word, every moment of our waking existence.

Even asleep we are experiencing dreams. The only way to stop experience is to die. And it seems most of us are trying our hardest to avoid that, most of the time. Or are we?

Looking back, it really feels like I was really looking for it a lot of the time. Some of the hikes I did alone in the Alps and some of the times I was out surfing alone I really pushed things and it's hard not to think I was flirting with that chap in the black cloak. But one way or another, for better or worse, I survived and made it here to tell you all about it.

Right now, I'd like to share some more of my own personal philosophy with you and it's very possibly the wisest thing I've ever said. So far. During the last winter, 22/23, A good friend of mine had fallen very sick with cancer and complications. He had been close to death several times although he was a fit young man and otherwise healthy. This was the first time that someone I know and care about had been in hospital in this kind of condition.

We found ourselves text-chatting on a few occasions and one night he was facing a very dark night ahead. We were discussing the treatment and how it might pan out and these words came to me. I'd like to make it clear that I have no idea if this helped him. But he did recover and is once again back on the water. Go on, son.

'Some things in life you can control, other things you can influence. The vast majority of things will do whatever they want to do and there's absolutely nothing you can do about it. Being able to tell the difference and knowing when to act accordingly is the key to success in anything.'

The fact of the matter is that, if I'm honest, I cannot hold my hand up to being successful at anything. Yet. To my mind being successful means achieving something. Now what ranks as an achievement is a very debatable subject and I guess the fact is that it's just subjective. However, I think we can all throw a few common denominators in there and one of the first would have to be simply to be happy.

How many of us do we think are actually happy? Are you? Really? If you really look deep down inside yourself and ask yourself some uncomfortable questions, you know the ones you hide from, then are you actually happy? Maybe you said no right away and if that's your response my immediate reaction would be exactly the same. Why not? Are you really not happy? What's actually so bad that's making you unhappy?

This is all so subjective and what it all really boils down to is how we interpret, react and respond to that which is occurring in our immediate reality. As I said before, there are some things we can control and one of those things, believe it or not, is how we Interpret, React, and Respond.

This is actually one of the very few things that we have the option to control. And I say option because that's what it is. We can control or we can be controlled. The choice is yours.

The good news is that in order to help you control or navigate your way through life we are all equipped with what's called "the moral compass". Yes, that's right we all have one, like it or not.

It's that voice that says, 'You really shouldn't be doing this, you know.'

Well at the same time being, another voice that says, 'No one will ever know so don't worry about it.'

You know the one? How well-tuned is your moral compass? Or rather how closely do you follow it? Because we all have one of these and the question is simply how much attention you pay to it. I only came into contact with the term "moral compass" a few years ago but it's stuck and it fits much better than other analogies like the angel and the demon on each shoulder.

It's all the same thing though really. The fact is we know what's right and wrong without anyone having to tell us. The only question is how well it fits with what we want.

I think we are all very good at lying to ourselves more than anyone else. How often do you find yourself thinking *Oh well, no one will ever know, so it doesn't matter or it can't come back to hurt me.* If you are a person who thinks that often, then I have bad news for you.

There's this thing called karma that's gonna come and bite you on the ass at some point in the future. Maybe not soon but it's coming at some point. One way or another.

It is my sincere belief that every single thing we do in our lives is recorded like on a CCTV that follows you around wherever you are for your whole life. When we die, we are going to be sat down in front of an audience of everybody we ever encountered in our life.

We are going to have to sit through every second we lived through, and have it scrutinised by a team of beings who lay out every thought, feeling and emotion you ever experienced. All for the audience to see and judge. How does that sound to you? Are you ready for that?

My experiences with karma have been many and varied but at some point, it started happening in a very immediate sense. What I mean is that things that I did had an immediate comeback. Both good and bad. It was so vividly striking that at one point when I was making a lot of music I titled a track "Insta-karma".

I framed an unshakeable belief that it makes no difference at all who apparently sees or knows what you do. Everything you do must be balanced and will be accounted for one way or another. Maybe not in this lifetime but at some point in your spirit's existence then its karma will catch up with it. In my experience, this has been an unshakeable truth and I try to live my life accordingly.

Alright, I think it's time we headed back in the direction of the story. More or less. What you need to remember is that the 22-year-old Bobby is largely oblivious to the vast majority of what I have just explained. The simple fact of the matter is that at the age of 22, I knew very little about not a lot. And I didn't really understand that very well.

To my advantage was the fact that my parents had done a reasonable job of installing a fairly rigid moral code in me. Largely a Christian-based one I would add but I don't think there's anything wrong with the main basis of Christianity and that's because it is simply "let's all be nice to each other". I mean how can anyone argue with that?

I certainly didn't and I had grown up with a firm belief that I should treat others as I wish to be treated myself. I hadn't always fulfilled this to the letter but for the most part, I'm happy to hold my hands up and say I did my best.

I feel like this has been born out in my karma and the fact that I am still alive and well and in fact sitting here writing this. The big problem, as I was about to find out, was that my idea that everyone else would be taking this same approach was sadly very wrong. Very wrong indeed.

For me, a large part of treating others as I wished to be treated myself revolved around sincerity. Something which remains of the utmost importance to me. However, it's my considered opinion that sincerity is actually viewed as a kind of sickness or disability in our world today.

Despite this, I had been brought up to think that it was vital, to tell the truth about all things at all times and that everyone else was on exactly the same page. It actually took me a very long time to realise how badly wrong I had got that. By age 22, I had already had a few lessons to the contrary and I'll tell you where I stand in this subject right now.

Most people lie about most things most of the time. Not more to anyone than to themselves. As technology steadily takes over and we become more digital this will only get worse as the facilitation of falsity becomes more deeply embedded in thoughts, words and actions.

This is something that I currently struggle with on a daily basis but to a 22-year-old Bobby I was completely oblivious. I honestly believed that every word everyone said to me was more or less the truth unless they were joking around in some way. Which was also a common way of saying stuff you didn't believe but making it sound like you did.

My time on Favonius had done me proud and I was well on my way to becoming a fairly alright sailor. Naturally, I now assumed I was "top-flight, pro level, as good as it gets" but I was a 22-year-old boy having his first taste of the big wide world and I think we could allow me that.

Nevertheless, I was nervous as hell waiting on the dock in Dubrovnik for IKRA to arrive after their passage down from Antibes where I had seen them last. This was to be my first proper job on a yacht where I would have a full-time position and salary. I also knew I would be doing a lot more than just sailing and it was that side of things I was a bit nervous about.

Bernard had called me up one day, shortly after we returned to Antibes and told me that I needed to go to the shipyard and find a guy called Luigi because he was looking for a deckhand for the summer season. I duly dashed round to the yard, found Luigi easily enough and got the job after a quick chat right there on the dock.

Luigi was from Milan and in his early 30s. He's a super fun-loving man and we hit it off right away. His first mate was another Italian by the name of Donny. Luigi and Donny both took a big shine to me in more ways than one and right away started making sexual jokes and references to me. They were both as straight as an arrow but in their culture, it was funny to joke about this.

It was not in mine and to start with I was really quite confused. They would both come up to me while I was working or reading and just lurk grinning.

Then they would say, 'Hey Robertina' (they had started calling me Robertina by now) what I want to know are you active or passive?'

I honestly didn't know what they meant as in my culture homosexuality was still quite taboo (in Torquay it was anyway) and it was most certainly not something men joked about with each other. More likely to start a fight in all truth.

So, when confronted with this question, 'Hey Robertina, are you active or passive?'

I just didn't know what to say.

Sometimes I would say, 'Well today, I'm quite full of energy so let's say active.'

In this case, their eyes would light up and they would walk off grinning saying, 'He's active. Ohhhh yes.'

36

Other times, I would be tired and say passive and this would provoke more or less the same response. It was all good fun and even later when I worked it out I didn't care and really engaged with them in all the humour.

Luigi would come up to me at random and say, 'Hey Robertina, you know what I love about you?'

I would blush and fidget and sort of say, 'Errrr no.'

Then he would burst out in a flamboyant Italian accent, 'EVERYTHING Robertina. I love EVERYTHING about you.'

These first few months on IKRA were by far the most fun I had on yachts at any point. Maybe largely due to my naivety but I think if you ask any of the other people on board at that time they would fully agree that there was a magic vibe and as working on yachts goes it was about as good as it gets. I guess you could say I landed on my feet. But I'm getting ahead of myself here.

At this point, I want to tell you about how I had just arrived on IKRA in Dubrovnik. Just previously I had a small complication called my sister's wedding which required me to return to the UK for a few days. Luigi and IKRA needed to make their way down to Dubrovnik from Antibes which was a couple of days sailing so a plan was hatched for me to meet the boat down there.

In the end, this worked perfectly and I was in fact waiting on the dock for them when they arrived.

All was not well on board. The chef Luigi had hired for the season had been seasick all the way down and had not been able to cook for the crew. He was an English chap who had basically bullshitted his way into the job and Luigi had hired him out of desperation as it was getting late and he needed a chef.

Accordingly, the vibe wasn't great which I found a bit of a shock. I was still thinking that everybody who worked on a yacht would just be so happy to be there that they could not possibly be upset about anything. Turns out I was wrong about that.

Luigi put me to work washing down which was something I did a lot on Favonius and Bernard had really taught me well. Plus, I was naturally a hard and diligent worker so as soon as Luigi saw me going at it he chilled out and the rest of the day passed quite uneventfully.

By sundown, the beers and vino came out and before long we were off to town to find somewhere nice for dinner. By now, I was quite tired as I had not slept well at all the previous night and had had a really long day by that point. The level of alcohol consumption was also at a standard yachty rate so…Full tilt.

So, by the time we made it to a restaurant, I was pissed as a fart and falling asleep. Not a great look on your first night out with a new crew but I was doing my best to hang in there.

Let's recall that the year was 1999 and in fact, the Yugoslavian civil war had only just finished a few years previously. Dubrovnik was still full of holes. Literally, bullet holes and bomb damage were still evident in many places. The menu that was thrust before me did not have a word of English and I was simply too shy to ask for anyone's help.

I saw one thing that I recognised and that was scampi. Now scampi in the UK and scampi on the continent are two quite different things. I was under the impression that what I had ordered was going to be a plate of little bread-crumbed prawn tails that would be ready to eat.

What I in fact got was a platter of mini lobsters still fully encased in their shells. As everyone else dug into their various dinners, pasta, pizza, steaks etc I just stared at my plate of mini lobsters. I really had no idea what I was supposed to do so I picked one of them up and just tried to take a bite out of it.

Of course, they were cooked so the shells were quite soft and I was able to actually chew through several of these little beasts before the others couldn't contain themselves any longer and the lot of them nearly fell off their chairs laughing at me. In fact, it spread to the other tables around us and I just had to sit there and blush.

What doesn't kill you makes you stronger, they say. I'm sure that there's a large element of truth in that but I'm afraid that my experiences in life have taught me that what doesn't kill you might make you stronger, but it can also make you bitter and twisted. Or at least it can if you let it.

We continue as the great man says. A couple of months later I would meet Ariel who would go on to be my first love and girlfriend for the next four years. That first season on IKRA will be a fascinating chapter all of its own in a later work but for now, you are going to be hearing a lot more about Ariel and the adventures we got up to together. Let's get into it.

4

The Domino Shack

It was mid-January 2000. What a time to be young, dumb and full of…enthusiasm. I was working on the sailing yacht PKB as first mate. My girlfriend, Ariel, was working as the stewardess. Ariel and I had met the previous summer while working abroad in IKRA. As you know I had spent the summer working on IKRA as deckhand.

I was literally living the dream and having the time of my life on a daily basis. Ariel had joined IKRA as chef mid-season and had been an immediate success as she had a good personality and her food was amazing. She slotted right in with all the madness created by Luigi and Donny and we became good friends very quickly.

There were several things that drew Ariel and I together right from the off. Firstly, she was from the town right next to my hometown back in Devon UK. In fact, she hadn't been born there but owned an apartment there at that time.

She had in fact been born nearby (in a posh part of Devon) but spent most of her childhood growing up all over the world as her father had been a pioneer of field anthropology.

Another thing we shared was that she seemed to love cannabis almost as much as me. In fact, I was to quickly work out that she loved it even more than me. Something I couldn't conceive of at that time. I suppose the fact that she was beautiful might have had something to do with it and it didn't take me long to find my way into her knickers.

So, we became a couple and for me, that was the icing on the cake. Now not only was I travelling the world on superyachts. I also had a beautiful woman to warm my bed, cook my food and roll my joints. There was only one problem. Ariel was 11 years older than me. That wasn't a problem as such but the way it panned out it was more the case that I warmed her bed, rolled her joints and in the end even cooked her food.

At the end of the season on IKRA, Luigi moved to another bigger boat and was looking for crew. Ariel and I didn't fancy staying on IKRA without Luigi and when he invited us to join him on his new yacht PKB it seemed like a match made in heaven.

The deal was done and we flew out to Las Palmas in the Canary Islands to join PKB. She had her previous crew on board for the crossing and we were to slot in with them to deliver PKB across to Antigua. We had some epic sailing and caught tons of delicious fish. We ate sushi almost every night.

Or the rest of the crew did as I was still a snotty-nosed little twat who couldn't stand the idea of eating raw fish. Let's remember I had grown up in a little seaside town in the UK in the 80s and 90s. Sushi was most certainly not an everyday thing back then.

At this point, I should mention Magda. Magda was Luigi's partner and she was joining us in Antigua to be the chef on board.

'Hang on,' I hear you cry. 'Wasn't Ariel the chef?'

Yes, she was and in fact, Magda was not a chef but a stewardess who has always wanted to be a chef but has zero training or experience. For some reason (well it's not hard to work out), Luigi had decided that it would be a good idea to have Magda working as the chef and Ariel working as the stewardess.

If Magda and Ariel had been good friends, this might have worked but would have still been very tricky for everyone involved. In reality, they hated each other from day one and it was a disaster for everyone involved. So, let's just say that things were a little tense onboard.

We had arrived in the Caribbean in mid-December and everything had been going wrong since the start. It was one disaster after another. The boat was taking a lot of damage and we, Ariel and myself that is, were struggling with the stress. At this point, I should be clear about something. Ariel and I were both full-time cannabis users.

These days we are called patients, but this was way before that sort of enlightenment. What this essentially means is that we are both a certain type of person who simply functions much better with regular doses of cannabis throughout the day. What it does is just slightly adjust how we perceive the world around us.

It's a little like putting on a pair of glasses that help you see things just slightly differently. It's only a subtle difference but it changes how we interpret, respond and react to the world to a great extent. I have met many people who share in this and none of them were in any way dysfunctional. In fact, most of them have been very successful in their chosen careers. As long as they have access to their medicine.

Back in those days, the options for consuming cannabis were, errrrr, rather limited shall we say. Combusting it in a rolling paper mixed with tobacco was by far the easiest and most popular method. What's generally known as a joint, a spliff, a dubi, a phat one, a number, a sly one and so on.

It wasn't my personal favourite way of consuming, but it was often the only option I had when out and about. Now it's fair to say that this form of self-medication presents a few problems when living and working as a crew on a super yacht.

In international waters, all illegal drugs are strictly forbidden on any kind of vessel. The penalties for being caught by the authorities are completely different to what they are on land and are generally severe. Luigi knew about our cannabis use and although he was far from happy about it he valued us both as crew and was doing his best to tolerate it.

However, he had told us both that we were not to smoke it on board but it was okay to go ashore and find a quiet place. If we were at anchor, he told us to take the tender and do the same. However, he was not at all relaxed about it.

He had freaked out several times when he caught us smoking it and told us that if Customs came on board then the whole yacht could be seized and become property of that country. Also, he said that all the crew would go to jail for years. So far this season there had not been any issues and at the point, we join the story PKB was berthed stern to on the dock at Nelson's dockyard, Antigua.

We had been working hard preparing for our charter which had arrived that day. This was an unusual charter in that it featured an elderly American couple and their four grandchildren. Three girls and a boy aged 7–12. They had arrived that day with no issues, and we were planning to leave the next day and sail a short distance over to Guadeloupe where we would spend the next few days.

That evening Ariel and I had the small issue that we needed to resupply with cannabis. Our normal source, a taxi driver, had not been seen for a few days and we needed to pick up before we departed for this charter. Back then the way to obtain illegal substances in this location was somewhat unique in my experience.

All yachts are required, by maritime law, to carry and use a VHF radio. These short-distance radios worked by having an open channel, 16, which all yachts kept always switched on 24/7. As maritime law dictates. If one yacht wishes to contact another, then they simply call the yacht's name out on the radio and as long as someone on that yacht is within hearing distance of the radio then they can respond.

The protocol is to then switch to another private channel and have the convo. The only issue with this is that you have to say the channel number you are switching to on the open channel. Obviously, this means anyone listening can follow and switch to the other channel. Normally this was a means of communication used only for navigation at sea. But here in Antigua, it was used for a lot more.

Many of the big yachts that go to the Caribbean for the winter actually end up sitting on the dock for most of the winter and the crew end up with a lot of time to chill out. Especially in the evenings. They also have a lot of spare cash and are generally quite hedonistic people.

The Caribbean in its raw form is quite an alien place to most Westerners and it's simply not possible for Westerners to blend in with locals as it is anywhere in the Mediterranean or Europe. These crews needed a way to engage with the local community and this was done through the taxis. The Antigua taxis were like a kind of mafia and they were very much in charge of supplying the entire yacht network with everything they needed. Everything.

Different drivers were known for their ability to supply different things and this occasion we wanted cannabis. We knew that one particular driver was very well-connected and so we called him up.

To call this man we had to use the open channel which is just hilarious because it meant that everyone in the community knew that we were calling up to get drugs. However, this was normal because we would listen to everyone else doing the same thing every night so it just didn't seem like a big risk or anything.

The call went like this, 'Red Rose taxi, Red Rose taxi this is yacht PKB' repeated several times.

Red Rose was listening and replied, 'This is Red Rose taxi, switch channel 72.'

We switched and arranged for Red Rose to come and pick us up. It was evening and dark when Red Rose arrived and we jumped in his minivan. We explained that we were proper smokers and we didn't want a pissy little bag but a decent-sized bag of good weed.

Red Rose considered this for a moment and then said, 'Okay, we go.'

We headed out of the dockyard and after a couple of minutes he took a turn off the main road and we disappeared into thick jungle. This was new territory for us yachties as we never normally left the coastline so we knew we were in for an adventure.

We drove down this single-lane road for about 10 minutes. There were no streetlights and just a few large houses set well back behind fences. Then we came into a street with a couple of smaller houses and some lights and he pulled over.

He turned to us looking serious and said, 'Okay you,' pointing at me. 'Come with me and you,' pointing at Ariel. 'Stay in here.'

I looked at Ariel with horror because the idea of leaving her alone in this place went right against all my instincts of protecting my girlfriend. However, Ariel had lived and worked all over the world and this was child's play next to the sort of things she'd done in the past.

She was a very experienced woman and she just said, 'Go with him, I'll be fine here.'

One of the reasons I liked Ariel was because of her worldly experience and so I trusted her completely. More importantly, I really wanted a smoke so Red Rose and I set off down a muddy path and immediately disappeared into blackness and jungle.

Now at this stage, I should point a couple of things out. The entire economy of the island of Antigua revolves around yachts and tourism. The safety of the yacht crew when ashore is a big deal and if anything, were to happen to me the whole island would know that it was Red Rose because we had called him up on an open radio.

So that same open radio that made it so obvious what we were doing was also a source of protection and security. The fact is that I never once felt at risk and never was in fact at risk.

After a few minutes, we came out of the jungle and started walking up a hill, now by moonlight alone. I could see a sort of shack on top of the hill and as we approached I was greeted by the strong smell of cannabis. Entering the shack, I beheld something I'd never seen before or after. A single open space with a kind of enclosed bar at one end and a large table filling the rest of the space.

Sitting around this table were around 15 Rastafarians, a variety of ages but all with long thick rich dreadlocks and all smoking massive joints. There was quite a dense fog in there. Red Rose led me to the bar and he had a conversation with the bartender, another massive, middle-aged Rasta. They appeared to have a bitter argument which was quite normal when listening to locals talking to each other. Then Red Rose ushered me to the bar.

The Rasta glared at me and said, 'You want the rough or the smooth.'

I was just blank and stuttered, 'Errr, I've got a hundred dollars.'

The guy's eyes nearly popped out and Red Rose jumped in saying, 'Give him the rough, the rough man.'

The guy went to a dustbin and pulled a couple of handfuls of bushy weed out, stuffed it in a brown paper bag and thrust it at me. The exchange was made and Red Rose promptly led me out and back to the waiting Ariel and eventually back to our yacht.

We gathered the necessary means for joint construction and headed to our spot on a little beach just around the corner from the dock. The cannabis was exceptional. The best we had ever scored in the Caribbean. We smoked a joint and chatted away quietly about the adventure we had just had. Now fully relaxed and in our comfort zones. Or were we?

As we finished our joint we became aware of movement down at the far end of the beach. We could see a lone figure moving quietly along the edge of the beach. We froze. The smoke from our joint was wafting down that way. This was normally what we wanted as it was away from the yachts. The lone figure slowly came closer until he was perched on a rock nearby.

We couldn't see his face but it was clear it was a local. The joint was nearly out but there was one last toke and I thought fuck it and took the toke. I exhaled the smoke and it wafted down the beach and over the shadowy figure.

Who turned and said quietly but loudly enough for us to hear, 'Hmmmmmm, yachties smoking weed, hmmmmmm, risky business that, hmmmmmm.'

Then he stepped back and was gone. I must admit that he did sound a little bit like Yoda. No bullshit. Ariel and I both had simultaneous panic attacks and just sat there not knowing what to do or say. Then we both just got up and without saying a word to each other walked back to the yacht.

Looking back, I simply can't see how that was connected to what was about to come. But who knows? It could have been. But nevertheless, he was right. Yachties smoking weed like that is a very risky business. As we were about to find out.

5

The Sniffer Dog and the Cake

The good ship PKB sailed out of Nelson's Harbour on a fine January morning. Captain Luigi at the helm with first mate Robert running the deck assisted by deck/stewie Ariel and chef Magda. The six charter guests consisted of a couple in their 70s and their four grandchildren. Three girls and a boy aged from 12 to 7.

I don't recall their exact home but they were Americans and I'm pretty sure they were from the East Coast. All my memories of those guests are positive. They were lovely people. Unfortunately, they had been sold a holiday on a yacht crewed by a bunch of reprobates. Although I'm pretty sure they left the yacht happy, they were most certainly going to have an interesting time.

The guests did not arrive until quite late in the day meaning that by the time we got to Guadeloupe, it was dark. We dropped anchor in the bay outside the main town, Pointe-à-Pitre, and then did the usual dinner routine.

Once they were taken care of we finished work for the day and then it was time for Ariel and I to sneak off in the tender and smoke a joint. In fact, Magda also enjoyed cannabis and on occasion would join us for a smoke. On this occasion, she decided to come along.

It was a very still night and we didn't really go that far from the yacht. While we were within easy sight of it, I killed the outboard engine and let us drift while Ariel and I both rolled a joint. It turned out that 100 dollars bought us a lot more weed than we were expecting. That combined with the increased potency meant we didn't need as much.

We were happily discussing this, while staring at the stars in this stunning location when I became aware of another small craft coming from outside the bay and heading in towards the town. As usual, I had been paying close attention to the direction that the smoke from our joints had been blowing. This was an essential skill when subversive smoking.

The smell of cannabis has got more people into trouble than any other clue so I always took note of the wind direction and chose my spot for a smoke accordingly. The problem, I had just perceived right now, was that although our smoke was drifting away from our yacht it was instead drifting right into the path of this approaching craft.

Sure enough, to my horror, as the craft was passing us, maybe 50 m away, it suddenly came off the plane and slowed right down. We three froze. For a second, there was no sound or movement from this mysterious craft. We also sat in silence. Then the motor roared into life once more and off they sped. We breathed a sigh of relief, took some last tokes and headed back to PKB.

Back onboard Magda disappeared into her cabin while Ariel and I convened in the galley. We didn't actually discuss what had just happened but instead, we decided that we needed to do something about this massive bag of smelly weed we had.

There was enough for the next month and it was way more than we were comfortable keeping onboard so Ariel decided to infuse the bulk of it into butter and then bake a cake with the butter. She went on and did that the very same night. It was a bloody good thing she did as we were about to find out.

The normal thing when a yacht arrives in a new country is for the captain to go straight to the local Customs office, together with the passports/visas of everyone on board. As we had arrived too late for this, Luigi elected to get it done ASAP the next morning and while Magda, Ariel and I were busy serving the guests breakfast he took the tender and headed into town with everybody's passports.

Breakfast on a charter yacht is no simple affair and usually takes a couple of hours for the whole process to be completed before the crew can switch tasks and get the boat ready to move again. Everything had been ticking along smoothly as usual and I had been enjoying some light-hearted banter with the kids. Being a big kid myself I was happy to joke and play with them and I had been explaining about some of the superstitions sailors have.

This is of course no joking matter and saying the word rabbit to any old-school sailor is a seriously taboo thing. Sailors are a highly superstitious bunch and this is in fact just one of a variety of things you should not say or do onboard a vessel of any kind.

I'm sure this sounds a little silly and the fact is that it is. But I still rolled with it (and still do) and I had been trying to convince the kids that although it seemed funny I considered this to be very serious and would prefer them not to say the word rabbit. If you are curious about the origin of this superstition, then I suggest you do a quick Google search.

This was of course like a red rag to a bull and they had been teasing me periodically through the charter so far. It was all light-hearted and in gest. Or was it on my part? Anyway, at the point when things got spicy this morning I was down below in the saloon when I noticed, out of the porthole windows, a small RIB (Rigid Inflatable Boat) passing rather close to us.

So close in fact that I decided to venture on deck and tell them to bugger off. Once on deck, I saw that they had passed round the bow and were heading down the other side. There were three scruffy-looking adult men and a rather pathetic-looking dog. I couldn't see any names or identification of any sort but as they got to the back of the yacht they started moving in closer and I realised they were planning to land on the bathing platform at the transom.

This was strictly against maritime etiquette so I started shouting, 'Hey, hey, hey! You can't come here.'

But as they arrived at the platform I saw that on their T-shirts, in very faded letters it said...*Customs*. FUCK. This will become a familiar expression during the course of reading this book. I can assure you.

Anyone who has spent any time around yachts will know that getting on and off the bloody things is seldom an easy thing. So, I had a quick minute to assess what was happening and realise that we were in serious shit.

It's actually quite a unique experience to be in a situation where you are face to face with authorities who are there to do a job and their job, if they manage to do it, is going to mean you losing your freedom. Now if you know full well that you have what they are looking for then it's a very interesting game one gets to play.

Personally, I'm an outright disaster at this game as generally, you can read my face like a book. My stomach plummeted the second I saw Customs on the T-shirts and revealed why they had a dog. It was a sniffer dog and it was there to sniff for drugs. Drugs that we had. Smelly drugs that we had.

So, once they had got their RIB tied up the lead guy turned to me and said, 'Hello, we are Customs and we are here to search the yacht. We need to see everybody's passports right now.'

Of course, Luigi had gone ashore with all our passports so I explained this to them and also that I had no way of contacting Luigi (this was pre-mobile phones) and we would just have to wait for him to get back. They didn't seem too impressed with this but didn't have much choice but to accept it.

It also gave me time to poke my head down into the galley and inform Ariel and Magda that Customs were here to search the boat.

Bear in mind that all the while the charter guests are sitting in the cockpit happily munching away on their breakfast not really aware of what was going on. I wanted to maintain an air of cool so did my best to pass this information on an almost conversational tone.

Ariel being the smart woman she is, immediately grasped the situation and dashed to our cabin where she grabbed the bag of cannabis and went to the bathroom where she started trying to flush it down the toilet.

Unfortunately, Red Rose taxi had told the man to give me the rough meaning that it was full of sticks and sticks don't go too well into a macerator. The toilet immediately jammed with the bowl still half full of weed. At this point, something odd happened.

Ariel swears she looked up at this moment and standing above her on the deck, looking right down through the skylight hatch, was one of the Customs men. Fortunately, these skylights had a slight tint and somehow it was enough to deflect his gaze as he didn't react and just walked on along the deck. Phew.

Meanwhile, I was with the other two guys and the dog, who was mostly cowering and didn't seem at all happy to be there, much to my relief. I was trying to stay cool and sort of entertain them while we waited for Luigi and somehow they just waited around until he finally returned about 30 minutes later.

Once briefed Luigi showed them the passports and the Customs stamps to show we had legally entered the country. He then led them on a quick tour of the interior, with the dog which had to be dragged along the floor. By now, I was starting to relax a little but there was just one last place they wanted to look. The galley.

Ariel's Cake was still sitting on the side just inside the galley door and it hadn't even crossed our minds.

As the door to the galley opened the dog suddenly perked up, as you might expect, and trotted happily in with its nose in the air. Ariel and I both watched this and looked at the cake and then at each other with horror. Sure enough, the dog caught the scent of cannabis from the cake and went off barking at the cake. Magda, Ariel and I froze.

Luigi and the Customs people just looked confused but the dog kept howling at the cake until the lead Customs guy whacked it on the head with a rolled-up document. Everyone winced but it didn't deter the dog who was now attempting to make up for his poor performance earlier and inform his bosses that he had found them a bust.

As a dog owner myself, I often think about how it would be if my dog could actually talk and properly understand English instructions. I've reached the conclusion that it would be a mixed blessing and I think my dog sees it the same way.

On this occasion, this poor dog earned itself something of a hiding and had to be dragged off the yacht by the now highly apologetic Customs people. Luigi went to see the Customs people off and Ariel and I went to our cabins and just burst out laughing with nervous energy. So relieved to have dodged a bullet. Unfortunately, relief was the last emotion Luigi was feeling and we were about to get one of the bollockings of our lives.

When we told Luigi what we had had on board while they were searching us, he turned white. I'm not sure why we told him. I used to be obsessed with honesty but with situations like this I slowly learnt there's a time and place for a little white lie and this should really have been one of them.

He didn't fire us. It was the second time that season he should have fired us both. In fact, as it happened, I was about to get a punishment quite a bit worse than being fired.

We spent the rest of that day at anchor and even went ashore for a couple of hours. The plan was to set sail early the next morning and head on down the island chain. I recall feeling a sort of empty stunned sensation all the next day. No doubt I was aware of what a close call that had been with some serious problems with authorities. Something at that stage, I was yet to experience. Running amok as I was, inevitably it couldn't be far away.

6

The Good News Is, He Does Have a Brain

Early the next morning, around first light, we lifted the anchor and set a course for Dominica. This would be new territory for me and although in theory this should all be super exciting it was, in fact, very far from that. It would be easy for a layperson to imagine that living and working on a luxury 89 ft yacht in the Caribbean would be pretty damn close to living the dream. Right?

In actual fact, the things which make life fun and enjoyable and dream-like are actually very far from what a naive young man like myself might have imagined. Just to deviate from the story a little here, I would like to share some knowledge with you if I might be so bold. Which clearly I am. Both literally and…yes, yes, get on with it, Bobby.

In order to establish why we go to work, its first necessary to question our base motives and priorities. Most people, not everyone, but most people go to work to earn money. That is the single most important reason to be there. Accordingly, how much you get paid in relation to how many hours you work, what exactly you are doing i.e. level of responsibility/accountability absolutely has to be the single most important factor when considering work options.

Although on PKB I was on a good salary, if you referenced it against the hours I worked and what I was doing then suddenly it didn't look so good. But I told myself this didn't matter because I was working on a big yacht and living the dream. And that was a big mistake. To think that what I was doing was more important than how much I was getting paid.

Clearly there are exceptions to this and I'm not trying to say that your wage is always going to override anything else. What I'm getting at is that getting paid should be your first reason to go to work. It wasn't for me. My first reason was that I wanted to sail around the world on big boats. For me, getting paid was just a bonus.

With hindsight, I see this as a big mistake and I advise anyone else not to follow my footsteps. Instead work hard at getting a good job that pays well and then buy your own damn boat.

I've come to think that the second most important element of work selection is who you will be working with. Again, for some people this is not so much of an issue as they are generally able to get along with just about anybody. But some people are simply toxic and if you find yourself forced to work alongside a person like this then it can make a working day long and tedious.

If you then combine that with the fact that you have to live and work together in very close confines, then things start to get extremely difficult.

Magda was the first person I found myself working alongside who I deeply disliked. Yet she was by no means the last. In one of my last actual "jobs" (I won't go into details here and now), I was forced to work with people I disliked so much that I ended up headbutting one of them. Yes really. The people you work with can and will make or break a job.

They can turn an awful day into an awesome one and vice versa just as quickly. The problem is that you have no way of selecting them or generally even meeting them before starting the job. So, all I'm saying is that be aware that your colleagues will play a large role in your ability to be happy at work.

The third most important aspect of work selection is where you will be working. Some people, like myself these days, prefer to work from home. However, the majority still make a short commute, of some sort, to and from a workplace. Both the commute and the workplace itself are significant factors and can easily make or break a job even if the first two factors are sorted.

Later in my life, I would make a decision to live in a beautiful place with really cheap rent but work over 45 minutes away. This journey depended on a ferry crossing a river and there were often delays causing massive queues. If everything went super smooth and no issues, then it was possible to do the drive in 45 minutes. Still a long time when you have to come back again but on the face of it manageable.

However, the reality was that it was one in 10 days that it took 45 minutes. The ferry often had problems and the route also had a variety of other potential hazards. Add to that the cost of the fuel and the wear on the car. The commute took over our lives and ruined them. Often by the time we got home it was too dark to enjoy the location anyway.

I had to work extra hours and often did weekends so in the end we spent very little time in the place we lived. Instead, we spent a hell of a lot of time driving and sitting in queues. To live in that place with a long drive to work was one of the worst decisions I ever made. Please don't ever take a job with a long commute. You will regret it in the end.

So, this brings us to the fourth factor in job selection. And that is exactly what you will be doing with your time. I spent the first 20 years of my working life fully convinced that the last and least important factor was by far the most important. As such I found myself in a kind of waking nightmare that was about to take another turn for the worse.

All was not well aboard the good ship PKB. Fortunately, Ariel and I were still getting on really well and actually very much in love. Despite the age gap we had found a real home in each other's hearts and in many ways were just exactly what each other needed.

But with hindsight I can also say that, in the long run, we were as badly matched as it's possible for two people to be. For now, at least all was good between us.

Unfortunately, Ariel and I both hated Magda and the animosity was very much reciprocated. Luigi and I were still getting on okay most of the time but he had exploded at me more than once and the fallout from my various fuck ups was still evident all over the boat. To make things worse Magda was heavily pressuring Luigi to turn against Ariel and I. So, Luigi was fighting with Magda a lot and…Well yes, I think maybe you're starting to get the picture.

Whenever possible Ariel and I would get off the boat and then we were generally able to have a lot of fun. We got to know the owner of a local bar who would score cannabis for us. I'm sure he only helped us because he fancied Ariel but one night we went to see him to score some weed and the bar was empty except for him.

We asked if it was still possible and he said yeah if I didn't mind tending the bar while he went to get it. Now I was a fairly experienced bartender so I tentatively said yes but I was still a bit nervous about being left in charge of a whole bar in the middle of the Caribbean. However, once again my desire to get weed overcame my natural caution and we sent the man on his way to get our smoke.

For the first 10 minutes or so, all was well but then in walked the first customer. A big local man who immediately started complaining about everything. He ordered a pint and as I was pouring it he was giving me verbal about everything and getting right on one. I was sort of trying to pacify him but panicking a bit as well when the owner walked in with our bag of weed.

When the two men saw each other, they burst out laughing both with their heads down on the bar crying. Turns out the owner had first stopped in at his best mates house and asked him to come and make sure the stupid little white man didn't burn the bloody bar down while he was gone.

So anyway. Back to the story. By now, Ariel and I had done a fair bit of sailing together. We'd met and hooked up on the previous yacht IKRA 2 where she was chef but as an active sailor herself, and also boat owner back in the UK, she was on deck at every opportunity. As a fun person to be around this generally worked well. It was also a large part of what I found attractive about her.

On PKB, we had the job of working the deck and sailing the boat together. In theory, a dream job and in practice we made a damn good fist of it. Except on this occasion. Where one tiny little indiscretion on my part led to me receiving a serious injury. As is the way with sailing big yachts. As a yacht gets progressively larger so the loads get greater on all the ropes sailors use to control the sails.

By load what I mean is that there is a strong force pulling in the opposing direction to the rope one is trying to hold in one's hand. It's a bit like a tug of war. The wind is pushing the sail which in turn is trying to pull the rope and the sailor pulls back against it. To moderate and control this force sailors use winches and if you want to understand better how this system works I suggest you do a quick Google search.

So, you see it's all friction-based. Which to start with is quite terrifying because there is often no actual mechanical lock and the only thing stopping the rope pulling back through your hand is the number of turns around the winch and your own ability to grip. More turns mean more friction. *Great,* you think. I'll just keep lots of turns on the winch and then it won't possibly be able to pull through my hand. Oh, if only it is that easy. And this is where it gets complicated.

The number of turns around the winch must match the load the sail is applying. When the rope is wrapped around the winch, once it's called a "turn". If you have too many turns, then as you try to pull the rope through you get what are called riding turns which are basically a kind of knot. These are loathed by sailors universally and are the enemy of all things fair and true.

Riding turns jam the winch and tangle the rope and can be the cause of personal injury, dismasting, capsize and even the bloody yacht sinking. Sailors don't like riding turns. Is that clear?

So, when a sailor has control of a sheet or a halyard by way of a winch they must apply a considerable level of observation to what is happening as any slight change in the amount of load will mean they may need to either add or remove a turn from the winch. This is one of the core skills a sailor learns and the need for this skill and its importance becomes more significant on larger yachts.

Now a halyard and sheet are both ropes but differ significantly. A halyard is attached to the top corner of the sail and is used to pull it up the mast whereas a sheet is attached to the bottom corner of the sail and is used only to control its shape. With a halyard, the load will generally only increase as the sail is raised.

Therefore, the person on the winch will start with just one turn and as the sail is raised and the load increases they will add more turns accordingly. Like this, it's quite simple and if the winch is located on the deck it's also much easier because the person can sit with their legs around the winch and watch the sail while they pull or tail the halyard.

On PKB, there were a lot of winches. The way Ariel and I worked was for me to power the winch using either a pedestal grinder, winch handle or button and Ariel would tail. She was good at that job and generally always knew when to add or lose a turn. However, one particular sail, the staysail, had a different system.

For this sail, there was a large stainless-steel, mast-mounted winch. This meant it was at 90 degrees to the deck. The staysail was comparatively small and we were generally able to whizz it up with no issues. One small issue was that it needed a lot of winching to get it all the way to the top.

Luigi had some funny ideas on how to sail a yacht and liked to get the boat fully powered up and leaning right over before calling for the staysail. I swear he did this just to be a cunt. It makes no sense to sail a boat this way unless you are racing which we never were.

On this morning, just after daybreak, with a decent-sized swell that we were heading into, Luigi was in every mood to be a cunt. Considering what had happened the day before in some ways I don't blame him but putting other people's lives at risk just because you are annoyed with them is a very questionable thing to do.

Once the mainsail and the headsail were set, sheeted home and we were healing right over and slamming into the approaching swell, Luigi called for the staysail. Without question, Ariel and I sped up the deck to the mast and set to work preparing for the hoist.

Once the bag was off and the halyard and sheets were attached, we commenced hoisting the sail. Despite the haphazard motion of the deck, we were skilled and used to this and it was actually one of the few parts of our work that we were really enjoying.

There was nothing particularly different about this morning except maybe what had happened over the last few days. We set about hoisting the sail and as the load came on the halyard Ariel asked for another turn. I had to remove the large, heavy, stainless-steel handle so that she could carefully wind another turn onto the winch.

On a mast-mounted winch, this is not a simple thing to do. In fact, it was a pain in the ass. But it was just part of life on a boat where everything was a pain in the ass.

It was normal to add three turns during hoisting the stay sail. At each turn, the load was greater and the process of adding another turn was riskier. If Ariel lost her grip on the halyard, then it would instantly recoil at high speed and try to pull itself back through the winch and up the mast thus dropping the sail again.

Dropping the sail wasn't a problem as such but what would actually happen is that the halyard would instantly ride up and jam on the winch meaning you would end up with the halyard wrapped and knotted tightly around the winch drum. The net result would mean that you have a half-hoisted sail, flogging noisily and dangerously, which can neither be winched up nor lowered down.

I believe this is the technical definition of a cluster fuck. In fact, this had never happened to Ariel and I while sailing together. We were both good sailors who took our jobs very seriously.

What happened on this occasion was that I made just a tiny mistake. The winch handle has a locking pin where it fits into the top of the winch. When it's pushed in, it clicks and locks in preventing the handle from slipping out when under load. On the third time removing the handle for another turn, I failed to notice that the pin had not located and I began to wind on the handle.

After a couple of turns, as the handle came around level with my face, the pin slipped, the shaft came out, the handle swung around and the end struck me full force about halfway between my right temple and eye. Remember the handle was made from solid stainless-steel. Which is quite hard. Harder than me anyway.

The blow smashed my sunglasses off and knocked me to the deck but I didn't lose consciousness. We're made of sterner stuff, us Dazzlers yes, yes. Ariel screamed my name but fortunately held on tight to the halyard. I regained my feet and in the same instant realised the stay sail was still not fully hoisted. Ariel was saying something but I just shouted that we had to finish hoisting the sail before anything else.

I was starting to piss blood out of a big hole in the side of my head but at that moment my only concern was to get the sail up. Once that was done I had to get myself back to the aft cockpit without getting blood on my precious teak deck. I spent half my life on that boat scrubbing the teak to keep it pristine and if anyone went near it with grease or worse then I growled at them.

As Ariel dragged me back to the cockpit I was screaming, 'Not the teak. Not the teak. Don't get blood on my teak.'

Then I saw the kids as Ariel dragged me past the main cockpit where all the guests had been watching the whole thing. You might recall the ongoing discussion I was having with the kids about sailing superstitions and the need not to say certain words.

The kids were just staring at me in wide-eyed horror and as I pissed blood all over my precious teak deck I screamed at them, 'I told you not to say that word (rabbit) and now look what's happened.'

Just to be clear that was a little harsh on my part as it was not at all their fault but…

Let's just backtrack a little and consider the situation again. It was about 09:00 am and we were about five miles off Guadeloupe, heading to Dominica, with a charter of six guests on board. Not a good time and place to smash your head open really. Fortunately, it was only a flesh wound which soon stopped bleeding.

However, I had taken a substantial blow to the noggin and was severely concussed. I think we must have dug out the best painkillers on board and then I just curled up in the corner of the cockpit until we got to calmer water. Then I got into my bunk while the rest of the crew managed to sail the boat to Dominica.

In fact, that wasn't too hard. All Luigi had to do was to get Magda to hold the wheel while he helped Ariel instead of me. Magda never helped me and Ariel so losing me wasn't an immediate disaster. But looking ahead to the rest of the charter…With a crew of four losing one was going to mean…Well, you do the maths.

Once we got to Dominica we dropped anchor and Luigi took me straight to the biggest town and went to look for a doctor. Dominica is just a tiny island in the middle of a big ocean so things are not quite as you might expect in a western country. I remember sitting on the dock with a severe headache for what felt like an age. There were baskets of fruit everywhere and it was very hot.

In due course, Luigi returned and led me to a house where a doctor gave me a quick check over and announced that I seemed fine for now but I must get a CAT scan ASAP to check for internal bleeding and swelling. The nearest place where this could be obtained was Antigua which was a couple of days sail away.

There was no way around this so I simply had to stay in bed for the rest of the charter, or until we got back to Antigua where the charter was concluded a few days early.

I was taken to the main hospital in the capital, St John, and left to wait in a big room with lots of colourful people coming and going. There were big cracks down the walls. This was probably about as close to the third world as I ever got and it was an odd feeling being in a hospital and looking at massive cracks in the walls. I was thinking how the hell are they going to look inside my head if they can't fix a cracked wall?

After some time, a door opened and a doctor appeared and I was beckoned into a room which would have been at home in any western hospital. In the middle was a CAT scan machine.

In due course, the scan was completed and when the doctor appeared with our results he announced with a massive grin, 'Well, the good news is he does have a brain and as far as we can tell, it seems to be intact.'

Although I was physically basically okay, I was in no fit state to continue working and this did not do wonders to improve Luigi's mood. We had another charter booked in just a couple of days and it was clear that I was not going to hack it.

The next morning, Luigi announced that I must take a flight back to the UK for a two-week break while they would take on a temporary crew member for the next charter. I was told curtly that I had to pay for everything and that I would be reimbursed at a later date. I never was but that's another story.

Truth is that I was more than happy to go home for a while. I arrived back in London and obviously, it was January but this had not occurred to me. While I was standing on the outdoor train platform in board shorts and flip-flops looking at everyone else wrapped up in great big coats, it occurred to me that I might put some more clothes on.

Two weeks later, I would be back on board sweating it out and things would not get any better. In fact, I was about to have my first really close brush with that chap in the black cloak.

7

Top Three Close Calls

No. 3 The Lee Rail

If you were to ask any professional sailor what their greatest fear is, then I think that for most of them, falling overboard would rank right up there. If not taking the top spot. It's an ever-present threat. Mostly for those on smaller sailing yachts. It occurs to me that I often refer to size when talking about yachts. I talk about smaller and larger yachts. Let me put this into perspective for those unfamiliar with the world of super and mega yachts.

The first yacht I worked on was Favonius. A Swan 651. She was accordingly 65 ft overall. To put this into context let me point out that prior to this the largest yacht I had been aboard, back in my hometown of Torquay, was 35 ft. So, to me at this point, a 65 ft yacht seemed big.

However, I joined Favonius in the port of Antibes where she was surrounded by literal giants and in fact Antibes was a good place to begin to understand the scale of superyachts. Even back in 1998, there was no shortage of large motor and sailing yachts. Many of these dwarfed Favonius and it gave me a good frame of reference to understand the scale of the superyacht fleet.

In the last 25 years, things have changed a lot. I don't think it would even be possible to estimate the number and size of all the big yachts today. The industry has been booming for several decades now. Regardless of worldwide economics or events.

So, the smallest yacht I worked on as a full-time crew was Favonius while the largest was Al Mirqab which came in at a whopping 113 metres. That's 370 ft. At the time I was working on her, she was officially the third largest private yacht in the world. We now have what I believe is called a frame of reference. Small for me means under a 100 ft and large means over 100 metres.

Professional sailors tend to be something of a macho breed. Even the women generally are of this cut and it's largely due to the brutal nature of spending a lot of time at sea. In my career as a professional sailor, I covered approximately 35,000 NM. If I'm totally honest, I would say that I enjoyed less than 5000 of those miles.

The ocean is a brutally hard place. The first thing you learn about it and the thing you remember at all times (if you want to stay alive) is that the ocean will kill you in a second if it wants to. The moment you let your guard down for even just a millisecond you can be gone.

Now it could be argued that this is always the case in life in general and of course, in a literal sense, this is true. However, I think it's fair to consider the level of actual relative danger that a person is in when engaged in an activity. A person sitting at home is only at risk from a medical emergency or domestic disaster.

The odds of suddenly being killed are relatively low. A person on the deck of a sailing yacht is, at all times, regardless of the weather or the motion of the vessel, in a considerable amount of relative danger.

Let's consider the number of things which can go wrong. First of all the person's entire safety depends on the structural stability and integrity of the vessel. If it is not watertight and seaworthy, then it's going to sink and the person is going to end up in the water.

I'm just going to stop for a second here and point something out. Just typing those words sends a shiver down my spine and makes me stop and give thanks for the fact that in all my time at sea, I never ended up in there.

There was a point somewhere in my first Atlantic crossing where it became clear to me that the only way to stay alive out there was to think of the ocean as the enemy. Now this might seem a little extreme but when you are at sea at night and you are looking at the black water the very idea of finding yourself in there is simply horrific and it's really not that hard to think of it as something threatening.

Since the infamous Fastnet tragedy things have changed a lot in the superyacht industry. When I joined Adela in the early noughties, I was lucky enough to be put through the STCW series of sea safety courses and qualifications. This included a module on safety at sea and sea survival. Part of this involved lengthy lectures about the chances of survival for anyone falling into the water. It's low. Very low.

I had also spent a fair bit of time driving RIBs and had my powerboat qualification. During the assessment for this ticket, great stress was put on the importance of staying out of the water.

It's very difficult to make it clear just how much danger a person is actually in when they are on the deck of a sailing yacht in open water. Let's consider a number of scenarios. If we start with the best possible situation, then we can easily work backwards and see how the danger levels increase as things change. Let's take a 65 ft sailing yacht that is motoring along at six kts with a light headwind and no swell to mention.

Firstly, I should point out that there is always swell at sea. Out on the open ocean, it is seldom flat calm. In all my miles at sea, I only recall seeing a complete flat calm a handful of times and that was always only at dawn. Let's put a crew member on the deck of this yacht. If the crew member does not move to any other place on the deck, then they remain at a relatively low level of risk.

Relative that is but simply by stepping foot on a vessel you are basically trusting your life to the integrity of that craft. Should that craft have any kind of major problem, that major problem is going to be yours as well.

So, we see there are a number of inherent hazards just by being out on the water. Firstly, the vessel may fail in some way and start to take on water. In a serious situation, this could result in the yacht sinking. Assuming the yacht has life rafts the person would expect to make it into one of these and avoid the worst fate but it's still a very dangerous situation to be in and one I have been fortunate enough to avoid.

If the yacht itself is absolutely bombproof, then the next thing that might go wrong is either a change in the weather or a navigation mistake. In a serious instance, either of these could be enough to sink the yacht and put the person in the water. I've been in various situations where the weather has changed suddenly with no warning and also seen navigation mistakes that could have easily resulted in disaster.

But for now, let's consider that the yacht is sound, the weather settled and the navigation in hand. As a crew member on said yacht you have jobs that are many and varied. Some involve moving around the deck while at sea. So our person is not going to be sitting in one place but actually moving around the yacht on a fairly regular basis.

In general, small yachts do not really have any kind of handrail or protection around the outside of the deck. What they have are stanchions (metal posts usually coming to just below waist height) and two wires running down the line of stanchions. This is a sailor's sole protection against falling over the side. There is a gap between the deck and the lower rail of about 0.3–0.5 m which is easily big enough for a person to roll through.

I nearly did several times. But only nearly. Otherwise, unless you are wearing a harness and clipped in, there is nothing to stop you falling from the deck into the water. Nothing except your own ability that is. And that is all most sailors need and want.

You might be wondering about harnesses and thinking surely you can just wear a harness and always remain clipped in. In theory, yes but in practice being clipped in can be as dangerous as it is safe and only a handful of times in my life have I chosen to be clipped in. I should add though that on one of those occasions it did save my life. Being clipped in presents two issues.

Firstly, the moment you need to move around a lot the lanyard becomes a potential trap just waiting to snag or get caught. It is always dragging and causing irritation at best. Second if you do fall in then you will likely still be drowned and this has happened to a fair few people. If the boat is moving along at a speed, say seven kts, then the person might be pinned between the side of the boat and against the flow of water.

A lot like being stuck against a rock in a river. Boats don't have brakes. A fully powered-up sailing yacht can take minutes to slow down and longer still to actually stop. If you end up in open water, then being dragged along at seven kts is still a horrible thing and very hard to get your head to the surface for air.

It's my idea of hell. I would rather end up in the water and take my chances swimming. Or at least that's what I thought until a harness saved my life. But that's coming later and believe me it's a good one. Close call number two.

Let's return to our hypothetical situation with the small yacht motoring along at a steady six kts in calm conditions. Our person who has been sitting in relative safety now has been given a task which involves going to the forepeak, retrieving a sail, and setting it. Without going into all the details this involves a fair amount of movement around the deck.

To a skilled and experienced sailor, this is standard working practice and in calm conditions, this can be carried out with very little fuss. However, the decks of all sailing yachts, the world over, are fickle places. Any experienced sailors will be nodding sagely right now. A task that is simple 9 days out of 10 can suddenly become a massive cluster fuck at the slightest whim.

This happens. It usually happens when you are already having a bad day. (more nodding). Sailing boats are incredibly temperamental things and on a regular basis, they throw curve balls at you that catch even the most experienced sailors off guard. However, I think most sailors would agree that it's actually one of the things we love about them. The unpredictability.

I'll give you an example of how things can go. Let's think about my situation in the previous chapter where I was struck with a serious blow to the head. On that occasion, I simply fell to the deck but if the blow was from another angle I might have staggered back and fallen over the side. Even without having been hit in the head, at that time and place falling over the side would have been a death ticket.

It terrifies me just to think about it. You might be thinking that the yacht could just turn around and go back. I already explained that it takes time to slow a yacht down and that's with a full crew. It takes even longer to turn a sailing yacht 180 degrees and in fact, it's just not possible to turn around and go back.

Add to that the fact that once a person is in the water they are very hard to see even very close up. It's terrifying how quickly a person will disappear even in relatively benign conditions. So even without a serious injury, it could be something as simple as tripping.

There are so many ways that a person can go from being on a yacht to in the water that if you think about it too much you would never even step a single foot on a yacht.

I chose to live and work on them for the better part of two decades…Somehow, I survived and so yes I'd better get on and tell the bloody story of my third closest call with death. But before I do I will just say that a couple of years after this event a guy I knew in Antibes was washed overboard and lost.

He was a popular guy that everybody knew and liked in the Antibes community. He was washed off the deck of a 70 ft sailing yacht during the night by a wave that no one even saw coming. I'll say no more.

So, I think by now I've provided the required context to properly appreciate the gravity of the situation I was about to find myself in. Life as crew on a charter yacht can be very hard work. In fact, it generally just is hard work. That's not to say it can't be fun as well.

On the previous yacht, I had worked on, IKRA , with the same captain, Luigi, we had managed to work hard but had a really good time as well. Work hard to play hard was to become something of a motto of mine.

However, everything had changed now. Everything. Not least of all the fact that on IKRA Luigi had been a single man and as such always on the lookout for any bar with women in it. Now he was in a relationship with a woman with whom he wasn't getting any sex. The fallout from this was plentiful and varied. One thing was that it meant that Luigi was grumpy almost all the time.

The playful, almost flirty, relationship I had with him before was gone and now we seldom joked or even spoke when we didn't need to. This simply doesn't work in a professional dynamic where you have four people working closely together and regular, accurate communication is essential to smooth operations.

We were having one problem after another. Between me and Luigi we had done some considerable damage to the yacht and ourselves. A rift had grown between us and was getting bigger all the time.

On any busy charter yacht, it's usual to have to work some silly hours. It's just part of the job. What is also usual is to have to make some long passages, usually between the end of one charter and the beginning of another, when all the crew are super tired and should really get some downtime.

Dates are set and given to the captain who is left with no option but to eat them…No sorry…Do his best to try and be in the right place, with a presentable boat and crew, at the right time. This can lead to some really dangerous situations and on this occasion, it very nearly cost me my life and shortly after…Well, you'll see.

I don't recall the exact point in that fateful season where this event took place but what I do recall is that we finished one charter very late in the day in St Martin. As soon as the guests were off we basically had to leave and set sail, through the night, to be in Antigua the next day. This would give us one day to prep the boat for the owners who wanted to use the boat the next day.

What should have happened is that the broker who dealt with the owner should have told him to wait one more day. But he didn't and as such we had to set sail into the night in a state of near exhaustion. To add to that the trade winds were blowing hard and a good swell was running. The wind direction would mean that we would be fighting our way into it for most of the passage.

As a crew of four, two couples, it was natural for us to split into two teams or watches and we elected for two on two off. So basically, Ariel and I would spend two hours on deck and then have two hours below before being back on deck for another two and so on. It's hard to explain how long two hours can seem when you are holding onto the wheel and struggling to keep your eyes open. Then how quickly two hours can pass the moment you are back down below.

We departed shortly after dark and went straight into the watch system with Luigi and Magda taking the first watch. It was impossible to sleep before our watch as I was nervous about how I would cope with driving for two hours.

I was right to be nervous because it was really challenging. It was rough and windy and cold and very hard to steer the boat as it was overpowered with the amount of sail we had up.

Luigi had one way of sailing a boat and one way only and that was the equivalent of sticking it in top gear and putting your foot down. This is all fine and good when impressing charter guests but as an approach to getting a boat from A to B, it's stupid, ignorant and dangerous to all involved.

It was one of the things that was really starting to piss me off about Luigi because it often meant that my job was far more difficult and dangerous than it needed to be. I also felt that he had been pushing this more and more as our relationship had been failing and that he was taking his overall frustration out on me through this.

All through the night so far it had been really difficult to steer the boat and make a decent course. We still had a full mainsail and we were overpowered meaning the boat couldn't find its natural rhythm and making it hell to steer.

The net result of all this was that we were going slowly and in the wrong direction meaning that we were not making our way to St Martin but instead just fucking around in the middle of the ocean for no good reason. I was dreading seeing Luigi because I was so angry with him and I knew that he was mad with me and I also knew we had made very little progress on our last watch.

Sure, enough, as soon as I got to the cockpit Luigi ripped into me but I wasn't in any mood to take it and for the first time ever I ripped back into him and shouted that we needed to reef or reduce the size of the mainsail.

This was something Luigi hated doing although I had to do all the work so he argued with me until Ariel freaked out and told us both to shut up or she would do it herself. This was enough for Luigi to succumb and it was agreed that we would take a reef.

Now there are a number of ways that a crew might go about reefing the mainsail of a sloop. It all depends on the wind direction and the vessel's ability to be turned into or away from the wind. Ideally, you will bring the vessel to point straight into the wind so that it is not blowing hard onto the sail. The sail can then be lowered with relative ease and reset in its new smaller position.

However, this should have been done before we left and we all knew this. Once you are out in the ocean and thus at the mercy of the swell the whole situation changes because the boat will behave differently. This whole situation was a result of Luigi not calling for a reef before we left and we all knew it.

The problem now was that if we went head to wind we would also be head straight into the swell and this would cause such a pitching motion that the whole boat would become like a bucking bronco and it was likely to do a lot of damage to the interior.

The general solution to a situation like this is to employ a downwind reef. So instead of turning into the wind the vessel turns away from the wind and the mainsail is eased out enough to allow it to depower and again it can then be lowered and reset.

Without discussion, we knew this would be the course of action and I set to preparing for the reef. The first thing that needed doing, as we turned away from the wind, was to walk the leeward runner all the way to the shrouds where it was fixed in place and held out of the way while it was not needed. Actually, taking the runners forward was a normal job while sailing PKB as it is with any large sloop. However, it's far from a simple thing to do as I shall explain.

The runner is a large stainless-steel double turning block, attached to high on the mast with a static cable and with thick ropes running from it to a winch on the deck where it is controlled. To walk it forward I had to grab the ropes near the block and another person had to man the winch and make sure the rope could run through as I walked forward with the block.

This was always hard work as there was always a lot of drag from the ropes. So, in a normal situation, it was a tricky thing to do. Add to that the fact that it was a leeward rail (the side further from the wind), meaning that it was generally down close to the water level. When the yacht was healed right up, as it often was, the water level would be lapping up around your ankles as it washed over the deck.

Luigi loved to push the boat right over on its heel at every opportunity. Several times when I had been taking the runners forward he had pushed it harder and the yacht had heeled over so much that I was submerged up to my knees in water rushing by. This made an already difficult task much more difficult and again it was for no good reason.

There was no reason to heel the boat up when taking runners forward. All you needed was someone on the mainsheet to ease a little as the runner went forward. Ariel was always there and able to do so but only if Luigi ordered it. Which he never did. I'm sure he loved watching me struggle.

So, let's just reset the scene here. We are all super tired and angry. It's around 02:00 am and we are about halfway between St Martin and Antigua. The wind is about 15–20 kts and there's a decent-sized swell rolling through. There was a little moon and a mix of clouds.

As I set off down the leeward rail hanging on tightly to the runner with one hand and taking grabs at the guardrail with the other the yacht started heeling more. It was already well over enough for the waves to be washing down the scuppers but this was normal.

However, this time as a big wave caught me a little off guard the deck seemed to drop beneath me and all of a sudden I was almost completely submerged in rapidly rushing water. The load came on my hand holding the rail and I had to hold on with all my strength but somehow I held fast to both the rail and runner.

I was seriously pissed off and managed to scream at Ariel to ease the mainsail. Thankfully, she ignored Luigi and she gave me a good ease meaning the load came off the sail and the boat sprang upright again clearing me from danger. I completed my task and secured the runner then headed back to the cockpit.

Before I even got there, Luigi started shouting at me that I was always whining about stuff like this and I just needed to man up but this time I lost it and started yelling back at him.

Luigi and I yelled at each other for a moment until Ariel screamed at us to shut up. But not because she didn't want us to argue. Because she could hear something that she should not have been able to. It was the sound of breaking waves. Luigi always took complete charge of navigation and although I knew how to do it he never wanted to get me involved.

Somehow he had made an oversight and it transpired that we had strayed to within sight of a well charted reef with open rocks and breaking waves. It was only Ariel's keen hearing and presence of mind which saved us from being wrecked that morning.

By now, it was just light. We were all utterly exhausted but somehow we made it to a little bay on the north side of Antigua and dropped the anchor enabling us all to climb into our bunks and lick our wounds for a minute. But only for a minute. In only just over 24 hours, we had the owner arriving. The boat was a mess, we had no provisions and we were all ready to kill each other.

Well not all of us. It was shortly after this event that Ariel told me that she loved me for the first time. It was the first time any woman had told me that and it had always been one of the only things I had ever really wanted out of life.

Perhaps it's because she knew, as Luigi and I also did, that if I had not held fast and I had in fact been washed over the side then I was gone, see ya, adios, thanks for all the fish. The chances of them being able to turn around and come back and find me, at night, with a decent swell and only two competent sailors on board, was exactly zero. Still, I was young and in love and in many ways still living the dream. So, in the words of the great man himself…We continue.

8
Chased by a Barracuda

I think it would be fair to say that by the end of the season, the crew of the good ship PKB pretty much hated each other. But not Ariel and I whose relationship had not only survived these last few months but had somehow flourished. We were very much in love and as such never actually that far from living the dream. However grim it might have been at times.

By the end of the season, Ariel and I had decided that we wanted off PKB ASAP. ASAP in this case meant the moment the last charter guest was off the boat we were close behind. We had both been on a good wage for some time now and with all our living expenses covered that money had been accumulating in the bank. Add to that the tips. Wealthy people love to tip and on yachts, the tip is a big part of the charter game.

There is an expectation on the part of the captain and crew that the guests will tip. It's an expected norm. However, it's not written into any contract (or at least it wasn't in my time) and is entirely at the discretion of the guests. To put this into context I'll give you a couple of examples of how things might go.

In one instance, I was tipped 500 euros for four hours work. That was on top of my wage. To be clear I wasn't working as a crew member exactly at that point but I was actually a DJ for a small private party on a large charter yacht. I was reminded of this by the foxy stewardess who was keeping an eye on the guests and hanging out close to where I was DJing.

I asked her where the crew usually smoked on board as I fancied a quick puff and she said, 'Well, we go to the aft deck but you're not crew, so, you can smoke wherever you want.'

My wage for that gig was similar to the tip so I can say that that was the most I've ever been paid per hour.

On another large charter yacht, I worked on, the crew decided to throw a party the evening after one of the charters was finished. We (the crew) had confirmation that a nice tip had been received and during the course of the party, two bottles of the yacht's very expensive champagne were opened and consumed. It was me who got them out of the fridge, but I didn't open them.

When we received tips from the captain, we were informed that five grand had been deducted from the overall amount to cover the cost of the champagne…Ouch. I don't think anyone even cared. I was so hungover when I got the news it just seemed to blur into all the other noise. What did get my attention, however, was an envelope full of cash from the other charters.

The third example was from the last charter of the PKB season. It was an Italian family who were lovely people. Unfortunately, by this stage of the season things had reached rock bottom between the crew and on a charter yacht, this is a very poor state of affairs. The charter was okay but there were several incidents including Magda serving them a cake which had come out of a packet.

They could tell by the taste it wasn't a real cake and asked her for the recipe which she obviously didn't have…whoops. Luigi also found himself alone with the family's adult daughter in the saloon one night after everyone else had gone to bed. They were caught making out by her parents a little later. Double whoops. The good ship PKB received zero tips for this charter.

This hurt Ariel and I as we had worked hard and not put a foot wrong. But this is the way with tipping. The tip has to be awarded to the whole crew or not at all. In truth, it's the only fair way but in this situation, it seemed very unfair to Ariel and I.

It would be reasonable to say that by this stage we had our sights very firmly fixed on what was coming next and that was to be a holiday for us. Yes, an actual holiday for us right there in the Caribbean. We didn't have a plan exactly because this was before the internet became more accessible and we had no way to find out what our options would be once we got off the boat.

What we did know was that we were going to be on an island which was full of amazing places to stay and things to do and we were CASHED UP. We also knew it wouldn't be hard to find some cannabis so we were ready to let the good times roll. Do you see what I did there? Roll? No? Never mind. All the stress from the last four months was ready to drop away the moment we got ashore.

To start with everything went according to plan. The only problem was that by now we really didn't even want to see or speak to Luigi but he was still captain of the yacht we were officially crewing on board. We did not have visas or permissions to be on the island as tourists and although this wouldn't present a problem in the short term we would not be able to leave the island without first checking out with the boat.

It was standard practice for the captain to hold on to all the crew's passports and just when we were leaving the boat to start our holiday this didn't really seem that important.

We each packed a bag of clothes, the sort of thing we thought we'd need for a Caribbean holiday, but all our main possessions remained on PKB. This did not amount to a huge amount of stuff as crew on charter yachts don't really need much. However, it was all we had and as such very important to us. As were our passports. Without which we could not leave the island.

Luigi took us ashore in the tender and as we departed he grunted something about seeing us back there in a week or so and was gone. We didn't care. All we wanted was to see the back of him and find ourselves a bar to have a drink in and a man to buy some weed from. As it was to happen we were to find everything we were looking for…And quite a bit more.

After a couple of beers, which tasted just about as good as any I've ever drank, and a quick chat with a couple of locals, we were in a taxi and on our way over the hill to a campsite we had been told about on the other side of the island. Being the year 2000 cannabis was still quite illegal and we always gravitated towards quiet places where we could smoke joints without having to worry. Too much.

It was always a worry. Everywhere we went and in everything we did. We were both perfectly able to function without cannabis but the simple fact is that we were both much happier people when we were able to consume a small amount on a regular basis. No matter where we were or what we were doing.

This obviously presented certain problems when travelling around the world. Ariel, however, had been doing this for about a decade already and had developed a very good sixth sense for buying or scoring cannabis.

The process was quite difficult for me to get my head around to start with as it basically involved finding the dodgiest part of whatever town we were in and lurking around there until we saw a person of a quite specific type. Shifty but not too shifty. Is that clear? Good.

Because it wasn't for let me tell you. Ariel was really good at this, however, and could just tell who to speak to and she never ever got it wrong. Without fail, wherever we went she always managed to get us cannabis in one form or another.

On one occasion, we had befriended a dealer in Vigo, Spain, near where we were living at the time and when we called him up, for about the third time that month, he informed us that he had had an accident on his scooter and was in hospital. However, it was still fine for us to go and see him.

Sure enough, he was up on the 10th floor of a big building but he had a private room and a bag full of cannabis and happily sold us some right there in the hospital. My most remote-ever score was actually in the middle of the Atlantic many years later.

I was doing a crossing as a crew member on the infamous Ramu motor yacht (we'll come back to that one later don't you worry) and about one week out on our way from St Martin to the Azores, we had run out of cannabis. We were getting towards the end of the bag of weed we had brought for the crossing and I mentioned this to one of the other crew.

A young man by the name of Chopsi who was from a small island far up a big river deep in the heart of Africa and Chopis was about as African as you get. Well maybe not but he seemed quite out of place on a yacht.

When I told him, I was running out of weed he gave a great big laugh and smile and said, 'Don't worry, I got plenty.'

He dashed off for a second and then came back with a carrier bag full and asked, with a massive grin, 'How much you want?'

We were over a thousand miles from the nearest land. I've always been quite proud of that score.

So back to the story. We had been told to ask for a chap called Winston or Whinny in order to obtain our beloved cannabis. So after we'd dumped our bags in the tents, just metres from a stunning Caribbean picture-perfect beach, we set about locating the said man. Now you might think that this was not much information to go on but you must remember that this is the Caribbean in the year 2000 and we were on one of the less densely populated islands.

Meaning that most of the island was jungle. There were only really a handful of locals and they all knew each other like family. So with hindsight, it's easy to see why Whinny came swaggering down the beach, strumming his guitar, within minutes of us arriving.

Whinny was about as close to a real Rastafarian as I ever got to know. I mean I didn't really get to know him as such but I know he saw something in us both that he admired and respected. One thing that he certainly respected about us was the vast quantity of cannabis that we consumed. The first time we chatted with him we said we wanted a lot.

He came back with enough to keep the pair of us going for about two days. Bear in mind we had just finished the season from hell and now had a chance to relax in paradise. We were pretty much chain-smoking from sleep to sleep.

The next time we saw him was the next day and when we told him we wanted more already he looked shocked and said, 'No way you guys must smoke more than I do.'

We were both deeply proud of that and took it as a compliment. After that, Whinny started coming to sit with us and smoke with us although he wouldn't smoke our joints because of the tobacco. He claimed it's against his religion because of the chemicals men had put on it.

Instead, he used his own tobacco he actually grew as plants. It was disgusting and I couldn't smoke his joints but it was fascinating to see how other cultures embraced cannabis.

Another interesting connection we made with him was through food. Ariel is a trained chef and she is really into healthy home-cooked food. This is actually something of a rarity in the Caribbean as it's mainly an American-dominated culture and most of the food we were used to seeing in supermarkets was processed American food which, frankly, is the stuff of the devil.

One evening Ariel had cooked us dinner, as usual, and as we were eating it Whinny came swaggering past. He was actually a very modest man but Rastas have this way about them which can come across as arrogance if you don't understand it. It's actually just a deep sense of pride and amen to that.

We called out to him and he came over to join us. Ariel naturally offered him some of our food as we had plenty and he shied away saying, 'No, no. I don't eat your food.'

Whinny was of the Rastafarian religion and as such he was forbidden to eat processed food, which he naturally assumed was what we were eating.

Obviously, this was quite offensive to Ariel and she jumped up saying, 'Hey man, don't judge my food till you try it. We have fish caught by Robert, rice and vegetables. Take it or leave it.'

Ariel's mother is a woman of colour and although Ariel's skin is as pale as mine she certainly has a robust character. Oh yes, indeed and that's what I liked about her. Well on our good days that was…

Whinny, however, was more than used to being shouted at by women and just looked curiously at the food. I encouraged him extolling the virtues of the Spanish mackerel I had speared the day before and that I was now eating. Without saying another word Ariel just dished him up a plate of fish, rice and veggies and thrust it at him with a fierce glare. Of course, after the first bite, he cleared the plate without another word.

He came back and ate with us several more times and he also played his guitar and sang for us a few nights. I recall sitting on the beach one night with Ariel in my arms, both of us staring at the stars while Whinny sang reggae love songs to us and we happily puffed on joints and made out.

At that point right, there all the months of previous stress seemed to fade into insignificance and I think that it's fair to say that it ranks as the most romantic moment of my life to date. To date, I said. There's still time and room for improvement.

And now, yes finally, we come to the story's namesake. One of the great things about working for Luigi, and yes I should point out at this stage that Luigi is, in fact, a good man who found himself in a difficult situation and did not deal with it very well. I think many of us can hold our hands up to that. I want to make it clear that I have no grudge against Luigi or anything like that.

I mean he did try to kill me several times but I think it's fair to say that many people in the past have wanted to do the same thing. They just didn't get the opportunity to try.

So yes, as I was saying, one of the good things about working for Luigi was his passion for free-dive spearfishing. I'd been introduced to this the previous summer in the Mediterranean. Being a surfer and strong swimmer, I'd taken well to the long deep dives required to find fish. I'd actually found I loved it.

In order to catch fish this way, one wears a camouflaged two-piece divers wetsuit. One also wears a heavy-weight belt, super long freedivers' fins, a knife, a torch and of course, a speargun. It's a lot to manage in the water and takes some time and practice to get under control. In the Mediterranean, there are very few fish these days and that's just a sad fact.

Spearfishing is still a popular sport but it takes much more skill to find fish. In the Caribbean fish of all sorts were plentiful, as were sharks, but out of all the hundreds of varieties of fish commonly found around the islands only a handful was edible. These were generally found in small caves quite deep down.

The approach was to lie flat on the surface, facing down and breathing very slowly and deeply through a snorkel. One steadily builds up more and more air in the lungs and also lowers one's heart rate to consume less oxygen. At the right moment, you commence your dive which is achieved by long slow kicks of the fins. No arm movement because you have a speargun in one hand and a torch in the other.

You need the torch because it gets dark quickly down there. Once you reach negative buoyancy (at about five m down) you just start to drop like a weight. It's an extremely frightening feeling the first few times but you quickly realise it's the only way to get down deep. You don't have to kick to go down and that way you are using the minimum of your supply of oxygen.

It is actually really quite stunning how long it is possible to hold your breath. Why don't you challenge yourself right now? I'm going too. It's been years since I had to hold my breath but I'm going to do a quick check now just to get a reference. Use your timer on your phone and do the same. Ready. Go. Well, I did 43 seconds. Not bad but I was just sitting still.

Any amount of movement will use the supply of oxygen quicker and so now imagine taking one big, long gulp of air and then diving. After a few kicks of your legs, you are then just dropping for between 1–10 seconds. I learnt how deep I could go through a steady process of practising. It wasn't just a case of throwing myself down a hole and hoping for the best.

All through the Mediterranean season on IKRA, I had been forced to watch while Luigi and his first mate Donny went off on fishing expeditions. There had been enough kit for me to gear up and go free diving at least and that way I had learnt the freediving side of the sport. Now, I was in the Caribbean. I was able to purchase my own speargun and it was time for me to catch some fish.

Sure enough, I had a whole range of adventures over the course of the season but somehow managed to stay alive and even catch some really nice fish. I was quite good at it actually and really enjoyed the challenge of something so physical that also involved both engaging nature and catching dinner. I really loved eating the fish I had caught this way and used to say that my favourite bit of the fish was the hole from the spear.

With hindsight, I can say that I think I was bloody lucky to come away unscathed. I certainly had some close calls, as I will elaborate on more at a later date. But I can say I saw a shark that was a lot bigger than me and I also came face to face with a massive barracuda.

I had brought my fishing gear with me from the yacht and had been waiting for a good time to swim out to the reef a short way off the beach and have a good dive around it. It took about 10 minutes to swim from the beach to where I could make out the reef by a series of rocks breaking the surface.

There turned out to be a maze-like series of corridors in the rock that were just teaming with fish. I shot a couple of Spanish mackerel quite quickly but what I really wanted was a Grouper as they were the best eating and our prize prey.

The normal system for keeping the fish that one catches in this way is to put them in a net bag which is attached to a float which is attached to oneself by a long thin floating line. However, in the Caribbean, there were a number of reasons not to do it this way. Firstly, blood from the fish will attract sharks and secondly, the float will alert others to the presence of a fisherman.

Great you say and isn't that what it's meant for? Well yes and no. The problem in the Caribbean is that spearfishing is not permitted on some of the islands. Luigi didn't seem too concerned about this and I only actually found out about halfway through the season. In fact, to put that into context, one time Luigi told me that in Italy it wasn't considered a problem to commit a crime.

The only problem was to be caught…As such he just always stuffed the dead fish up in between the two layers of the wetsuit in front of the stomach. Although a bit gross this actually worked well in practice and one could get quite a few fish up there. The only problem was they would continue to wiggle after they were supposed to be dead and this is one of the more peculiar sensations I have experienced in my life. It's a little like having something alive inside you.

I had already caught two Spanish mackerels and a couple of Red Eyes as well. It was a good catch and I should have been swimming back to the beach. But I wanted a Grouper so I was still out on the far side of the reef…Cruising…Hunting…Or maybe it was me that was being hunted?

After a deep dive and unsuccessful shot, I was slowly floating back to the surface surveying my surroundings when I saw by far the biggest fish I had ever seen. And most of it was mouth, well jaw really. It was a barracuda and a relatively large one. It was stationary. Just floating there staring. Staring at me.

Now, in a normal situation, a person wouldn't have any reason to fear a barracuda. They are not a threat to humans and although they have the potential to maim or kill they are not known to attack humans as we are not prey for them. However, on this occasion, I was stuffed full of juicy dead fish.

Juicy smelly fish. Smelly that is by its blood which predator fish can smell a long way off. This barracuda could smell the fish in my wetsuit and I'm pretty sure it fancied a taste as well.

I reloaded my speargun hastily which in reality would have been of little defence against a determined attack by a creature like this. Nonetheless, it made me feel better and I started to swim away from it while still facing back towards it with the spear gun pointing at it. It followed.

Fuck. I started to panic. Never before or since has something in nature taken this kind of interest in me. I can assure you it's not the kind of interest you want anything or anyone to ever take in you. Most especially when considering my current location.

I was on the far side of the reef meaning I was a fair distance to the beach and safety. I started swimming faster and the bloody fish did the same. I decided to take more drastic action and the only thing I could think of was to kick my fins really hard and make a big commotion in the hope of scaring it off.

This I did and as I continued swimming away I could see the cloud of bubbles slowly dispersing and there, yes there, was my mate Barry. I swear it was grinning and I can still see it clear as if it was yesterday. Well maybe not but it's pretty clear. Coming through the bubbles with a determined grin on its hideous face.

Now, I panicked and decided to just try and swim to the beach as quickly as possible. I turned to do this and came straight into one of the sort of stone corridors of the reef. It was like a sort of maze and in a proper fluster, I careered through those channels until I spat out the other side and was able to just swim like hell for the beach. I never looked back again.

Either I was going to make it to the beach or it was going to…well, I didn't think too much about that and just swam.

I crawled onto the beach and up a short way and just lay there panting for a few minutes. One of the local women who worked on the campsite was walking past. She stopped and looked at me and it was one of those looks that anyone can read a mile away.

She grinned broadly and cried out loudly, 'Stupid little white boy getting into trouble…Again…Ooh Lordy, help us.'

She walked off laughing loudly and left me sprawled on the sand. In my thick wetsuit, I was now rapidly overheating but all I could think of was what did she mean by "again"? Despite the scare, I was elated to have scored such a good catch and we really enjoyed eating those fish for the next few days.

After around a week of life on the campsite, we decided that we better think about locating Luigi. We took a taxi to the small port where we had departed PKB and hoped that they would be there. They were not and were nowhere to be seen. With no phones or internet, we had no way to contact Luigi and simply had to return to our campsite later that day.

Now, a sort of slow panic set in that would plant a big black cloud over the second week of our stay on the campsite. Each morning, we took a taxi to check and see if PKB was there but she was not. Each time we did this it cost quite a bit of money. Taxis were not cheap and it was a long ride.

There was another problem brewing. We were paying for everything with cash from our tips. Even though we had quite a bit we were going through, it quickly what with buying weed, food and paying for taxis every day. We both had a reasonable amount in the bank but also could not check this to be sure because our banks were on the other side of a large ocean.

The boat also owed us a large chunk of wages. However, at this point, this was owed and had not been paid. Added to that was the fact that I had been ordered to fly home for 10 days after my accident. Luigi didn't even give me a choice. He came to me and told me that I had to go home for a while and that I had to pay for all the flights myself and that the boat would pay me back at a later date. I never received a penny.

All these things added up meant that we were steadily starting to worry about money. Not a good thing when you are a long way from home, in a very expensive place to live with no income, friends or family. Suddenly we had gone from being super cashed up to having to worry about every expense. This was a pattern that was to be repeated in my life for the next 20 years.

Looking back, I can see how this was the first time that Ariel and I came unstuck. The problem was that we were very similar in many ways and one of those ways was that we both suffered badly from anxiety. Two people both suffering from anxiety make each other worse. Each acts like a catalyst for the other.

I've come to understand that what makes a relationship work is complementary differences. Ariel and I did have some of these but we also both suffered awfully from anxiety. When we both got it at the same time, it was not pretty.

Eventually, after about six days, when the taxi rounded the corner and the view into the bay opened up, there she was, PKB sitting at anchor. Looking back it seems so ironic that after being so desperate to leave the boat just a short time before we were now so happy to see it again. Luigi came ashore and we sat down with him for a very uncomfortable conversation. It was brief.

Luigi was never one for many words. There was no need to discuss anything now. It was an all-round mutual agreement that we were leaving. Our passports were placed on the table and Luigi got up and left without another word. A few days later we flew out of Tortola and it would be a few years before I would be back there again.

At this stage, I think it was fair to say that, Ariel and I had enough of boats for a while. Ariel owned an apartment close to my hometown back in the UK and we decided to head back there and lick our wounds for a bit.

Unfortunately, my vortex of chaos didn't seem inclined to stay in the Caribbean and followed me back to the UK instead. So don't worry. This story isn't about to slow down. In fact, it's just getting interesting.

9

The Beach Party

A few years later Ariel and I had relocated to the UK and had somehow ended up living on a 28 ft yacht in a grotty mud birth, down a dirty estuary in a dead-end town. Millbrook was a wonderful place in the early noughties. It was a really fitting place for a pair like Ariel and I to end up. Not because we were grotty, dirty or dead-end type people. Oh no. Quite the reverse.

Or so, we liked to think. Prior to moving onto the yacht, we had been living at Ariel's mother's house which was located in the country and was fairly sizeable. Ariel was from a good family and their estate was sufficient to accommodate us for a long enough period to work out that we did not want to share any kind of accommodation with her mother. No matter how commodious.

So, in typical Ariel and I fashion we had come up with the grand plan of buying a small yacht to live on and berthing it in Plymouth which was actually very close to where I was working in Ivybridge. At this point in my life, I had found myself working for Princess Yachts as part of a fit-out crew on an assembly line in one of their factories.

I worked there for around 18 months and my time there will be an extensive chapter of its own in later works. But for now, I'll attempt to give you a basic picture. The factory was manned by about 75 men and produced two powerboats. A 42 ft and a 49 ft speed boat.

While I was working there I did a number of different jobs but my main role, once settled, was cockpit fit-out on the V49. In fact, the term cockpit was a very loose label because I actually fitted everything on the deck. Well, most of it.

They taught me most of what I needed to know to be able to do this right there and then on the job. This meant a lot of stress and hard work for very little pay. Especially after coming from superyacht wages. I have a very mixed bag of feelings about that place when I look back. On the one hand, I hated every second I spent in the building.

On the other hand, I learnt a massive amount of boat-building skills and formed a decent understanding of how a production yacht is put together from start to finish. I also formed a number of friendships that I feel were a real compliment to me. The men who worked in that factory were some of the finest men I've ever worked alongside.

They had integrity and respect and all worked their asses off every day. One of them was actually one of the funniest people I ever met but that's another story.

In many ways, I was from a totally different world than the majority of the men who worked there. Chalk and cheese you might say. I'll be blunt and if you are from the UK, you will understand this. They were mostly working class and I am middle class.

Add to that, the fact that they were almost all from the Plymouth area and I was from Torquay, then add to that the fact that all of them were skilled tradesmen for whom hard work was just a way of life. Whereas I knew nothing about building boats but was claiming to have sailed all over the world on big fancy ones.

Now, you might think that this was going to be a recipe for disaster but in actual fact, the reverse seemed to be true. Somehow this tight-knit team of hard men really warmed to me. I'm sure a large part of it was simply because of my work ethic. It's been something that has carried me through hard situations in life many times and won me some good friends.

To put it in a nutshell, I am a grafter. When I am at work and on the clock, I am there to get the job done. There is one simple reason for this and that is that when one takes this approach to work the day generally passes much more quickly.

Before you know it, you are drinking a beer and smoking a joint with a day's wages in the bank or pocket. Of course, it's not always as simple as that but in general, I think it's fair to say that applying yourself to your work and finding ways to derive satisfaction from it is one of the keys to a successful long-term career.

Listen to me sounding like I know what I'm talking about. Ha…Successful long-term career…What would I know about that? Well actually, I did build one of those and it was only mental health issues that took it away from me. But I digress.

So, I was working in Ivybridge building these yachts and we had been living just a 15-minute drive away at Ariel's mums in South Brent. Bear in mind that at this point I didn't drive and Ariel had to drive me to work every morning and pick me up again. When we moved onto the boat in Millbrook, that commute became anything from 45 minutes (fastest possible) to an hour and a half depending on how the ferries were running and the traffic was flowing.

Both there and back were mostly done early morning and early evening. So, it was usually dark. For at least half the time I was working there, I didn't see daylight from Monday to Saturday as I would arrive before dawn and leave after dusk. I always worked Saturday morning overtime. I had to. I didn't have a choice about that.

This was the first, but not last, time I willingly put myself in a position of having to make a long commute to work. Let me give you a bit of advice. Don't ever do this if you can possibly avoid it. This commute will take over your life and ruin it. It certainly did ours.

Now if I was to write a comprehensive list of the reasons why my whole life situation was a complete disaster at this point then we would be here for some time. I will get to it later but for now, we have a story about a beach party to enjoy. So, let's get on with that.

Ariel had grown up all over the world but she had spent a lot of her teenage years around south Devon and still had some friends in the area. James and Elly were an amazing couple who lived in a stunning cottage way up on Dartmoor with their two kids.

Elly had been one of Ariel's best friends since school and one hazy August day Ariel announced that Elly's brother's mate's sister's friend's neighbour's cat was having a beach party somewhere near Salcombe. A plan was hatched to give Elly and her whole entourage a ride with us on Florence (our little yacht) from our base in Southdown up the coast to Salcombe where the party would be.

Elly had still not visited us on Florence although we were regular visitors with them and we all got on really well. So it all seemed a jolly good idea. Yes, yes.

Ariel and I had been taking Florence out on expeditions as often as possible although it was almost always a horribly stressful experience for us both and usually ended up with us fighting. Despite that, we kept going back for more at every opportunity. Perhaps it was the fact that we needed some justification for living on this tiny yacht miles from anywhere. Whatever it was, it just made things worse every time we did it.

We did have some success and covered a fair few miles together. We never had a major problem either. Just a couple of very close calls and a hell of a lot of minor ones that we were fairly evenly to blame for. This resulted in a lot of fighting but also a sort of stalemate that kept us thinking for a while that we might make it work.

Let's just consider a couple of things though. I was aged 26 by now. Ariel was 37. Yes, 37. Frankly, an age at which she should have been making a lot better decisions about a lot of things. I was still a naive boy and although I'm happy to hold my hand up to a great many mistakes I was still just a naive young boy.

However, that naivety was largely responsible for getting me into a great many adventures which have made me into the man I am today. Also given this book its content, so, I guess I can't complain. I will though because I'm British and it's my God-given right don't you know.

So, the party was on a Saturday night. The plan was for Elly and co to come to our berth at Millbrook and join us for the passage to Salcombe. Florence was 28 ft and very seaworthy so in principle there was nothing wrong with this plan.

However, one major difference between this trip and the ones we normally made was that we normally looked at the weather and tides and then, based on that information, a decision would be made about where we would go. This time we had a plan and weather and tides be damned we were going to Salcombe.

Florence had a good strong engine that could normally push her along at a steady seven kts. That is in calm conditions without any headwind or excess passengers. Ariel and I had been using the engine a fair amount in our trips but generally, we wanted to sail so we never actually motored all the way to a destination.

Accordingly, we didn't really have much of an idea how much fuel to expect her to use on a long passage like we were about to make. Add to that the fact that the wind was blowing quite hard from the direction we wanted to go into.

This meant that Florence's engine had to work harder to push her through the water. Add to that the fact that instead of two adults on board, we were going to be four adults and two children. Fortunately, they were quite a skinny family.

Before setting off, Ariel mentioned that it would be a good idea if I checked the fuel level in the tank. To be honest I wasn't that worried about this and only gave it a quick look. That was all I needed to see that it was just over halfway full.

As we hadn't filled it since we arrived on Florence and had done a lot of miles with her already this seemed like it would be more than enough for the coming trip. So, I declared that we didn't need to worry about fuelling up before leaving. Bad Bobby. Bad, bad, bad. Oh dear, oh dear. What had I done? Have I given any clue as to what's coming next? No? Not really? Okay, good. Then I shall continue.

We departed our berth under a sunny sky and the passage up to Salcombe was really quite pleasant and uneventful. The site of the actual party was on a normally inaccessible beach a few miles around the coast from Salcombe. The party would have DJs and a sound system and when we arrived a very serious team of people were working hard on lowering speakers and amplifiers down a cliff using ropes.

Yes really. We dropped anchor and by now the sun was already setting and it was quite late as it was mid-summer. Elly contacted her friends while we sorted our little RIB out and then we went ashore with Elly and her family. The beach was quite busy with people already and I have to say that arriving at a beach party from a yacht is most certainly the only way to arrive at a beach party.

Drinks were obtained and also ecstasy tablets. We swallowed them straight away as we both loved these kinds of party drugs. It wasn't long before Elly appeared asking if we could help get some of the sound equipment around from another beach using Florence's little RIB.

I was happy to help and spent the next couple of hours assisting with the whole process of setting up the sound system and tent. Yes, I was high as a kite while doing this but it didn't deter me in any way.

The party was an odd one. The sound system was at one end of the beach and from the moment it fired up it was just banging out the beats. Hard and fast. Just how I liked it. But nobody was dancing. Nobody except me that is. I love to dance and in clubs when I was high I would always seek out the stage or a podium.

This night was no exception and I danced alone, pilled off my tits, for most of the night. I didn't care that I was alone. The music was a bit too hard for Ariel's taste and she was with her friends so I just let go and went for it.

As is usually the way with parties like this the latter stages are somewhat blurry. Somehow we made it back to the boat and woke in our forward berth to full daylight and some quiet voices coming aft from the saloon. It transpired that some of the new friends we had made the night before were still high and swam out to the boat to wish us good morning. Only they had been polite enough not to wake us.

If you're not familiar with attending parties like this, then you will probably not be familiar with the way your head feels the morning after. We had only consumed a very small amount of alcohol so we were not hungover but instead, we had been munching on ecstasy pills and hash truffles. Yes, that's right, hash truffles.

Some of Elly's friends specialised in the production of these delicacies and generally, wherever there was a party they were there selling them. They were two, very well-to-do, middle-class ladies who you would never expect might get up to such naughtiness. I thought they were both hot and loved the truffles, which were strong and Ariel and I couldn't get enough.

Actually, at the end of one Glastonbury festival, they had a little surplus left over and we took what they had left for a very good price. As it happened we stopped at a friend's house on the way home and left some for him as he wasn't home. We just didn't think to tell him what was in them and…Yes, well, I'm sure you can work that one out. He had an interesting couple of days.

One of the good things about these truffles was that they seemed to work on a slow release. So basically, I was still high the next morning. I was probably also still a little high from the pills so yes…Not great as we actually now had a long passage home beckoning. However, it was the middle of summer and there was a clear blue sky and zero wind. So, in theory, it should just be a very simple passage motoring home.

It was Sunday morning now. Around 9:00 am. We needed to be back in our berth in Millbrook by that evening and we had a long passage to make. Add to that the fact that our berth was tidal which means that we had a time window inside which we must arrive in order to make our way up the estuary with a sufficient depth of water to keep Florence afloat.

Florence needed about five feet of water to stay afloat. The channel we had to navigate was bare mud for about half of every tide. Do the maths. Or try at least. Tidal navigation is a dark art and although we had the channel pretty well dialled it was always a challenge and always at the end of whatever adventure we had just had. But at this point, that channel was still a really long way away.

The good news was that there was not a cloud in the sky and it was already getting hot (that's good in the UK by the way). There was also no wind which was good in that it meant we didn't need to think about actual sailing but…Well at that point it only seemed good that we didn't need to worry about actual sailing.

We hung out with our new best friends for a while and then dropped them ashore. By now, I was feeling very hazy and also quite jealous of those that were carrying on the party. My thoughts were already set on work the next day and as such my state of mind was declining rapidly.

However, we were still vibing from the night before and had no reason to be concerned about anything untoward so once back on Florence we made ready for the passage.

The first thing we had to do was start the engine. This was a traditional-style diesel engine and had a key to start it just like with an old-style car. You put the key in and I think you had to turn it one way for about five seconds and then the other way and it would fire the starter motor which would fire the main engine. I turned the key like normal and nothing happened. Like nothing.

It didn't make a single sound. Ariel and I just stared blankly at the bulkhead where the key fitting was mounted. I tried again and it was the same. Nothing. Just dead. This was the first and only time Florence did this to us and we never found out why.

After a couple of minutes of just sort of trying the same thing, panic started to set in. For now, the weather was calm and we didn't need the engine for safety but that could change very quickly. Not to mention the fact that we had a long passage to make.

By now, it was around 10:00 am. My mind was blank but one thing that did occur to me was to try and disassemble the key fitting to see if I could locate a poor connection or something. In reality, it was a fool's errand but it was all I could think to do. Ariel suggested I try calling my uncle Pete who was a marine engineer on merchant ships.

He lived in Torquay which wasn't that far away and we knew that if we really needed he would come and sort it out for us. But that would take hours and we needed to get moving ASAP. We were already pushing it with our estimated arrival times for the channel.

What exactly happened next has always confused me but the simple fact is that it just suddenly started working. I tried the same thing I had been trying over and over and it just suddenly worked and the engine roared to life. Many prayers of thanks were offered and we were on our way.

Now we could relax a little Ariel sorted us some coffee and food while I rolled a joint. It was an absolute flat calm. One of those hazy summer days where the sky and horizon blur into one and you feel like this sunshine must last forever. We both sank into a relaxed sort of coma and I manned the helm while Ariel retired to the cabin for a nap.

This was by no means a normal thing for her. We both took equal responsibilities on the deck and would never leave the other alone up there for long. But on this day, with no wind and a clear blue sky, it seemed fine and we were motoring along happily enough, a couple of miles outside Salcombe when there was an almighty bang and the engine abruptly stopped.

In an instant, Ariel appeared and glared at me saying, 'I told you to check the fuel.'

I jumped below, lifted the steps, grabbed the torch and got down on my belly to get the angle to see the level indicator for the fuel tank. It was empty. At that moment, I couldn't comprehend how we could have possibly used all our fuel but the very clear and obvious fact was that we had.

Fuck, double fuck. In our favour was the fact that we were right at low tide meaning that there was zero tidal flow at that particular time. This was very lucky because, at the same location, there can be anything up to a six kt current running in either direction up or down the coast.

Not something you want to be at the mercy of. There was also still not a breath of wind. So, any idea of sailing home was right out.

What saved us was that it was a busy summer's day and there was quite a bit of other water traffic out and about. It didn't take us long to see a speed boat cruising up the coast not that far away so we started waving and shouting as loudly as possible. As luck would have it they saw us and immediately altered course to intercept us.

Once within hailing distance, we explained our predicament and a plan was formed to take me and a jerry can into Salcombe to fuel up while Ariel would stay with Florence. I was none too happy about the idea of leaving Ariel alone but there didn't seem to be any other option.

First of all, I had to get from Florence to this other boat. This is actually a very difficult thing to do out at sea as the two different vessels will always have different motions with the waves and will likely crash into each other causing major damage. Even in a flat calm like this, it was going to be a challenge and so we quickly decided that I would jump in the RIB and row over to them.

Unfortunately, I had my head on backwards and rather than getting into the RIB which we had been towing behind I just untied it and let it go.

Ariel just stared at me and said, "Robert WHAT are you doing?"

While the people on the other boat (a middle-aged man and two younger women) just looked bemused.

Somehow I managed to get the RIB back and make my way over to the other boat. They sped me into Salcombe where the fuel barge was thankfully open and filled my jerry can up with more than enough to get us home. Our saviours refused to take any money from us and once we had the engine going again they sped happily off leaving me with a very pissed-off girlfriend.

To say, I was unpopular for a while after this would be a minor understatement. However, we still had to get home and now we were right on the edge of the time window for making it up the channel.

The rest of the passage home was uneventful but we both had a rising panic about the approaching channel navigation challenge. Since arriving at our mud berth in Southdown marina every single time we had been in and out we had had some sort of issue. We never actually got stranded high and dry but we had more than a few close scrapes and this was certainly one of them.

The problem was that we needed to get up the channel to get into our berth to be able to go back to our normal work routine the next day. I needed to be in Ivybridge by 7:00 am, Monday morning. I took my job seriously and although I did pull the occasional sicky I was generally always on time come rain or shine.

Let's consider the process of getting up the channel. At high water, Millbrook basin is like a little lake with an open end which is out onto the river Tamar. There's plenty of depth of water for Florence to go anywhere in the basin. However, the moment the tide starts to drop this changes quickly. By the time the tide is halfway out, 50% of the basin is bare mud and there is only a very narrow strip of deep water remaining.

This winds up through the mud basin to the Southdown marina complex. This whole marina dries out and all the boats there are in mud berths. Depending on the tide and the draft of the vessel it is usually possible to get in and out a few hours either side of low tide. However, Florence drew a bit more than most craft her size and added to that she had a traditional long keel.

This meant that in the event of her grounding and drying out, she would end up leaning hard over on one of her hulls. If this happened on a flat bottom, it wasn't a massive problem except that the whole boat would be over 45 degrees on its side for the whole duration of that tide.

If the bottom was rocky or uneven, then who knows what might happen. It's not a scenario anyone really wants to be stuck in and fortunately, it wasn't one I ever did end up in. However, on this occasion, we came very close.

Considering all this it wouldn't have been a bad idea to have cancelled going home that night and instead just take a berth in one of the Plymouth marinas before then going home on the next high tide. But Plymouth berths were expensive and this would also mean me missing work the next day. So, we had a double incentive to try and do something that we should really have not.

The major risk in this event is that you miss the channel and ground. Then as the tide is flowing out the boat becomes more and more firmly stuck. Once there is no chance of moving and the water continues to drop away the boat will have to find its own home on the bottom. The channel has a steep bank on either side meaning that there is a risk of the yacht's keel getting stuck and the yacht ending up sitting at a very bad angle.

One which could damage the vessel or even mean it would be firmly stuck and would be engulfed by the next incoming tide. Clearly, the sensible thing would have been not to attempt the channel in the dark that night. But by now you are probably guessing that Ariel and I did not really ever do things the sensible way.

No, instead, we liked to make things as hard as possible most of the time. Not deliberately I should add. We wanted things to be easy but we made bad decisions that ultimately made our lives a total pain in the ass. Some people might call this a stoner mentality.

To start with it went okay and we were quietly creeping up the channel but then there was a slow thump and Florence came to a halt. Ariel always drove when we were manoeuvring as I was much better at handling the lines and securing the yacht once on the dock. We'd had a fair bit of practice by now and usually managed okay. She tried going hard in reverse but it was no good.

We were stuck. We were still towing the RIB so a plan was quickly formed for me to get into it, locate the channel and try to drag us back into deeper water because we were in pitch black by now and actually had no idea where the channel was.

The outboard was not even attached so we first had to get that out and fitted and then I sped off with a lead line (a weighted rope used for measuring depth manually) to try and work out where the water was deeper. All the while the tide is flowing out faster and faster and Florence is settling deeper into the mud.

I can't believe I actually managed it but somehow I did work out where the water was deeper and somehow I did actually manage to tow her off the mud and back into the channel and shortly after we were finally back on the dock. Safe and sound but utterly mentally and emotionally exhausted.

In the end, I was too tired and stressed out to go to work the next day anyway. Looking back, it was just another day in the life of Ariel and Robert. We careered from one disaster to the next until in the end I had enough and returned to France to find work on a big yacht.

Over the next few months, things went from bad to worse. Ariel and I had grown to hate each other by now. We fought bitterly every evening and both of us were drinking a lot more than was healthy. Our time was through. It was time for me to move on. I still had friends in Antibes so I made some calls, booked a spot on a sofa and flew back to the Cote d'Azur to look for a job on a big boat.

The only problem was that I had a severely broken heart. A large part of me had still been in love with Ariel. She was my first love and we actually both believed that, despite the age gap it could work and we could be happy long term.

Ultimately it was the age gap that forced us apart. We were simply at very different places in our lives but despite that, I hadn't wanted Ariel and I to actually break up. In my naivety, I imagined that once we had been apart for a while and I had earned a load of money we could get back together.

Ariel didn't see it that way. I found a job without a problem but shortly after she informed me that she didn't want me back. So, in the end it was a sort of mutual break-up and was very much for the best for us both.

Just to put things into context. I found out later that Ariel had started another relationship within months of my leaving. Actually, with someone who had been a mate of mine. That really hurt but at least I knew she was with someone I liked. However, for me, the break-up left me so heartbroken that it took me years to recover. Literally.

At this point in time, Ariel and I are not in touch. I've tried to contact her several times but I've not had a reply. What will be will be and it is what it is.

However, for some time, I've had this feeling that I will encounter Ariel again at some stage in the future. My feeling is that we may even find ourselves in competition of some sort. Who knows. Stranger things have come to pass.

10

Top Three Close Calls

No. 2 Adela's Bowsprit

After separating from Ariel and moving back to France, it took me just a couple of weeks to find my next job. In fact, I was to stay on this next yacht for two and a half years. The yacht's name is Adela and in my humble opinion, she is still to this day one of the most exquisite yachts afloat. I said something along these lines to the captain during the interview and he gave me a smile that was priceless.

I got the job as he could see that I would be a valuable addition to the crew. I was a fairly well-skilled marine carpenter/joiner by then as well as an experienced sailor. I'd worked with a few shipwrights as their assistant and had picked up a lot of useful skills along the way.

I joined Adela in the early noughties in the port of Cap-d'Ail. Cap-d'Ail is a strange place and hard to describe really. It's a sort of town located next to Monaco. It's not actually part of Monaco and is technically in France although the city of Monaco and the town of Cap-d'Ail merge into one and there is no border as such.

All I seemed to be able to see was a lot of luxury apartment tower blocks and a football stadium. There's also a marina and a large docking space for big yachts.

Adela most certainly qualifies as a big in terms of sailing yachts. Her length overall is 55 m. At the time, I worked on her that made her one of the largest private sailing yachts in the world. To this day she is still one of the most exquisite yachts afloat. I am deeply proud to have spent the time working on her that I did.

Although unfortunately for a large part of the time, I was crew onboard Adela I was very unhappy. It was another lesson for me that what you are doing is nowhere near as important as where you are doing it and who you are doing it with.

Actually, in this case the other crew on Adela were a damn good bunch of people. All except the captain and chief stewardess/chef who was also his wife. If you've spent any time around professionally crewed yachts, you'll know that this is an unpopular arrangement for those who work below them.

Again, my time aboard Adela will make an extensive chapter (or several in fact) all of its own in a later work. However, for the purposes of this story, I will give you some context.

Adela was (and still is I believe) owned by an elderly American couple. At the time I worked for them, they were officially very high on the Forbes list. Like most seriously wealthy people the vast majority of the general public have never heard of them. They were actually able to walk on and off the yacht without any attention.

Nobody had a clue who they were and despite being two of the world's uber elite they were able to walk down a busy city street without looking any different from anyone else. And they did. They didn't take on airs or graces or feel the need for any kind of security which with hindsight is pretty mind-blowing really. It was something that, as crew and essentially their servants, we liked about them.

As deck crew, in general, I had very little to do with them. Our responsibilities were to maintain the deck and drive the tenders. Note I didn't say anything about sailing there. That's because the only time we sailed with them aboard was during the Maxi Cup. We would often see them and say hello and Missis would sometimes stop by for a brief chat but I never exchanged a single word with Mr other than hello.

However, I will share this with you. One day I was fixing the sill of a door on the deck near to where they were sitting. I could hear them but they could not see me and were unaware of my presence. They had their "business manager" with them and they were discussing the price of a company they wanted to buy.

I never heard the actual total price but they were discussing the price going up or down 40 million dollars. It sounded like how we might discuss something going up or down 10 or 20 dollars in price.

Their general practice was to use the yacht for two trips each summer. One in the mid-summer and one in the later part of the season which always culminated in the Porto Cervo Supermaxi Cup. I raced on Adela twice in this event and the whole experience ranks as one of the most mind-blowing things I was ever a part of. To witness this spectacle alone is awe-inspiring.

To be right at the heart of it, an integral part of the crew on one of the biggest and most stunning yachts, was a dream come true. One of many dreams that I managed to achieve as it happens.

Unfortunately, as is so often the case, the reality was nothing like the dream. The good thing about memory is that it's very good at blurring out all the crap and only recalling the good bits. For the purposes of my writing, you'll be pleased to know I recall it all in vivid technicolour detail.

In fact, this would be a good time to have a quick chat about memory and if you'll allow me I'm going to give you some of the philosophy I've formed for myself over the last few decades.

You see, I'm not really too interested in what other people say. I'm very interested in what they do but not so much what they say. Even less so if it's not first-hand. The fact is that you generally find that the two things are not the same. Accordingly, I've gone through my life looking at what other people say and then working out for myself if I find there to be any truth in it.

The fact is that the vast majority of the so-called knowledge I was given as a young man was utter rubbish. *Utter rubbish.* About 10% of it is true I would say. The paradigm we have in place around the western world at this time is very good at taking 10% truth, adding 90% lies and then presenting it as fact. The 10% truth is all that most people need to be carried along with it.

Without meaning to sound arrogant, I am not like most people. Every single person who has ever gotten to know me has said that I am utterly unlike any other person they have ever got to know. I used to see this as a failure but now I've come to cherish it. So, it didn't take me long, as a young man, to fall off that particular train.

'What particular train, Bobby?' I hear you cry. 'What the devil are you talking about man?'

Well, I'm not going to go into it too far right here and now but maybe this is a good chance for me to share what I have derived as my own personal philosophy on life, the universe and everything. It goes like this:

'Learn as if you will live forever,
Laugh as if it's your last day alive,
Trust nobody
Question everything
Dive deep,
Reach the bottom and keep digging.
Make a hole in the heart of things,
Only the Fool is Free.'

For some time now, I've had a strong belief that our brains are in fact recording every sensory input they receive. Every single one. In exactly the same way, a computer would. They are all logged and filed away for potential future use. To my mind, it stands to reason that if we can remember some things then we must actually be able to remember everything.

I know that our "so-called knowledge" about the brain says that there's a system by which the brain decides what to record or not. But if that were true, why then are some people so much better at remembering than others? Or more specifically they are able to access the information more readily.

Some people have what's called photographic memories and are able to look at a whole page of text and be able to recall it all at will for a given period after. Apparently, one of my cousins is one of these people and has this gift. As far as I can see (which I admit is not that far) this goes right in the face of what science says about this subject.

If you think about it, then it's clear that a lot of our whole paradigm revolves around the use of memory. It's the key to our education system and in many fields, it's essential to be able to remember massive amounts of knowledge in order to be able to perform one's profession. So, we certainly have an understanding of the relative importance of memory.

All of our schooling revolves around it. We are taught to remember information and then tested on our ability to reproduce this data. Those of us who show capacity for this are rewarded with qualifications and given careers. If that's what they want.

However, I feel something is missing and, as usual, there is an imbalance. If so much importance is based around memory, then why are we not actually looking at the function itself and working harder to improve this specific skill? Maybe that happens in school today? Do they now have a class for English, a class for science, one for maths and a class for memory? I seriously doubt it.

Obviously, at this point in history, we are moving into a time when we are quite happily using our memories less and less and letting technology do it all for us. Let me give you some important information. *Memory is a muscle. Use it or lose it.*

The more you allow your technology to remember stuff for you the less you will be able to do it yourself. If a trend like this is allowed to continue, then before long nobody is going to be able to remember much more than their own name.

At this time though, as far as I'm aware, schools still expect students to be able to remember large amounts of data and then to be able to recall it again under exam conditions. But why are we not working harder on this skill of memory more specifically? Well, if I was to answer that question then we would be opening a very large can of worms and it's most certainly not going to happen here and now.

Humour me and allow me to propose a hypothetical scenario. What if we all could remember everything we ever said, did and heard? With no effort. It's all right there. If you were asked what you had for lunch on this day 10 years ago, you would be able to know exactly in an instant what you ate, what the weather was like, and what you watched on TV that night.

Just as you can for the day before. Think about how this might change your life. It's quite hard to really because the concept is so alien. Yet we do it in dribs and drabs, here and there all day every day.

I find that the more I try and use my memory the better it gets. Which fits with the muscle analogy. Clearly, for the purposes of writing this book, it's my principal tool and it's been really interesting, so far, finding what I can and cannot recall. It's so curious how some parts of the stories are as clear as if they happened yesterday yet what happened just five minutes later is a complete blank.

I think our brain must have a system of prioritisation as and when it receives new data input. In fact, the more I think about our brain in this way the more it starts to appear as though it is often working, just like a computer, in the background, doing all sorts of tasks without the conscious part of our brain having any awareness.

Sorry I keep saying this but this will be a topic I come back to much more later because I think every single human on this planet is walking around with a supercomputer in their skull and very few people have even the vaguest concept of it. Instead, we all go to work all day to earn money to buy a computer to do it all for us. There now. I did say I might give you something to think about.

So yes back to Adela. I covered a fair few sea miles on her but almost all of them were under the motor's power. Despite having six able crew to sail the yacht, the captain very rarely let us hoist more than a stabilising head sail. We were all keen sailors which is why we had chosen this career path so this was incredibly frustrating.

If anyone reading this is young, really enjoys yacht racing and is thinking about a career on superyachts then let me give you a bit of advice. Don't do it unless you already have no other option. You don't need any school qualifications is one bonus, however, my advice would be this.

If you really enjoy sailing, then work hard to get yourself a good job so that you can buy your own boat. Then you can sail it where and when you want with whomever you want. If I could wind back the clock that is most certainly what I would do.

The sad fact of life as a crew on superyachts is that you spend all your time living and working on stunning yachts. Also being surrounded by them. But you actually do very little sailing. Instead, you spend most of your time preparing other people's yachts for them and very rarely spend any time sailing yourself.

Unfortunately, in my experience at least, many of the owners of big sailing yachts are not actually that fussed about sailing them and the captain is often of the same mindset. Sailing a big yacht usually involves a lot of hassle and a lot of potential risk of damage to the yacht itself and also to its crew. From the captain's point of view, why would they risk this unless they have a good reason? Fair enough when you think about it.

So, the vast majority of sea miles that I covered on Adela were under motor and I can confirm that once you've done a few miles offshore and out of sight of land, motoring along becomes very boring. An autopilot steers and the only role of the crew is as lookouts. The likelihood of seeing other traffic varied from certain to almost zero depending on where you were.

When passing through a busy shipping lane, you might need to alter course many times during the course of a watch. However, out in the open ocean, a vessel might cruise for a week or more without seeing a single other craft. I can confirm that the ocean is a bloody big place and once you've been out there for a while it gets very boring. That is until the weather gets bad and then it becomes scary instead. I hate to say it but I think about 99% of my time spent on passage as a professional sailor was either mind-numbingly boring or really frightening.

At this point, I don't feel like I'm painting a particularly good picture of life as a crew on superyachts. The simple fact is that it really can be an incredibly mixed bag. In any walk of life, there are pros and cons and I find that a useful thing to do is to try and look at a situation and do a realistic appraisal of these two opposing factors. Especially if you write them down, I find this to be a good way to weigh up the options.

Now, I promise you at some point soon I'm going to stop waffling and actually get on with the story and I suppose this is as good a time as any. The first summer season that I was crew on Adela we completed a voyage touring around the Baltic Sea. We actually left France in the Spring and cruised to Falmouth UK where the boat had been originally built.

We spent around a month in the shipyard there and then continued up the English Channel and around the top of Denmark. We then stopped in Helsinki for a couple of weeks to finally prepare the yacht for the owner's arrival in St Petersburg shortly after.

We cruised all around the Baltic for around two weeks with the owners on board and then made our way back to Falmouth before finally returning to France, mid-summer. We had around one month before the owners would return for another two-week trip before finishing the season at Porto Cervo. Sounds glamorous doesn't it? I was bored out of my brain for most of it. Most but not all.

During the return leg of our trip, while we were attempting to pass through the straits of Dover, we experienced the biggest waves I've ever seen at sea. And I've seen a few big waves. We found ourselves attempting to make our way into a large seaway that was wind against tide. Now I won't go into a lengthy explanation here and now of what this is but let's just say it creates big steep angry waves.

It reached a point where we actually buried the front of the yacht, almost up to the foremast, into an approaching wave. Take a look at a picture of Adela and just try and imagine the size of the wave that would have buried the front third of this yacht.

It was big and steep and on this occasion, the captain ordered us to turn around which was in itself no easy thing and run before the waves until we found shelter in a little cove nearby. All we had to do was wait a few hours and then the tide had reduced and we were able to motor through with no issue.

After Falmouth, we had to make our way through the notorious Bay of Biscay and then down to the straights of Gibraltar and then through the western Mediterranean up to Monaco where we would be berthing. We actually had a really nice trip after departing Falmouth. The captain was relaxing after all the stress of the Baltic and we managed to persuade him to let us get a few more sails up than usual.

We had a large but gentle following swell and the wind on the beam which made for very nice sailing with a big schooner like Adela. Actually, one of my favourite memories from all my time as a professional crew was at this time.

As we were making our way down the Portuguese coast the swell increased and Adela was able to take off and surf down each wave. It's really quite impossible to try and describe this with any degree of accuracy but I'll try. Despite being a 55 m yacht, this Atlantic Ocean swell was large enough to pick her up like a toy dinghy. Superyachts look so big in port but it's amazing how small they seem once out at sea.

As the wave would approach from behind it would actually tower up behind the boat, quite terrifying when viewed from on board. However, not being a breaking wave, it would pick the yacht up in a way that would expose the whole rig to more wind and as such the yacht increases speed and then starts to actually surf down the wave.

As this happens the yacht's natural tendency is to turn side-on to the wave. This is very dangerous and if allowed to happen can actually capsize a yacht.

Even one the size of Adela. Out on a big ocean swell, even a 55 m superyacht is just a little toy.

To counteract this turning the helmsman must put the helm hard over to keep the yacht in a straight line. As she straightens up she also increases in speed and we would watch the speed go from 11–12 kts right up to 15, 16 and 17 kts. That's really fast on something the size of Adela. She has a lot of volume below the waterline which equates to one hell of a lot of water being pushed aside. As the yacht becomes faster than the wave she reaches the trough in the bottom.

At this point, the helmsman must let the wheel go and allow it to spin back through his hands until it centres up again. This needs to all be done in exact unison between the yacht, driver and swell. As a helmsman, it's your job to be able to do this several times a minute for the duration of your time on the wheel.

It's a delicate skill and the penalty of getting it wrong could mean the yacht capsizing and the potential death of everyone on board. I'm totally serious about that. A mistake on the helm of a yacht that size in a situation like that could have catastrophic consequences. No pressure right?

Nevertheless, that watch when I was helming Adela down those swells is one of the best memories of my entire life. Not just my time as crew. I was totally confident in my ability to steer her and I would not have been there if I was not.

The feeling of controlling something that size and that powerful with so much at stake is quite a unique one and a memory I will always cherish. Was it worth all the months, no years, of bullshit? If you genuinely want to know the answer to that you'll have to find me and ask me yourself.

By the time we reached the bottom of Portugal and the corner of Spain, we had to turn into the wind to head up towards the straits of Gibraltar. Some of the non-sailor types amongst you may even have heard of the fearsome reputation of the Straits of Gibraltar. I've made my way through them five times and never actually had any bad weather in the straights themselves. It's all a question of timing really.

On this occasion, however, there was a large swell coming out of the straights with a solid blow pushing it along. As we were headed for Gibraltar this meant that we had to punch right into the teeth of it. When a yacht is motoring into a swell, it produces what we call a pitching motion. So basically, it's rocking back and forth, pivoting at a point around the middle or mid-ships.

So, in the middle of the boat, there is very little up or down motion but at either the front or back, bow or stern, there is a rising and dropping motion. As the boat is generally forcing its way forward with either power or sail it generally results in the front part of the boat raising up out of the water, as the wave passes under, and then slamming down into either the trough or the wave in front. Depending on the relative size of the boat and swell.

The first time one experiences this slamming it's easy to think that the sky has just fallen upon your head. Certainly, something must have broken the hull in two and we must surely sink. Actually, yachts are designed to absorb this impact (well some are in theory) and in general, although it's avoided where possible, a certain amount of slamming is just part of life on sailing yachts.

It's no secret that Adela has a very long bowsprit. The purpose of the bowsprit is to allow the yacht to set more sails. Often when those forward sails are not actually in use they are tied or lashed down onto the bowsprit to keep them tidy. Not just for the sake of neatness.

The sails are still attached to the yacht at one end but a large part of the sail remains free to flop over the side into the water where it would become a dead weight and be very difficult to retrieve making the yacht immobile until sorted.

Lashing sails down was everyday work for the deck crew. It's quite literally what we were there to do and as such we were all highly skilled with a range of knots and techniques for getting the sails under control, even in desperate circumstances.

So, we were approaching the straights of Gibraltar and I was on watch with Paul. Although Paul was a far less experienced sailor than me, he had been on Adela longer and as such was the watch captain. In reality, we didn't get on that well but in fact, did make a good watch team as we both took our job very seriously and that was all that really mattered. We were in good spirits after sailing the day before but this watch was starting to be a hard one.

It was just after midnight, there was no moon and despite the time of year and location, it was cold enough for us to be wearing full wet weather gear. We had been steadily slamming into the swell through the past few hours and, as was my regular habit, I went for a quick walk around up forward to check a few things. As I was flashing my torch around from the safety of the forward mast we did a really big slam.

The whole yacht shuddered for a second and then a flash of white up forward caught my eye. I shone the torch up there and yes, as I suspected, a couple of the lashings had come loose on the sail which was lashed down to the bowsprit. One had come off completely and the end of the sail was already flapping around which was steadily working the other lashings free.

In a situation like this, things can escalate very quickly and the key to fixing it is quick thinking followed by immediate appropriate action. In a split second, it was clear to me that the sail would need to be tied down again completely by hand. This would require at least two people who would both have to go out on the bowsprit to do so.

Now ordinarily, this was something we enjoyed doing. We had zero fear of the bowsprit. It had a large and well-maintained net for us to stand on as well as a rail along both sides that was easy to hold onto or could be clipped into in a worst-case scenario.

I got back aft rapidly and told Paul what I'd seen. Needless to say, he was not thrilled as we both knew it was going to be him and I that would have to go out there and sort it out. However, we couldn't do this alone and somebody must remain aft to hold the wheel while we worked up forward. The standard practice in this event was to wake Alex up, the first mate, who was currently in a deep slumber below in his cabin.

I went below and woke Alex up. I can tell you that being woken up with this sort of news does not go down well with anyone. After a short pause, he duly made his way on deck but as you might expect was far from alert or tuned in to the situation. We explained that the forward sail had come loose and we would need to re-lash it.

Alex made the call to back the revs right off while we were going to be up there. The thinking behind this was that it would mean that we were slamming into the swell less. It seemed like some sort of measure should be taken as we'd all seen the bowsprit punching through the waves the day before and it was clear that Paul and I could not be exposed to that.

On a big yacht like Adela, we had never once previously had to wear a safety harness. Adela has a waist-high, solid bulwark all the way around the deck so she's really quite safe, relatively speaking. However, the moment we stepped outside that and onto the bowsprit we would have only a thin net between ourselves and the water. A thin net and our ability to hang on tightly. An ability which already saved my life on a few occasions by now.

But this time we were going to be working on a sail which was going to need both our hands so, despite the inconvenience, we both donned the chest harnesses, got psyched up, climbed over the rail and out onto the netting. I can tell you that right now just thinking about it is making my hands sweat.

We both clipped the end of the lanyards to the rail on the bowsprit, made our way to the sail and started working on getting it under control. Adela had powerful foredeck lights so we had good visibility of what we were working on. What we could not see was the ocean beneath us and I suspect if we had we might not have even been there. The only thing that gave away what was about to happen was the motion of the vessel.

When you reduce the revs, the boat will slow down and come to a virtual stop. However, this does not in any way stop the pitching motion. Rather a new one starts slowly at first and then builds up as rather than punching into the waves the boat is just sitting there and riding them.

As I was working on getting a knot as tight as possible I became aware that we were rising rapidly. A bit like the feeling when an elevator starts going up. A part of my brain actually registered this but I couldn't react.

The rising stopped and very shortly after we started to drop rapidly back down. Right then Paul and I were hit by a solid wall of seawater that fully engulfed us and the whole bowsprit and we were both hurled bodily backwards until the lanyard came tight and stopped us right at the back end of the netting. Easily 10 ft back. Stunned, it took me a second to register what had happened.

I managed to get back to my feet just as Paul did so as well. We both looked at each other but didn't say a word. We still had a job to do. The sail wasn't yet fully lashed down so we both climbed back to the front end where the final lashings were needed and worked hard to get it done.

Just as the final lashing was in place the rising sensation started again but this time worse. Again, we didn't even see it coming but were struck by a solid wall of fast-moving cold sea water. This time the impact slammed Paul and I into each other and our heads banged together.

Again, we both found ourselves right back at the far end of the netting with the lanyard tight back to the metal rail where it was clipped. That rail was made out of 10 mm stainless-steel and the force of the impact created a big U-shaped curve in it which was still there when I left some years later.

Having actually finished the job we quickly climbed back into the safety of the deck. We looked at each other but didn't say anything. We headed back to where Alex was waiting at the helm but from all the way back there he had not even seen what was happening.

Had we not been wearing harnesses or if something had broken then we would have been gone without a word or a sound and Alex would not have even been aware for a good long while. We didn't tell him right then what had happened. It was the end of our watch by then anyway.

Once back down below I was stripping off my soaking wet clothes and I said to myself very clearly. Never ever again in my life will I put the safety of a sail over my own. Of course, I did. I had to on a daily basis. All sailors do. It's just an inherently dangerous job.

Looking backwards it's easy to point the finger at Alex and say he should not have sent us out there. But the fact is that the sail needed sorting. It was a job that had to be done. It didn't matter if we woke up all the rest of the crew and had them help. Two people still needed to go out and do the work and there was only one other way to prevent the pitching motion in a seaway like that.

To prevent pitching the vessel would have to turn "beam on" or sideways to the swell which would instead cause a rolling motion. This can be just as dangerous and in the situation we were in was just not possible. We were approaching the straits of Gibraltar at night and there was shipping all around us. To turn the vessel beam on would have required waking the captain and then explaining to him that his crew were too scared to go out on the bowsprit.

That's simply not going to happen. So, you see the situation was, in effect, unavoidable. Well, it could be argued that the bloody sail should have been lashed down properly in the first place. But anyway. Let's not get into that right now.

Next up we head to Portofino, one of my favourite places in the world, and I'm going to be having my first serious encounter with the weather. Despite all the miles I've sailed, the worst weather I've seen by far has all been in the northern Mediterranean. It's an area of water that is so benign so much of the time but when it gets mad, oh lordy it gets mad.

As I was about to find out. Did my vortex of chaos have anything to do with it? In this case, I actually think not. But I'll let you decide for yourself. See you there. Oh, and dress smart, please. It's quite posh there you know.

11

Brown Sky in Santa Margherita

You may recall that in the previous chapter, I said that I was unhappy for a lot of the time I spent on Adela. Now I really need to balance that statement out by saying that I also had one hell of a lot of fun during that period. For one thing, I learnt to snowboard and for the next three winters, I would spend every available moment in the mountains. Plus, every other unavailable moment absorbing movies, magazines and any other media I could find on the subject.

I also started playing regular DJ gigs at a very cool and trendy bar in Antibes that some of you may have heard of...The Blue Lady. I was actually the first person to ever DJ live in that venue. I'd been working there periodically for a few years already but now I had some money and I'd invested in a Mac laptop.

This had led to me discovering the world of digital DJing which blew my mind as to the creative potential the platform offered.

Prior to that, I had been a vinyl-only DJ. Saying vinyl-only is a joke because when I started DJing there was only vinyl. There were some very basic CD mixers around but if you wanted to be a DJ and play out in public you needed a collection of vinyl.

And good vinyl because in my hometown alone there were three specialist vinyl record shops catering to a large community of talented and active DJs. To get a public gig you had to have good tunes and know how to mix them with old-school beat matching.

When I went off to work on boats, my DJ career was really taking off but simply had to take a sabbatical. At the point when I left, I was actually in a position where I could have pursued a career as a professional DJ. I'd been working in a local bar/nightclub for a couple of years and had built up a very good range of contacts and a solid reputation as a good DJ who always brought the bangers.

Fortunately, my desire to travel the world was far more pertinent than my desire to be a hometown hero. Considering how my life panned out later I think it's a very good thing I chose the path I did.

So, life on Adela should have been, well, living the dream and in many respects it was. The only problem was that I was broken-hearted. For the first year (yes year, I took this very hard) after breaking up with Ariel, I just desperately missed her and wanted her back. Once it finally settled in that that wasn't going to happen I just sank into a deep depression.

I spent all day, every day, surrounded by people I really liked doing a job I should have loved but I was totally miserable. I had a higher wage than ever before in my life and was living on a superyacht in the south of France. Yet somehow my spirits were at their lowest since my mid-teenage years.

My way of coping with this was to drink, smoke, swallow and snort whatever I could get my hands on at every possible opportunity. Except when snowboarding that is. Well to be honest I was usually high when I was doing that as well. Literally and metaphorically. I never actually got drunk while I was riding though…Well that's not entirely true, is it Bobby? No…Okay so I had a hip flask with cognac, and we would always have beer or wine with lunch.

Add to that the fact that no day on the hill is complete without a cigarette box full of PRs.

'Hey Bobby, what's PR?' I hear you ask.

Well, a PR is a "pre-rolled" joint. During a day of snowboarding, one finds oneself spending a lot of time on chairlifts. Often while enjoying stunning views of the mountains. To me that represented the best possible time and place to smoke a joint and I took advantage at every possible opportunity. However, joint construction in said location would be, err, challenging to say the least.

Now believe me, I have constructed joints in some very precarious situations. It's one of the core skills of any serious cannabis consumer. But all things considered, even attempting to roll one on a chair lift was just taking things a bit too far. Therefore, the PR was the solution.

Cannabis also made the perfect companion to snowboarding. Alcohol takes away a person's sense of consequence and as such they lose a lot of their fear. This might help some people to ride better but it will also impair your mental and physical ability. Cannabis on the other hand makes you a little more cautious but it also makes you a lot more relaxed and that's what helped me.

I'd picked snowboarding up quickly having been surfing and skating most of my life. I couldn't believe how similar it was. However, this meant that I was also pushing myself into some situations that I wasn't really experienced enough to be in considering I was in the mountains which is a specialist environment all of its own. Cannabis helped me to chill and take a more relaxed approach to riding which, with hindsight, probably saved my life on more than one occasion.

Therefore, the tradition, the night before a day on the hill, was to roll a bunch of joints that were ready to be smoked on the chair lifts the next day. PRs. There's nothing quite so satisfying as charging down a run, jumping on a four-man lift with your mates, pulling out a PR and sharing it between you all as you reascend for another run.

In fact, many new friends were made this way, cannabis being the social thing that is. So, you see I would have had to try pretty hard not to enjoy that. And I did enjoy that. Very much indeed.

So, life on Adela was a mixed bag. During the off-season (October to June) the yacht generally stayed put in one spot and the crew took care of maintenance. I spent three off-seasons on Adela. One in Cap-d'Ail, one in Cannes and one in Falmouth.

For the deck crew, the bulk of the work for this period was varnishing. Adela is covered in stunning teak joinery which is all covered in many layers of golden varnish. A large part of the crew's annual work is the maintenance of this varnish.

Now as much as I love varnishing, and in fact became highly skilled at it, it is also incredibly boring and requires about as much thought as farting.

The crew worked a regular working week meaning 8–5 Monday to Friday. We also had to have a person officially "on watch" at all times and this was organised via a dreaded rota. It was the watchman's responsibility to remain on board and be "vigilant" for a 24-hour period.

During this time, you had to complete checks around the vessel, fill out logs, answer the phone, clean the crew heads (bathrooms) and mess (relaxation area) and tidy up after breakfast, lunch and dinner. It wasn't a big drama really but the main gripe was simply that you had to remain on board during the evening.

It wasn't like we all went out and got drunk every night. Not at all. Just most nights. We also didn't always feel like going out and so got drunk on board a lot and in general, as the watchman, it was considered the done thing to get as drunk as possible as a way of drowning your sorrows for being stuck on board when everyone else could go out and get drunk. As supportive crew members, it was often the done thing to remain on board and keep your poor-stricken watchkeeper company. What goes around comes around after all.

Of course, all the crew lived on board and so after getting drunk in a nearby bar or club they would then come back to the boat and usually carry on the party.

If you were on watch when this happened and had had the nerve to not get drunk and actually be in bed asleep when the horde got home, then you would be dragged bodily out of your bed by drunken thugs who would force feed you beer and cheese from the fridge. As such it really made sense to pre-empt this and just be drunk and ready for them when they arrived.

Actually, just writing this is making me cry laughing at some of the recollections of the shits and giggles that used to go on. High jinks don't even start to sum it up. I gained a solid reputation for being found in a drunken slumber in the most unusual places onboard. In the heads (there was a video of that which became legendary), crew mess, galley, pump room, nav station etc.

I also proudly laid claim to the fact that I had fallen down the main companionway ladder, which is quite a drop, with a full pint of beer that I'd carried back from the pub and managed not to spill a drop. Some feat I tell you, yes, yes.

The key to the harmony on board was the fact that we all got on really well and actually took our jobs very seriously. Despite all of this excessive debauchery, I don't recall a single serious argument. For sure, there were tons of minor scuffles and the odd harsh word but for the majority of my time on board, the crew were a super tight-knit family.

Credit for this has to go to the man who was responsible for all the rules that we hated and made life so tedious, or so, we thought.

Clive (the captain) might have been a grumpy old sod but he knew how to pick a crew and that's for sure. As a crew, we also faced our fair share of trials and tribulations when manning Adela. Not just when sailing her I should point out.

A yacht the size of Adela is quite simply one great big, massive cluster fuck waiting to happen at any time. Anyone who has spent any time around big yachts will be nodding sagely right now. The only time this is not true is if she is out of the water and on dry land. The moment a yacht this size hits the water she is at the mercy of the elements. With a massive schooner rig, Adela carries one hell of a lot of windage.

This means that the masts act like sails and when it's windy, even with no sails up, the yacht can be pushed around by the wind to a very alarming degree. When there is no wind and a flat sea and she is tied up safe and sound, then she is relatively benign. The moment the wind rises a little and/or a swell arrives the vessel's security is compromised and great care and attention must be paid to how she is tied to the dock.

In general, a yacht the size of Adela will be parked or berthed stern too. What this means is the back of the boat is tied to a dock with a range of ropes or mooring lines as we call them. The yacht is at 90 degrees to the dock so the front of the yacht must also be secured or there is no way to stop the whole front end swinging around.

There are several ways this may be achieved but the two most common are to drop either one or two anchors and or to pass lines out to mooring buoys. Many captains and officers will choose both if possible. Most larger ports have docks set up for this with mooring buoys already in place as the dropping and retrieval of anchors is a dark art indeed and the cause of a great many incidents in the world of yachting.

So, let's consider a large yacht tied up in this way as the weather deteriorates. It all really depends on the direction of the wind. If the wind is mostly in line with the yacht, from either the front or the back, then it's not so likely to be a problem. But if the wind is side or beam on as we say then it's much more likely to be a problem as it will cause a great amount of windage and try to push the yacht before it.

This usually results in the yacht leaning over a little but as long as the lines are set correctly to begin with and can be adjusted according to small changes in direction or strength, then, in general things should remain under control. In general, that is.

Portofino, a small town on the Italian Riviera, is one of my favourite places in the world. It is also one of the favourite places of many of the world's elite. Including Adela's owners who liked to park their yacht there for a week each summer. To put this into context Adela is right on the size limit of any yacht that can fit into this port. Portofino is also a very hard place just to get a berth in the first place.

In fact, unless you are well-connected with the local mafia then it's basically impossible to get a berth. Our spot for each year had been booked years in advance. I have absolutely no idea how much it would have cost to berth Adela in Portofino for one week but I think it's fair to say it's…A lot.

This was my first summer season on Adela and we had already completed the tour of the Baltic. After making our way back to France, we had a month to get the boat ready for the next owners trip. To be fair this was more than enough time but the problem with this kind of work is that you cannot do it too far in advance of the arrival of the guests.

Obvious really. To ensure the boat is perfectly clean it can only be washed immediately before arrival. Any time the yacht is just sitting in the elements is time for it to get dirty again. As such we had quite a detailed and rigid process for preparing for a guest trip and it all had to be done at the last minute.

We were due to pick the owners up in mid-August in Portofino. That is peak season in that part of the world and if you've ever been there at that time you'll know that things get a little crazy. However, everything was basically ticking along and going to plan.

While we were waiting the last few days for our berth in Portofino to come available, Adela was berthed stern too in a much bigger port, Santa Margherita, just down the coast. The plan was to motor around and take our spot later that day, ready for the owners to arrive the next morning.

As it was mid-summer the weather had been calm and friendly for a good long while. The danger with this is that it's just so easy to forget how severe and fierce it can suddenly become with very little warning. Despite sailing across the

Atlantic five times and completing a tour of the Baltic, all the worst weather I saw during my time as a professional sailor was in the northern Mediterranean. Where we were currently located.

Santa Margarita, the nearby port where we were currently docked, has no actual natural harbour but instead has a large, man-made breakwater, which acts as both defence against oncoming swell and a dock to berth on. Behind it is a small marina for local craft and a basin with moorings for a selection of local fishing boats. At that time, it was not a superyacht port as such and didn't really have any facilities.

In fact, it transpired that it didn't even have adequate docking space in the event of a…a…a…What exactly? I still don't even know what one might call such a storm. I suppose it was a squall of sorts but not like any other I've ever witnessed. Well, actually I did encounter another similar storm much later but we'll come back to that towards the end.

Out towards the end of the breakwater, on the inside, there was a docking space which afforded Adela just enough room to be able to put her stern against it and stick out about halfway into the port where we dropped two anchors amongst the moored fishing boats. In principle, there was nothing wrong with this setup. It was the same way we moored in a great many places we went.

However, there was one significant difference with Santa Margherita to the other ports and that was a large sign on the end of the dock that we were moored on. A large sign which said, 'Warning, dock UNSAFE in case of high winds.' It actually said this in English despite the fact we were in Italy.

When I saw this sign, I scoffed and said, 'Well, no bloody dock is safe in the event of high winds, is it?'

True enough. Yes, true enough, Bobby. Weren't you the wise old hand?

Now it's simply not possible that I'm going to tell a story about Adela without mentioning Sally. Sally (pronounced Sal-ayy) was the captain's wife, chef and chief stewardess. Sally, bless her little frilly cotton socks, had to be one of the most hated people I ever encountered while working on yachts. Although I ended up being quite fond of her.

For the first six months or so that I was onboard, I also hated her and this mutual animosity earned me the title of the "hated one". Sally would always have one member of the crew who she especially disliked and would bully. She would also have one who she loved and who was given treats and special privileges. This person was known as Golden Balls.

Sally was from Finland and was certainly more than a couple of sandwiches short of a picnic. In fact, you might say she was mad as a box of frogs. Having said that she had managed to marry a wealthy and successful man and come to think of it with hindsight she had actually done very well for herself all things considered.

However, to us, the crew, at that time she was stark raving bonkers and a real royal pain in the ass. She ruled below decks where we lived. On deck, she didn't have a word to say (although that didn't stop her trying) but down below it was her world and her word was law. Initially, I found this really difficult and rebelled against her.

This led to me becoming the hated one for the duration of the first trip to the Baltic. However, by the time the second trip came around this was starting to change and I quickly rose to be Golden Balls. A title I was to hang on too tightly for the remainder of my time on Adela.

The thing I worked out about Sally was simply not to argue with her. It wasn't possible to win an argument with her even if you were right. (Does that sound familiar to anyone?) Mainly because she was the captain's wife and as such had the captain's authority at her dispersal. Something she dearly loved to be able to exercise. And I can't say I blame her really.

The thing I learnt to do was to stop and to listen carefully and attentively to whatever she was saying. Certainly, no interruption or arguing. Oh no no. Once she had finished, I would agree wholeheartedly and change whatever I was doing to how she thought it should be done. As soon as she was gone I would return to whatever I was doing the way I was doing it before.

Even if she was to pass by again soon after she would likely not say a word. All she wanted was to throw her weight around a little and as long as she was able to do that she was happy. I recommend this approach to anyone stuck dealing with a similar situation. It worked wonders for me. The only problem is that you have to swallow your pride a little.

Once I worked this out then life got a lot easier. Although many of the rules were annoying and inconvenient, in the context of a superyacht with six young men and two young women living on board, these rules made a lot of sense. It kept an order that made life quite pleasant as long as everyone played ball.

What also helped was that Sally had sussed out that I was quite knowledgeable about food and quite happy to go off the beaten track looking for some local delicacy she might want.

Provisioning is a massive part of life for any yacht chef. It's one of the main and most important parts of their job. They cannot cook food if they do not have food to cook. When a yacht is cruising, this can become a big challenge and for many yacht chefs the whole provisioning thing is just a massive headache. So once Sally realised that I knew a bit about food she started sending me off on missions to find fresh local produce.

This wasn't for the main provisioning stock-ups because they were all done long before. Rather while we were away from our home port and cruising it became my job to go hunting. She'd give me a pouch of cash and a list, usually accompanied by extensive verbal instructions, which I would listen to attentively and off I'd go.

I absolutely loved doing this for a bunch of reasons. First and foremost, it gave me a chance to sneak off somewhere and smoke a joint and this is actually how and when this book got its title. Usually, I'd have time to get a coffee and a pastry as well. All while the other crew were stuck on board polishing the same bit of stainless that they polished the day before. It also gave me a chance to actually see and engage with some of the places we visited.

Unfortunately, one of the cons of life on yachts is that you often go to places but as crew, you don't even get a chance to go ashore and see the place. I have a long list of places I've been to but have not actually been to. However, on Adela, I got a chance to go on a few really fun adventures.

On this particular morning, I had a long and important list. Important because the owners were arriving the next day and she wanted to have some of their favourites ready for them. Local delicacies and so on. As usual, I'd been for a coffee and hadn't exactly been hurrying.

I'd also not been paying the slightest attention to the weather as I'd mostly been in small shops down dark alleys. As I was walking back around the quay towards the dock where Adela was moored I saw something I'd never seen before or after and I never want to see it again either.

Above the town, the sky had turned a shade of dark brown. The clouds were swirling around in a way that looked just like the sky at the end of the Ghostbusters movie when the evil guy was trying to escape the museum. If you're not familiar with the scene I'm referring to, watch "Ghostbusters 2".

Where I was in the town the wind was sort of swirling around from no particular direction but was already really powerful and it was just starting to rain. At this point, it occurred to me that perhaps I might make some haste and sure enough, as I got to within sight of Adela I saw her pushed hard over by the wind already in a bit of a dicey spot.

I ran the last 100 m to the end of the dock and I could see all the rest of the crew were already on deck getting ready to get the hell out of there. If a yacht finds itself in this sort of predicament, then there are two main options. First, you sit tight and trust that your lines, anchors and moorings will keep you from breaking loose.

The second option is that you drop everything and get out of the enclosed port area ASAP. Out in open water, there is far less relative risk from a short-term hard blow. It's things like breakwaters and docks that are the hazard in that event.

This second option is dependent on a number of factors. Firstly, the current position of the boat relative to the wind direction simply may not allow for this. Secondly, you may not be able to just drop all the previous points of attachment. Anchors, in particular, are often a nightmare to retrieve even in calm weather. Lines can get jammed or broken resulting in all sorts of damage to both boat and crew.

The whole process of a yacht the size of Adela leaving the dock would normally take an hour or so as all the various lines would be removed in a specific order to make sure the yacht remains as safe as possible at all times.

As I reached the passerelle, a horizontal boarding ladder attached to the back of the yacht, it was very clear that Clive had opted for option two. The moment I was on board the full force of the storm hit. I cannot estimate how strong the wind was but I could not look into it with the force of the rain as well.

Alex (the first mate) and most of the deck crew were up forward working on retrieving the anchors. Clive (the captain) was at the wheel with the engine on and he was already motoring hard to try and hold Adela back as the wind was pushing us both down and into the dock. Dazza, the engineer, saw me and yelled at me to let the port spring off.

I jumped over to where the spring line was secured to a cleat and started unwrapping the rope from where it was wound around it. Just like winches, cleats work by friction alone. Once the top locking knot is removed then it is only the number of turns around the cleat that gives its resistance to the pull coming on it from the other direction. Looking back, I think these next few seconds could easily rank as one of my close calls with a serious injury.

This particular rope was under a massive amount of strain at this point. Both from the wind pushing it one way and the yacht trying to motor back the other way. I have an average-sized man's hands and if I put my first finger and thumb together at the tips then that is about the diameter of the rope that we are talking about. There was so much load on this rope that it was bar-tight like a rod of metal.

As I took the first couple of turns off this the load came on without me expecting it and the whole thing instantly pulled out of my hands and whipped all the way through in a matter of seconds. There was a fair length of rope behind me and it would have been very easy for this to have caught me or wrapped around me as it went thundering past.

The result could have been maiming or worse. It didn't grab me, which is incredibly lucky and in no way a result of judgement on my part.

The whole thing happened in a couple of seconds and in the middle of what was going on I didn't notice it any more than to say, 'Oh.'

I didn't have time. All around me, all hell was breaking loose. Now we had cast off our two windward lines and we had started drifting down the dock. Clive was giving it full revs with the wheel hard over to try and hold the stern of the yacht off the dock but the passerelle was still out. This was normally one of the first things we put away.

It took the whole deck crew (so six of us) to remove it from the back of the yacht and then move it forward to where it was stowed on the deckhouse roof. There had been no time for that as it didn't actually stop us being able to leave the dock and in theory, could just be left sticking out the back. This would have been fine. No problem.

But there was a problem, a bloody big problem and that was the bloody big sign saying in bloody big letters. 'Warning, bloody dock not safe in high bloody wind'

About a minute before it happened I could see exactly what was going to happen and I could also see that there was nothing any of us could do to prevent it. A curious state of affairs to find oneself in. In fact, the whole thing happened in slow motion as the force of the yacht motoring and the force of the wind sort of worked together to move the yacht steadily sideways down the dock.

The passerelle was sticking out about 1 m over the dock. The sign was positioned about 0.5 m back from the edge.

The passerelle was constructed out of carbon fibre but then covered in beautiful teak joinery to make it look like it was actually all made of wood. It was constructed as two long booms with bridges in between to join the booms and for the solid teak gratings to sit on. In the event, it was this that actually saved the thing from total destruction.

As it struck the sign and the yacht continued to move down the dock the booms just sort of crumpled together. The bridges in between all shattered but the gratings somehow all just popped out and into the water where they floated and were collected later. The end of the passerelle, where it sat on the back of the yacht, popped out of its housing but somehow with very little damage.

However, now the whole thing was only attached to the yacht by the rope which held it up and off the dock. This rope was secured high up the mast and now was the only thing stopping the passerelle from sinking as it was all hanging, in pieces, over the back of the yacht and in the water.

However, in that immediate moment, this was still the last of our concerns as we had two serious problems. First, we had not been able to retrieve either of our anchors yet as they had both fouled on the bottom. This was usual in this kind of port and we normally had to employ a local diver to get the anchor free for us.

For a moment, there was nothing that I could do and I stood there, pelted by the wind and rain, and watched. The second problem was that Adela was still moving along the dock towards the end of the breakwater. The shape of the end of the breakwater meant that we were going to end up right on it if something didn't give.

Something gave. The wind eased just enough for Clive to motor us off the dock and out into the port. If the wind had not eased, we would have ended up wreaked on that breakwater. Through a lot of hard work up forward one of the anchors was retrieved and the other one dumped and we were finally able to motor out of the port and to safety.

In fact, by now, the squall/storm thingy had already passed its worst and by the time we had dropped anchor again, just outside of Santa Margarita, it was all over.

However, the reality of what had just happened was in fact far from over as we now had to deal with the fallout. Let's consider a couple of things. On the plus side, nobody was hurt. However, it normally took us a solid week of work to get the yacht completely ready for an owner's trip. That included a lot of attention and detailing to the passerelle.

The same passerelle that was currently sitting on the deck in around eight pieces. The same passerelle that was the only way on or off the yacht when we were moored stern too. The same passerelle that the owners were due to use to board their yacht the very next day. Oh dear.

Not to mention the fact that the rest of the yacht had been trashed by the squall. There was no actual damage as such but she was filthy. Covered in brown residue everywhere. Somehow crew morale remained high and it's often the case that there's nothing like a good storm to pull a crew together. Not that there is such a thing as a good storm. But I think you know what I mean.

As the ship's carpenter, I found myself surveying the remains of the passerelle with Clive. Bit by bit we put it all back to where it should have joined together and it slowly became clear that in fact, it had not actually broken that badly in any one place. All the breaks were clean and in fact, the rest of the thing had survived relatively unscathed. I've always wondered if this was by design. I like to think it was.

During my time working for Princess Yachts I had done a lot of work with fibreglass. Hardly surprising considering the things are built out of them but it wasn't my job to actually lay up the moulds. My job was to fit the whole thing together and this often involved using small pieces of fibreglass as patches around the inside to join larger mouldings together.

As I was looking at all these broken sections it was slowly coming clear to me that I might just be able to patch this thing up and get it back into some kind of shape to allow us to receive the owners the next day. Bear in mind it was now around midday and we only carried a basic fibreglass repair kit on board. I was going to need a lot more than that to fix this but I could see it was possible.

Clive didn't have much option but to give me a wallet of cash and the keys to the tender and off I sped, back to Santa Margherita to see if I could locate a shop selling fibreglass repair products. Now this might sound like a long shot but in fact, I had a solid feeling that a town like this would have some sort of yachting store that would normally have the things I needed.

I knew this because I had spent a fair bit of time around this part of the med by now and most towns with a marina had one of these shops somewhere. However, I was in Italy, let's remember and I don't speak a word of Italian. This was also before the internet's widespread use. However, that hadn't deterred me in the provisioning explorations for Sally and my confidence was high that I would succeed. As in fact, I did.

It took me a couple of hours of walking around and I was starting to lose faith when I found it. There was a store with everything I needed and before long I was speeding back over the water to Adela. I was well chuffed at my success in finding what I needed but I was also now getting quite nervous about the task ahead. The owner is not a small man.

If I was successful in patching this thing up, then he and his wife were going to have to walk across it the very next day. I didn't think too hard or long about what might happen in the worst case here. Instead, I focused on the job at hand.

The rest of the crew were working hard on getting Adela back into some resemblance of order. They were making good progress as she had been pristine just before so it wasn't that big a job in the end. I enlisted Tom's help as it was a two-man job. Although Tom was an annoying cocky twat most of the time, he was also by far the most capable of all the deck crew and I simply needed another pair of hands.

We set to work and somehow, a few hours later, the passerelle was in one piece again. Considering what had happened earlier that day it just didn't seem possible and I confess I didn't sleep very well that night. I was up and down all night checking on the curing process of the new joints.

Fibreglass is normally allowed to cure for around one month before any load or stress is applied to it, however, if you use a little extra hardener it is possible for it to go hard in a few hours. Sure enough, it was solid the next morning.

Adela was already on the dock in Portofino by now and the next morning we tentatively pushed the new passerelle out and into place. All good so far. The owners arrived later that afternoon and although I couldn't watch, they were able to board their yacht without incident. I've no idea if Clive even told them what happened or if they noticed any of the damage to the passerelle or stern of the yacht. It didn't matter. They were onboard and all was good in our world again.

In the evening, we, the crew, were relaxing on the foredeck with a few beers, as was our custom. Clive never ate his meals or drank beer with us. He was a very old-school captain and believed firmly that the captain should retain a certain distance from the crew. I can see why now but at the time we just thought he was a stuck-up cunt.

However, this evening he wandered up with a beer and lurked around for a while. Our conversation sort of died and then Clive enquired what I thought about the music coming from the town. There was a jazz concert going on and we could clearly hear the music from where we were onboard. Despite being a music lover, I can't stand jazz and simply replied that it wasn't my cup of tea.

He just grinned and said, 'No I expect not.' Then wandered off shortly after without saying another word.

It was one of the few times he spoke to me about something unconnected to work. Shortly after Sally appeared with some ice creams which she handed out saying, 'Captain, thanks and compliments for your hard work today.'

That was life on Adela. After everything that had happened that day, the only thanks I got was to be asked my opinion on something trivial and then given an ice cream. To put it into context we were all thrilled with the ice creams because we never normally got treats like that.

I'm fond of the quote, "Only fools, jugglers and clowns require applause", and in fact, I got my reward when I received a pay raise the next month. (Author's note. Can anybody place that quote? Answers on a postcard)

Looking back at my time on Adela, many of the things that seemed unfair and without sense, in the time and place, actually made perfect sense and were, in fact, that way for a good reason. I like to think that it's possible to apply that kind of hindsight at any point in life. I wonder how I will perceive my life in a decade from now.

Will I look back at myself in the present now and say, 'The fool. if only he knew...' or will it be more like, 'Good Bobby, just keep doing that, Mate. Keep going and you will get there.'

Which do you think it will be? I have a suspicion it will be a little of both.

12

Top Three Close Calls

No 1. A Small Tumble in Chamonix

Alright, now it's time for something completely different. We're off to the mountains and not just any old mountains. Our next story takes place in the hometown of extreme sports and adventure. The place where it all began. And ended abruptly for many. As it nearly did for me.

Of course, any Frenchman will tell you that Chamonix is the centre of the extreme sports world and they would probably be right. At least, it was when I was there, and it blew my mind on a number of different levels. I was able to visit Chamonix on a number of occasions over the years.

This was my second holiday there and this time I had to travel from the UK to get there. At this point, I was still crew aboard Adela and she was in her home port of Falmouth for the winter. Being in Falmouth for the winter on Adela was supposed to be something of a dream come true. Once again, the reality turned out to be quite different.

Not long after I joined Adela hushed rumours began about the boat going to spend a winter in the shipyard in Falmouth. All of us deck crew were from the SW of England so what this basically meant was that we would be able to have a job working on a superyacht but live ashore in the UK. Keeping our expenses-free lifestyle all the time.

The way it works on yachts is that when a yacht must come out of the water for an extended yard period it's not usually possible for anyone to remain living on board. In this event, it is the responsibility of the yacht to find accommodation for all the crew.

The crew still need to be fed as well and sometimes this happens in a makeshift kitchen, sometimes in restaurants, sometimes takeaways and sometimes the crew are just given a budget and left to fend for themselves. On

Adela, it was the last option. Now you must understand that to us the crew this seemed very much like the definition of having your cake and eating it.

From the moment I joined the boat, these rumours had been floating around. In the event, it was cancelled, rebooked and cancelled again more times than I can recall. The whole thing became a saga of epic proportions but at the end of the day, we had sailed into Falmouth at the end of my second full summer season.

Most of the crew had left almost immediately. We had not had a good summer. Although I had remained Sally's Golden Balls the whole time, I really did not get on with Clive the Captain. I had, by now, worked out that a large amount of the bullshit on board was of his creation but that he used Sally as the monster to do his work while everyone thought he was the nice guy.

It was kind of like a classic good cop bad cop routine. Only that they were not really working together. Sally was being used as a disciplinarian to police and enforce all the many rules that were involved with us crew living on board. As such Sally was seen by the entire community as a monster and Clive as a super chap. We, the crew, felt that having to live with Sally and all her rules, was a real hardship and looking back that is just hilarious.

I'll give you an example of why. We, the crew, were not allowed to stay in bed past 08:00 pm on the weekends. Even when we did not have to work. So no matter what time you went to bed you could not sleep in at all the next day. Remember that fully crewed we also had two interior girls (sorry but they were always girls) and an engineer. So, with four deckhands, and a mate that made eight of us.

This no "lie-ins" rule seemed incredibly unjust to us. Remember that we were all into hard partying, so this presented us with something of an obstacle. This rule was policed by Sally who would periodically turn up around 09:00 am at the weekend to see what state the crew area was in. We hated her for this.

She busted me a few times in my first year on board but, by and large, we found ways to do what we wanted without too much inconvenience. The simple solution was just to find somewhere to stay ashore. Which was of course the whole point.

With hindsight, I can totally understand why this rule was in place and this again makes me think about many other situations where things seem unjust but later come clear. If we the crew had been allowed to sleep in, then for one thing the watch person would not be able to clean the crew cabins. By 09:00 am, the crew area had to have been fully cleaned up after breakfast just like on a regular weekday.

For whoever was on watch, it was essentially a regular weekday. They had to work all day as they would do normally. This was seen as the ultimate punishment but in reality, we all just had to take our turns.

One of the jobs of the watch person was to clean the crew area after breakfast and although the rest of the crew were allowed to eat what they wanted when they wanted this breakfast clean up still had to happen at the same time and in the same order. Next for the watch person was cleaning the two crew heads and then finally they had to quickly hoover around the floor.

On a normal working day, all the crew would be out on deck now and their beds would be made as was expected. Accordingly, the watch person could go about their duties as needed. If the crew had been allowed to do what they wanted when they wanted, then I can tell you that it would have been one long party most weekends.

Even with the threat of checks from Sally, it was usually one long party of one description or another anyway. But if you take away that rule about sleeping in and then how will the watch person perform their duties if the crew are still in their beds? It all makes total sense to me now.

Looking back, I feel like a stupid child for moaning about these things but hey you know I was 27 and living the dream. Young dumb and full of…well yes, let's move on, shall we?

So, Adela spent the winter in Falmouth and I, after dreaming of spending the winter in the UK for the last three years, spent most of the winter either wishing I was in the Alps or actually in the Alps. I did three trips to the Alps to snowboard that winter. It left me pretty much broke at the end of it when I quit my job. This wasn't quite as I had planned it but that's another story.

Right here and now we are going to pick up the story in Falmouth and into the picture enters Ron. Ron was a total legend of a man. He was actually much too good a person for me to keep as a friend for long as by this time I had turned into quite a miserable cunt.

Except when I was drinking and then I was the life of the party. The split with Ariel broke me in two and I just never really got myself together again. Not for a long time in fact. Well, it's still a work in progress I guess you could say.

Anyway, the point is that Ron joined Adela to do the passage from Cannes back to Falmouth. Ron is from a long-standing and highly respectable Falmouth family and was about five years younger than me. We ended up on watch together for the passage back and really hit it off.

You might have called it a bromance I suppose. He was broken-hearted as well and we just sort of fell into a man-love thing. There was nothing gay about it but we just got on really well and both were at a point when we needed that kind of companionship.

When we got back to Falmouth, we stayed mates and Ron became a regular visitor at the apartment I rented for the winter. God, we had some shits and giggles. A particularly debaucherous new year for one thing. Ron and I stayed in contact for a good few years after this and he will turn up again later in this book.

By now, it was late winter/early spring and the option came up for a trip to Chamonix with Ron and a couple of his friends. Ron was also a keen snowboarder and all winter we had been making plans to do a trip together. So, tickets were booked and Ron, three of his mates and myself arrived in a very nice chalet for a week's stay right in the heart of the Chamonix valley.

When we arrived, it had been snowing heavily for days and in extreme cases like this, the mountain gets closed because of avalanche risk. It hadn't been the best winter for snow and we had been more worried about there not being enough so when we arrived and found the whole valley shut down we were a little put out, to say the least.

The first day was a write-off and we were not able to ride at all. It was hard enough to drive around the valley with all the fresh snow and it was clear why they had to close the upper slopes.

However, the next day a lot of the lower slopes were opened and we were able to get some riding in. But not the sort I wanted. Not at all. By now, I had become quite skilled at snowboarding.

This was my third winter and I had done more days on the hill over the last three seasons than most people do in a lifetime of skiing. Well maybe not but we were up there pretty much every weekend all winter. I averaged about 35 days each season.

The thing I had come to love more than anything else was off-piste riding. The powder was where it was at as far as I was concerned and this trip to Chamonix was going to be my first taste of real off-piste riding. We had booked a guide to take us up the world-famous Aiguille du Midi cable car and then down the Valley Blanche. The night before we were more nervous than excited.

It had continued snowing and the fact was that we really didn't know if we were even going to be able to make the descent. Complete whiteout and avalanche risk were just two of the reasons it was looking sketchy. There was also a notorious ridge traverse that had to be completed before the descent could begin and if the wind was up this could be quite hazardous.

Quite hazardous would be one way of putting it. The fact was that there was a very long drop on either side and it was certain death if you fell. In the event, I never actually saw the ridge because when we got up there it was a complete whiteout.

When we met up with the guide in the morning, a local Frenchman, we talked through the options and a decision was made to ascend the Aiguille du midi cable car (worth doing alone to be fair) and see how it looked at the top. I'm sure the guide knew exactly what it would look like at the top but he wanted to stretch the day out as we were most definitely not going to be able to do the Vallee Blanche as planned.

To get to the very top of the Aiguille du midi there are two separate cable cars that must be ridden. There is a station midway where you change into a second car that ascends to a stunning peak where you have the Aiguille du midi station. It took about 10 seconds for us to look at the conditions and say no way.

We could not even see the ridge and it was blowing hard. The main reason for doing the Vallee Blanche is for the scenery. The riding is quite mellow after the first section. Apparently. So in whiteout conditions, this was just another reason not to go.

Instead, plan B was to ride the cable car back down to the midway station and then we could ride all the way back down into Chamonix. From there, the guide would drive us up to another station where we could access some other off-piste stuff that he knew would be open. I wish he had just taken us there first.

But he didn't and instead, we found ourselves departing the midway station into some really nice deep powder that we were able to ride for only about five minutes before it turned into a crappy cat track. Cat tracks are sort of roads that are cut into the hillside and through the forest.

They are usually in lower parts of the slopes where there are more trees and access paths made for the maintenance vehicles in the summer months. In the winter, they become covered in snow and often get very icy.

They are actually a pain in the ass to ride and very boring as it's not meant for riding but for normal vehicles. But with all the snow we had been having it wasn't that bad and we cruised along for a while before we came to an obstacle in the form of an old avalanche. Periodically there were clearings in the trees and down these had come some almighty avalanches.

They completely buried the cat track and we had to stop and remove our boards in order to carefully traverse across. This was done by sort of hoping between steps which had been dug into the 45-degree frozen icy slope.

Old avalanches are not soft snow as one might think. Snow is in fact mostly air and in the event of an avalanche all the air is blasted out when it comes to a halt and all you are left with is hard ice, rocks and anything else the avalanche has picked up.

In all the time I spent in the mountains, I was lucky enough to never see an actual live avalanche. I saw plenty of old ones but never saw one coming down. Thankfully.

I was about to reach a point where my inexperience in the mountains was to become really pertinent. It was not at all clear to me that these patches of steep snow were not really soft snow but in fact hard ice. Two quite different things on a 45-degree slope.

The first one we encountered had deep steps cut into the ice so it was easy to traverse but when we reached the second, much larger patch of steep ice I was getting a little impatient because this was really not the sort of riding we had paid the guide to take us to. All I was interested in was getting to the bottom as quickly as possible so we could get on with the rest of the day.

One of the best bits of advice I ever heard is you should be careful what you wish for. In this case, I certainly found a quick way down. To cross the mound of ice, as it appeared approaching it from the side, one had to first remove one's board and then sort of face in, holding your board against the slope, and hop from one step to the next.

Unfortunately, snowboarding boots are designed to be clipped into a snowboard and not to be used for mountaineering. In this kind of situation, my boots offered next to zero grip and in my haste, I got it wrong and slipped.

In an instant, I was sliding down a steep slope that was solid ice and offered no means of slowing myself. Rather I was gathering speed rapidly. I was still holding my board and I turned with it and tried to use it as a break but it didn't work as I was going too fast already.

I turned back to face the slope as I shot out over the edge. I have a clear recollection, still now, of being mid-air and looking down and thinking very calmly, *This is probably not going to be good.* I hadn't had time to be scared at any moment so far as when things are happening that quickly it's just pure adrenaline.

What I find amazing is that I still recall being in mid-air and having this moment of clear anticipation of what was coming. It's the last thing I remember for a while. I don't recall the actual impact but what's certain is that my helmet saved my life. I received a serious enough blow to the right side of my head to knock me unconscious. We think for about 15 minutes. I continued to tumble a long way. Well, pretty much all the way to the bottom as I had wanted.

Somehow in that tumble, the only injury I sustained was to crush the tips of two vertebrae as my spine compressed upon impact. We think the impact must have been with a deep drift of powder snow because I was otherwise unscathed. Despite surviving this initial impact, I still fell a long way after. A long way through a lot of large trees and boulders yet I somehow didn't hit anything.

At the point, my memory kicks in again we find me sitting upright in the snow on a relatively flat section of the slope. That's because the slope was finished. It was levelling out into the valley by then which was why I came to a stop. I had my goggles in my hands and was looking at them pondering why they were broken.

They were badly smashed and for the life of me, I couldn't tell why. As I sat there contemplating this and my newfound surroundings, my phone started ringing. This was actually the fifth time it had rung but the first time I heard it. I removed it from my pocket and saw it was Ron calling.

I answered and said, 'Hellooooo,' as I was quite slurry and still had no idea what was going on.

Ron and the others were in a state of shock and panic and the moment I answered they were all just massively relieved I was alive. They had watched me go. Just disappear over the edge. Gone. See ya. Thanks for all the fish. And then nothing for about 15 minutes. By this time, they had started working their way down to me but still had no idea if I was alive or dead.

Ron started jabbering at me and I was just like, 'Hey man, yeah it's all good. I'm fine just my back hurts a bit. Where are you? What's going on?'

As I was talking to Ron I was slowly coming around and at that point, I turned and there was the guide standing behind me just staring at me with wide eyes.

He gave me a quick check over and I don't think he actually said, 'Sacre bleu,' but it was clear he was quite surprised.

By now, the others joined us and they helped me make my way across the short meadow to the road where a car had been arranged to whisk me down to the hospital. X-rays were done and as I was lying on the bed stretcher thing a couple of doctors came in with the results and put them up on the light board.

Despite having spent years living in France, I still understood very little of the language. What I did understand was that they were pointing to one place a lot and that didn't seem like a good sign.

They duly announced that my back was broken in two places and that I would have to be flown back to the UK on a stretcher. Up until now, I had been putting a brave face on the whole thing, stiff upper lip and all that yes, yes, but at this news I broke down in tears.

However, it didn't turn out to be as bad as they first thought and after a couple of days in the hospital, I was released with a packet of paracetamol. Literally. My insurance didn't cover any actual treatment so it was adios amigos. That's private health care for you.

My back still really hurt though and I spent the rest of the holiday lying in the chalet in a lot of pain. I didn't have any weed to smoke either and I must admit that lying there, while the others were off enjoying the slopes was not a high point for me.

In fact, you could say that relatively speaking it was a low point. No pun intended. Another example of the dream turning into a nightmare. Are you seeing a pattern here yet?

The flight home wasn't much fun either as I hadn't been prescribed any kind of painkiller and the only thing I could get was over-the-counter stuff which just wasn't cutting the mustard. My back hurt a lot right in the middle and there was simply nothing that could be done except wait for it to heal. Added to that were the after-effects of the concussion.

It's thought that I was unconscious for around 15 minutes. My right eye turned black. All the white part of it turned black. I could still see okay but every time I went from lying down to an upright position it felt like someone picking me up by my feet and swinging me around and around. It stayed like that for months after.

After two and half years on Adela, it was time for me to move on. In fact, by this point, I was the longest-serving crew member as most of the crew had left when we arrived and the rest had all left over the course of the winter. So, by the early spring, I was actually the only crew member left out of the eight that had arrived in the autumn.

This was one of many reasons I was leaving. Clive and I hated each other by now. I saw through his use of Sally and actually felt quite sorry for her in the end. I despised his attitude of superiority over us and I'm quite sure he felt an equal animosity to me.

It had always been my plan to hand in my notice when I returned from this latest trip. In my contract, I had a standard one-month notice period that I was obliged to give. This last month of wages would also give me something in the bank as I was now going to be job hunting for a while.

The day I was due to start work again I had my letter of resignation ready and I went to find Clive in his office to get it done. The problem was going to be that I had been told I needed a minimum of two months off work for my back to heal. So, when Clive read my letter he roared at me that there would be NO notice period because I couldn't work it and so that was that and I might as well just fuck off.

He didn't actually say fuck off but he might as well have. I was done and finished right there and then. After two and a half years, I walked out of the office without another word. Sally just looked at me with a deeply sad expression. I walked to Adela where she was in the dry dock and took one last long look at her. She was a mess with no rig and half covered with protection.

But I could still see her gorgeous lines and I suddenly felt deeply sad to be saying goodbye to this beautiful lady who had been my home and workplace for two and a half years. In the crew cabin, I collected the last of my things and that was it. I walked away and was once again a solo entity in a big wide world.

Shortly after all this I moved back to Antibes, found myself an apartment there and took up residence with an inflatable alligator, named Zilla. Shout out Zilla. Now if you think my life so far has been interesting then you ain't seen nothing yet. The next few years in Antibes would be some of the most hedonistic so far.

As you might guess there are more than a few juicy bits and our next adventure takes place in St Tropez so grab your Gucci sunnies and let's head on over there. Oh yeah, by the way, I forgot to mention. My vortex of chaos will be waiting on the dock with cocktails so hurry along now.

13

Party with the Madman in St Tropez

Now I'm sure most of you will have heard of St Tropez and I'm sure many of you have also been there. However, you'd be forgiven for wondering who, or perhaps more to the point, what, is the madman? Well, don't worry we are gonna get to that. Yes, yes. Naughty chuckle, wink, wink, nudge, nudge, if you know you know, innit.

But before we get to all that as usual I must first set up my easel and arrange my palette, brushes and canvas in order to create some context for you good people. There now. I'm ready. Are you sitting comfortably? I hope so. You'd better hold tight because this is gonna be a spicy one.

By now, it must have been the mid-late noughties. After leaving Adela, I moved back to Antibes just as the summer season was getting into full swing. It was a bit late to be looking for a job but it was a great time to get caught up in all the massive parties that would happen around the various bars every night. Yes, every night.

If you don't know Antibes in the summer months, then I can tell you that it is a big party every night. Much like any other holiday destination. Why would they have a night off with a town full of tourists all desperate to part with their cash?

By now, I think I have probably established the fact that I had, err, well…A taste for the party shall we say? I now also had no job which had two significant impacts on my life. Number one I had no income and number two I had no reason to get up in the morning. Meaning, more importantly, that I had no reason to go to bed at night.

Now, you might think that I would have prioritised these two things this way round but in fact, a young Bobby did not see it that way. Oh no. Instead a young Bobby, well not so young by now as I was 29. So yes, a not-so-young Bobby thought that not having to get up was the perfect reason to stay out late every night. Steadily drinking away what little money he had arrived with.

What always happened in these situations is that I found work. Usually well-paid work. In this instance, I picked up a job as a deckhand on a busy 55 m charter motor yacht. I spent most of the rest of the summer onboard and earned a shit load of money.

There are some serious stories to tell from those few months I can tell you. But they will have to wait for now. You might recall me mentioning the two bottles of Crystal champagne that got drunk by the crew. That was there.

So anyway. After that, I was cashed up and a plan was hatched to rent a car and drive back home to the UK and pick up all my personal stuff I had in storage at my parents. I would then drive this back to France and furnish my new apartment. Oh yeah. I forgot to say.

I also managed to rent an apartment through a local agency. This was something of an achievement and cost me a large chunk of the money I had earned that summer. But it gave me a home which I could call my own for the first time in my life really.

I booked a nice hire car for a week and also the ferry across the English Channel. The day before I was due to leave Ron turned up out of the blue. He had been working on one of the big classic yachts that live in the Mediterranean. However, it turned out he had just quit and was looking for a way to get back to the UK.

It seemed to make sense for him to jump in with me and take a share of the driving and so we made the trip together. As it happened he decided to come back with me as well and we had a proper adventure both ways.

Within days of getting back, I got a call from Banger. Banger had been one of the deckhands on Adela. He joined for the second season as a newbie to sailing as he had previously only worked on motor yachts. He was mates with some of the other crew and fitted in well. We hit it off immediately and were close mates while he was on board and remained so for a while after.

We remained in touch for a good long time after that. Right up until my 40s in fact. After one season, Banger had had enough of the bullshit on Adela and wanted to move on. He was a promising young sailor and did well at talking shit in the bars. He also had a taste for hard partying which was one of the things he and I did a lot of together.

He was offered a deck job on the prestigious J-class yacht Shamrock V which had been berthed just down the dock from Adela in Cannes. Banger had been chatting a lot with the captain and he got the job as soon as he left Adela which is quite remarkable considering he had very little sailing experience. Generally, J-class yachts only employ the most experienced and skilled crew.

However, he had earned a lot of respect on Adela as a very strong forward deck crew member. Banger is short, stocky and strong which makes for a good bow crew on big racing yachts. A yacht like Shamrock has a permanent need for strong bow crew so a match was made that was to be the Bangers home for a good few years after.

So, as we pick the story up, Banger was just approaching the end of his first summer season and Shamrock needed additional race crew for the upcoming series of regattas along the coast of the Cote d'Azur. I'd always dreamt of racing on the Js and it looked like I was going to get my chance as Banger told me they would definitely need extra race crew once they got to St Tropez.

However, before I got my chance to race aboard Shamrock I had to first be a part of the crew for the chase boat that was to accompany Shamrock on the passage race from Cannes to St Tropez.

Big racing yachts like Shamrock usually have a powerboat which acts as a support vessel. Known as the chase boat. This boat will carry all sorts of spare sails and equipment and also be available to collect crew members if they fall overboard. Which was not that unusual on these big classic racing yachts. Believe it or not.

By now, in the process of writing this book, I feel like I'm finding my feet a little in the field of writing. However, I'm going to really struggle to try and use words to describe what it's like to be aboard a racing yacht like Shamrock during an actual race. Just to be aboard is a mind-blowing experience in itself. In fact, for anyone who loves this kind of yacht (and there are many worldwide) just to be within sight of a yacht like this would be a special thing.

Racing on Adela was exciting for sure but Adela and Shamrock differ considerably in that one, Adela, is essentially designed for cruising and the other is 100% for racing. Just to be on the deck of Shamrock when she's powered up you need to really know what you're doing. There is no guardrail at all. Nothing. Remember that Adela has a waist-high solid bulwark all the way round. Shamrock has a toe rail.

I'll let you work out how high that is. Anything else is considered to be unnecessary and the crew are expected to look after themselves. Add to that the fact that you could be seriously injured just by standing in the wrong place.

Sails, booms, spinnaker poles, other crew and more fly all over the deck at regular intervals and these things do not stop to ask your permission to come past. They come through and you get hurt. It's a very serious place to be and if you don't know what you're doing you can and will get hurt.

You have to appreciate that Shamrock is in a special class of yachts. As one of the three original J-class yachts, she is actually untouchable in that respect. There are only three original J-class yachts still afloat and they date back to the golden age of sail in the early 1900s.

In recent years, the popularity of these yachts has boomed and at this time I believe there are 10 on the water. However, only three of these, Velsheda, Endeavour and Shamrock V still boast their original hulls and as such hold a status that is unique in the yachting world.

However, a yacht's reputation is as much based around its current captain and crew as it is the yacht itself. In recent years, Shamrock's captain had not been the strongest leader and this had led to something of a demise in the overall structure of the crew and the knowledge base around which everything depended. This was one of the reasons someone like Banger found himself on board despite having only a few months of sailing experience.

The fact is that no matter how much potential a new sailor might show there is simply no substitute for experience. Nothing. You have to put the hours and miles in to get that wisdom that makes one person able and another a liability. Mistakes on big racing yachts generally have two consequences. Things get broken and people get hurt. By now, I'd had my share of incidents, both breakages and injuries.

Never any serious injuries but I'd certainly broken some shit. In one incident, I'd be directly responsible for a large crash between two superyachts. One of the yachts sustained damage all down one side and it was just hours before they were due to have a charter turn up.

However, in general, by now I was a fairly capable sailor. I could hand, reef and steer which was the criteria for being able on the ships of old. The thing was that by now I was also sick to death of living on the yachts themselves. It might all sound very glamorous and convenient, and yes sometimes it was but the fact is that someone else's yacht is never going to be your home. It's only ever your place of work.

You sleep, eat, shower and shit all in the same place as you earn your income. If you've never done it, I can tell you that it becomes tedious very quickly. People in general are much happier when they are able to switch off from work and have a balance between work, domesticity and play.

On a professionally crewed yacht, the deck crew have very little domesticity as it's generally the work of other crew. To me back then as a young man, this was very appealing but let me give some advice to any young people reading this. Domesticity is an essential and unavoidable part of life.

At base level, we must all wash and take care of our own personal hygiene and that doesn't change on a yacht. However, all other aspects of caring for oneself are removed.

One way or another in life you are going to have to face domesticity and basically what I'm talking about is cooking, cleaning and laundry. Unless you are so wealthy that you can always at all times in your life get somebody else to do it all for you. Some young men might be thinking they can get themselves a wife to do all this for them.

Or perhaps servants for the lucky few. I suppose some people do manage to avoid it their whole lives but to me, it feels like you are just delaying the inevitable. The longer you delay things like cooking and cleaning the more difficult you will make your life in the present and future. These are basic skills that every human needs. But I digress. Where were we?

Ah yes. Shamrock at the point of Les Voiles des St Tropez. As we've already established the crew was not all that it might have been and the only reason the yacht was racing at all was because they had a charter. Actually, at this edition of Les Voiles des St Tropez, there was only one other J-class, Velsheda, who was racing in another class with the Maxis and Wally's.

At this point in the story, BigK enters the fray. Shout out BigK. One of the most top all-round blokes I ever met. I was lucky enough to be friends with BigK for a good few years. We'd met while snowboarding together the previous winter and had instantly hit it off. BigK had an equal taste for hard partying and hard play.

Just like me, we both loved to do nothing more than spend all day doing a sport we loved (mainly rock-climbing, snowboarding and surfing) and all night doing drugs we loved. Mainly beer, weed, coke and pills. Can't be that bad, can it? All I'm gonna say is balance and moderation…Anyway.

BigK had been employed as the chase boat driver and although he didn't need an assistant he created the need for one so that I may come along for the ride. After all, he needed someone to keep him amused with shits and giggles as he had a long and very boring job ahead of him. BigK and I could make each other descend into fits of giggles just by singing silly songs or saying quotes from movies we loved.

We'd become skilled at entertaining each other while waiting around for ski lifts or at the bottom of rock-climbing crags. We shared a childish sense of humour that was to get us through many hard times.

The passage races are not taken that seriously as the crews are usually totally shagged from the main events and just want a break. There was also very little wind that day so Shamrock motor sailed down to St Tropez with us just gently cruising along behind in the RIB. Not a bad way to spend the day. Once on the dock, I was asked to help with the wash down and then after, during sundowner beers, I was offered a spot to race with them for the regatta.

This was very literally a dream come true. I'd been looking at pictures of the J-class yachts since I had joined the industry many years before. To be someone who was part of a J-class program means that you are a cut above anyone else in the yachting community.

Or at least I think it does. To me, they are the pinnacle of yachting prowess and I know that a great many sailing enthusiasts would agree with me. As such, to be invited to race aboard one of the three originals was quite literally a dream come true.

The racing was bloody hard work and scary. Really scary as the first mate who ran the deck was out of his depth and there was not a cohesive crew structure as such. Still, there was enough muscle on board to get all the sails up and get the thing going full pelt. Then it was a case of let's see how to keep it under control. Sometimes we managed and sometimes not. No one got hurt but a few things got broken.

On the last day, we sailed the best we had sailed all week. It's often the way as the crew had by now had time to work each other and the boat out. Just in time for the majority of them to leave again. Alas, this is a tradition on yachts that always has been and always will be and that's just how it is. Crew come and go.

After racing, we did a quick washdown and then all headed together to the beer tent. Spirits were high as we had sailed well and the beers flowed like fountains. We were all still in the same clothes we had been wearing all day, encrusted with salt and sweat. At some point, it was proposed that we head to a local Mexican restaurant somewhere back up in the town of St Tropez.

Bear in mind that St Tropez is a very small place so we are only talking a couple of minutes' walk. There must have been about 20 of us but this was usual in these parts and the restaurant was set up to accommodate large groups. We all ended up down one long table, had ourselves a damn good feast and that's when the madman turned up.

The madman is code for MDMA. MDMA is the active ingredient in ecstasy tablets. I don't understand the exact science but what it basically does is synthesise dopamine. So effectively it makes you feel like something really good has happened. Like the best thing you can imagine. It gives you an enormous sense of well-being in yourself and towards everyone else.

It's very nice, I will confess, used in moderation and in the right time and place. As it happens this was the right sort of time and place. The only problem with MDMA is that it's way too easy to do too much.

It comes in the form of crystals and just a tiny pin-head size piece will get you high as a kite for hours. What's tricky with it is that the euphoria comes in waves. Often when you come down off the first wave you think that it's finished but then it comes back again and again for hours after.

The problems start when you are really fucked up on a cocktail of stuff and any form of moderation just goes out the window. When that first wave wears off, I often found I just couldn't help doing some more. So then when the second wave comes you get both together and it's double trouble.

Well, it's not trouble if you are in a good time and place. I can confirm that using this drug while having sex is simply mind-blowing. In the safety of your own home and in the company of a person you love and trust, it's quite safe to go down that rabbit hole and see what you find.

But if you take away that security then it's another kettle of fish altogether. Your ability to perceive and engage with the world around you is reduced to a few base elements. All you wanna do is hug, laugh, and fuck.

One gram of MDMA is enough to get about 10–15 people really fucked up for a whole night. It's that strong. Years later, I discovered that it's actually relatively simple to make. I was working with a guy who had a taste for it and one night we went to buy some. He took me with him and instead of going to some dodgy part of town we went to one of the big yachting ports located up and down the coast and we drove right up to one of the biggest motor yachts.

My mate jumped out and went to the passerelle of one of the yachts. One of the crew came out and met him and they went back in together for a minute. I knew the guy who came out. He was an engineer and a weirdo-nerdy type guy who never spoke to anyone but was always around in the bars.

When my mate got back to the car a few minutes later, I was stunned to learn that this guy made MDMA himself aboard his yacht. Presumably in the engine room which would be his own personal domain and a suitable place for such an operation. I was mind blown and I still am, to be honest.

That night in St Tropez a bag of MDMA had been passed round the table after dinner and we all took a dab. Taking a dab was effectively the same as dropping a whole pill except that the effects come on a LOT more quickly. Things got really twisted really quickly after that and I'm not too clear about too much.

Ron was there as he had been racing on another yacht and we found ourselves in another bar and another bag of MDMA came out. This time I took a big dab and that's about the last thing I remember. Ron later informed me that I had started talking about a beach party that was happening and had walked off into the night saying I was gonna get a taxi to said party.

Let's remember that this was St Tropez in the mid-noughties. There was still a taxi mafia in that part of France at that time. Taxis were extremely hard to find and extremely expensive. However, I was still cashed up, or so I thought and in my highly intoxicated state of mind I considered that getting to the beach wouldn't be a problem.

There is another small issue here. The beach, in the case of St Tropez, is not actually close. Not at all. It's about a 15-minute drive down a good fast road. There's no footpath. It's a drive-only thing. I do have a vague recollection of going to a cash point and so I think you can see where this is going. However, I seriously doubt anyone could have predicted what was to happen next.

I still don't know myself. What I do know is that I woke up staring at the sky. I was lying on a wall at the end of a country lane. There were no buildings in sight. Just a road that finished where I was with two large gateways (presumably leading to private villas), a short wall and trees. It was full daylight but not yet hot. I looked around and didn't have the vaguest clue where I was. In my pocket was my phone and my wallet.

When I discovered this, things seemed to be under control. However, the battery on my phone was dead. Completely. And my wallet was devoid of cash despite my trip to the ATM the previous evening. My cards were still there so I figured I was okay as long as I could get to a cash point.

However, I very literally had no clue at all where I was. There was nothing to give any clue except the sun and I was too befuddled to think that clearly. As it happened there was only one way to get out of there and so at this point it seemed like I might as well get moving.

It was then that I discovered that I was missing a flip-flop. Reefs were standard footwear back then and I must have lost so many pairs over the years that you could build a raft out of them.

Now I believe it's fair to say that an unshakeable truth of the universe is that one item of footwear is not much good without the other. But I was always a conscientious Cainer and wouldn't have dreamt of abandoning my solitary flip-flop so it was carried as moral support for the approaching journey.

Let's be clear at this point that I wasn't feeling too tickety-boo exactly. However, a situation was at hand and I needed to pull myself together as no one was going to come looking for me. Of that much I was sure. So I set off up the road and after some time walking (barefooted, obviously) I reached some sort of sand dune type small mound and found myself with a view stretching out over Pamplona beach.

This is not a small beach. It's actually a vast area and I was at the far end of it. The entire stretch of beach was between me and St Tropez and there was still a long walk to town at the other end of this beach. It wasn't as though there was just a road or pathway that runs down the side of it either. It's not really set up to accommodate pedestrians around there. As I tried to make my way along I repeatedly got lost in a maze of car parks, caravans and chalets.

By this stage, the sun was well up and I was now really missing my sunnies. Like all yachties, I wore sunnies all day almost regardless of the conditions. The only time they came off was if it was actually raining and that was rare. They were almost as essential as footwear really.

If I hadn't been feeling that good at the start of this trek, then by now I was really starting to feel the pain. But I had no choice other than to keep going in the general direction I perceived as being St Tropez.

The last few miles along the main road were pure suffering but at least I knew where I was now and that I would soon be back at the hotel where the rest of the race crew would be. That was where I would find BigK and Ron.

I literally walked through the gate as the lot of them were piling out. Heading into town for breakfast and saying farewell as most of them were flying out that day. I located BigK and he cheerfully informed me that the RIB was ready and if I was willing he'd really appreciate me keeping him company for the drive back to Cannes.

About a four-hour trip. At this point in time, this sounded like my personal idea of hell. However, I really didn't have much choice. As it happens St Tropez has no train station. Funny that. I can't imagine why not. The only way in or out of the town is by road and if you don't have a car then it's a bus to get to St Maxime and train back to Antibes from there.

I was good with the trains but never took buses and plus BigK had asked for my help. I couldn't say no. I was only there because he offered me a ride in the first place. Several times I complained to BigK about my lack of sunnies and he just grinned at me. I seemed to be able to cope okay without footwear but no sunnies was just killing me.

We met up with the captain of Shamrock for a coffee and a quick chat before departing. As we were getting ready to leave I asked him if he knew if anyone on board had a spare pair of sunnies I might be able to borrow for the passage home.

He just looked at me and said, 'What's wrong with the pair on your head, you stupid fuck?'

I looked at BigK who just grinned at me. I slid my sunnies from my head and onto my nose and it was never mentioned again.

That passage back to Antibes was as close to a kind of living hell as I had ever experienced in my life at that point. Well, that's not true but at the time that's how it felt. It was the first time in my life that I actually saw flashing stars in my normal daytime vision.

The four-hour passage had to be made upwind and against the swell. That meant that in a small RIB, it wasn't going to be a comfy ride. A couple of times a minute the bow would fall off a wave and the whole thing would slam so violently that you'd feel sure it was broken in two. Still, what doesn't kill you makes you stronger…Right?

The next day I went to the supermarket to stock up on provisions and at the checkout my card declined. I had about 200 euros in cash but that was all. I was thinking that I should still have about one grand left from my summer wages. When I called the bank the next day, they informed me my account was empty.

I still don't know where that money went but I have some theories. It didn't matter then. It was gone. Once again I was skint. And once again another job came up within days.

This time I was to join a crew of painters who had been given a whole motor yacht to repaint. One of the leaders of the team was Mason who had worked with us on Adela helping with all the varnish. Mason was one of the funniest, if not the funniest, person I ever met and the next six months were another rollercoaster of hard work, shits and giggles, all combined with a massive amount of debauchery.

But that's another story. Next up we are going to jump a few years ahead and rejoin the story while I was taking a break from yachts and working as a carpenter's apprentice. Every day is a school day around here you know. Let's get into it.

14

Monte Grosso/Brown Girl in the Ring, with the Dude

You may recall me mentioning my vortex of chaos that follows me around. Well, I think it's fair to say that by this stage in my life (early 30s) it had made itself very much at home. The winter that I spent working for Mason in no way deviated from this trend.

For one thing, we were working in a little shipyard on the Cannes islands. Yes, islands. Cannes has two little islands down at the Le Cannet end. On the closer of these is a small shipyard which is reputed to have been there since Roman times.

The shipyard itself has a small tugboat-type thing that they use to transport the workers and equipment back and forth. However, we had use of the yacht's little RIB which gave us freedom to come and go as we pleased but also put us at the mercy of the elements.

A small body of water had to be crossed to get from the mainland out to the island. There was no bridge or other way to get there. We were working out there all through the winter which meant that we often had to make the crossing in the dark and in very bad weather. It was often cold, windy and pouring with rain. Yes, even in the south of France it does that in the winter.

Sometimes the waves between the island and the mainland were so big our little RIB would disappear in between and we'd lose sight of land. This with up to six men crammed onboard with no life jackets or any kind of safety equipment at all. Often when we got to the shipyard dock we were soaked from the waves and the spray. And that was just to get to work.

On the plus side, the money was okay and we were certainly putting the hours in so I wasn't in a bad spot financially. However, rather than even considering saving any of it I focused on going snowboarding as often as possible and when I couldn't do that in my spare time I'd do drugs.

By now, I was starting to get really lonely. Living ashore in my own place meant that I had all the freedom I wanted but it also meant I had no company. Something that I thought I wanted but with no girlfriend that meant that I was spending more and more time alone at home.

Although the work with Mason provided me with an income, it also left me with no direction. I knew I didn't want to crew or paint yachts forever but I didn't really know what else I might do.

The project with Mason finished late spring and although I was offered more work with them I had found a new direction. I met John while I was working as a shipwright periodically after moving back to Antibes. John was an English, shore-based carpenter/joiner with a small business based just outside Cannes. He had found his way into a lot of lucrative contracts building walk-in dressing rooms and the like in countryside villas.

John was looking for an apprentice and I fitted the bill. I went on to work for John for well over a year and it was he who took my hand and led me firmly down the path of alcoholism. Here was my introduction to drunk driving and morning drinking. Inevitably this was to be the beginning of a very long slow end. Anyway, as usual, I'm digressing. Let's continue.

My work with John involved a lot of manual labour and at the end of most days, I would be quite exhausted. At the end of Friday, I would be feeling really beaten up but then I'd then usually have a massive night out drinking (and more) followed by a weekend of either snowboarding or rock-climbing. This meant that by most Monday mornings I was in a worse state than I had been in at the end of Friday but I'd have a big grin from the fun I'd had all weekend.

I've not talked much about rock-climbing yet but it has been a massive part of my life since the age of 16. In my hometown of Torquay, there is an abundance of first-class rock-climbing right here within the main town area itself. There are a number of old quarries and also some of the finest sea cliffs in the UK.

As a kid, I had seen this emerging sport on TV and was instantly fascinated by it. In later or recent years, this has become quite curious to me and I'll attempt to explain why. I'm going to go off on a bit of a tangent here for a moment if you'll allow me but please bear with me. This does have a point and context.

Despite growing up with Christianity as soon as I heard about the concept of reincarnation, I was sold. It just made perfect sense to me. Even though I didn't want it to. In some ways, I still don't want it to. Wouldn't it be better to just go to heaven and be able to live in eternal bliss forever after?

Do I really have to come back here again and again? It's really a question of perception, isn't it? What to one person would be the most amazing blessing possible would be to another their idea of hell. Isn't it interesting how so many things can be broken down like that when you come to think of it?

I certainly spent many years feeling as though my life was some sort of curse or punishment. I know many of us have and continue to do so. But it's also possible to feel like life is the most amazing gift possible and being able to repeat it over and over is the very definition of heaven. I guess it depends on who, how and where you find yourself in life and that, my friends, is where karma comes in.

Or at least that's where I think it does. You see, I'm not in any way proposing myself as a Buddhist or trying to put forward Buddhist philosophy here. I know next to nothing about Buddhism so how could I? However, the few things that I do know about Buddhism do make a lot of sense to me and I have seen the evidence in my life first-hand. Over and over.

But what I wanted to focus on here was more specifically past lives and reincarnation. In the West, we think this is all nonsense because we either believe in God or in science or for some people both. Which doesn't make a lot of sense but I won't go into that just now. It's my understanding that children under the age of seven are able to recall past lives quite vividly.

In other cultures, this is embraced and children are encouraged to talk about it. Of course, in the West children are taught specifically not to engage with such nonsense. If it's not in the Bible and you can neither measure nor replicate it, then it must be the work of the devil and should be burned in the fire.

Just on a quick side note. There are a great many things which science cannot measure or replicate and that are all around us all the time. Things that science doesn't like to talk about because it doesn't fit the paradigm. Do you want an example? I'll give you one. Ghosts. How many of you have had some sort of paranormal experience in your life? Most of you I'm guessing. At some point.

Whether you want to admit it or not. Personally, I have had a lot of experiences with ghosts (why does that not surprise you?) yet science tells us they don't exist. If science tells us that one thing does not exist but it clearly does then where do that leave us on the rest of it? Well, it leaves me in a lot of doubt. That's for sure.

As I said before, 'I'm not that interested in what anyone else <u>says</u>. I'm very interested in what they do but not what they say. The problem I find is that the two are not normally the same.'

I recently reached the conclusion that my most recent past life ended at my own discretion. Why do I think this? A pattern of thinking and a memory of a very early dream. A dream I had when I was still very likely under the age of seven. It involved a cliff and falling. I still often dream about being high on cliffs and sometimes falling off.

I was born with abnormally high anxiety. As a baby, I wouldn't let anyone pick me up except my mother. This seemed to ease as I got older but came back much worse later in life. When it did, I nearly killed myself. In the period after I finally stopped drinking, I became deeply depressed.

At one point, I found myself on the top of a sea cliff in north Devon in the teeth of a raging storm. I didn't even know it at the time but I was very close to throwing myself off. Forget my top three close calls. That was by far my closest brush with death.

I've now come to think that this was a turning point in the passage of my spirit through its lives. It's my understanding that one's karma is always moving in one direction or the other. Either up or down. Gotta give a shout out to the book "Jonathan Livingston Seagull" at this point.

If you've not read this book, go find it. It's short, powerful and might change your view of the entire world. It did mine and I have to thank Ariel for sharing it with me.

So, I feel like that point, a few years back, when I found myself on the cliff top, was a point where I had the chance to either continue the downward spiral or say no. No, no, no. Because I am most certainly not done around here and not for a good while yet. I have work to do and this book is just the start. You better believe it. So...sorry about that...writing about that made me quite emotional as you might have guessed.

At some point earlier in this chapter, I was talking about rock-climbing, I think. Perhaps we'll go back to that now but I think you can see why it's curious to me that I was drawn to this sport. I knew immediately that it was all about overcoming fear.

As a child, I had been fascinated and frightened of edges close to long drops. But the sport of rock-climbing looked so cool and glamorous that I just had to have a piece of it. The images coming out of Yosemite in California were just awe-inspiring and then I saw the movie K2. The movie itself isn't that amazing but it has a section near the start where they are training in Yosemite and it just blew my mind. I had to find a way into this sport.

Let's remember that this was the late 80s early 90s and so there was no internet and the media for this sort of thing was really hard to find. The newsagent WHSmith sold magazines about most sports but even they didn't have climbing magazines at that time.

I had to wait for a family holiday in Scotland to get my first taste and after that, I was hooked. The guide we hired in Scotland told me about all the rock-climbing back in my hometown of Torquay and so when we got home I set out to find it.

What I found was Anstey's Cove in Babbacombe which was already by then one of the most well-developed sport climbing crags in the whole UK. It's only a 30 walk from where I currently sit. Literally. So, I didn't need transport and I was able to buy the basic equipment I needed to get started with my parent's help. Before long, I met some local climbers who were super friendly and welcomed me into the circle.

It's a shame how elitist, conformist and unfriendly the scene has now become. When I started rock-climbing, it was very much a fringe sport. All the people I met down at Anstey's Cove were characters, oddballs, eccentrics and people who wanted something different from the mainstream. I fitted in perfectly and it was actually the first time I really felt at home in any kind of community.

Years later when I moved back to Torquay I attempted to once again find my way into the local climbing community. It had been a very long time since I had climbed at Anstey's and I had no idea who the local community were. Well, I found them and I'm not going to go into details about what I think about the current state of the climbing community but let me just say this.

Things have changed, A LOT. Gone are the oddballs and eccentrics and instead, the mainstream has taken a firm grip. Now please don't get me wrong. There are still plenty of wanna be oddballs and pretend eccentrics. But it's all so generic and off the shelf that it makes me either want to laugh or cry.

I look at them and just think *Are you serious? Like are you actually serious? Surely you must be going to a fancy dress party?*

The dress and style of the 80s was unique and new at the time. Replicating it is to me a fundamental faceplant in the evolution of our society and actually something that really pisses me off. Can you tell?

During my attempts to find my way into the current community the bulk of the people I met treated me like some kind of disease. I did not fit. That much was made very clear. I've since quit rock-climbing on the basis that I want no association with any of them. I feel that's a great shame but it is what it is. I'm 100% sure this suits them fine and that the animosity is entirely mutual.

But anyway, let's go back to the good old days, shall we? Anstey's Cove circa 1995. I was to spend most of the next four years at Anstey's Cove. When it wasn't raining that is. It became a second home to me and long before bouldering became a sport of its own I would go on solo bouldering missions to Anstey's at every opportunity. Bear in mind we had no crash mats back then. I used to use a little cushion my mum knitted. Seriously.

When I went off to work on yachts, this had to stop. To be honest, my interest in rock-climbing had declined while I was at university because I was spending most of my time surfing. Not studying. Surfing. Oh dear. Anyway...But Ariel was into things like rock-climbing and while we'd been together we'd managed to get out on the rock from time to time.

By the time I had rented my apartment in Antibes, it had been a few years since I had climbed. However, a bunch of the new friends I made snowboarding were also into climbing and we'd been making plans to go together for some time.

BigK was one such friend who I did many climbing adventures with. Another was "The Dude", as we shall know him. The third was Mush. We were all mates and often went on climbing trips together and much fun was had yes, yes.

The Dude was from California (naturally) and had a beautiful and super cool French girlfriend. Just on a side note, he was nothing like the original Dude (if you know you know) but it still seems like a fitting moniker. They were renting an apartment near mine in Antibes so little by little I became close with them both.

I was working all week with John and often on Saturdays as well but I always had Sunday free and usually it was spent with The Dude and his girlfriend. We'd meet up late in the morning, stop to pick up some supplies for lunch and then head off for the rest of the day to one of the many local sport climbing crags.

Within a one-hour drive, there were more than 20 separate sports climbing venues. Literally. The local guide was massive. Most weekends we would visit somewhere new and we had some truly epic adventures.

In fact, The Dude and I formed a really close bond that was to last for a good few years. In the summer months, his girlfriend was often away working on her yacht. The Dude's job didn't require that he did much actual work and I was often out of work during the summer as it was the quietest time of year in both the maintenance side of yachting and the local joinery trade.

So, The Dude and I often found ourselves spending long days together. Just the two of us. We became like the proverbial old married couple and used to bicker constantly. It was hilarious and everyone else thought the way we interacted with each other was really sweet. I guess you could call it another bromance of sorts.

I was coming towards the end of a long period of celibacy. Not at all out of choice I would add. Since my relationship with Ariel had ended nearly four years previously, every single attempt I had made in the direction of any female I found attractive had been a catastrophic failure or just a non-event. I was in the process of reaching the conclusion that I was really very unattractive to the opposite sex.

I seemed to relate really well to women and had lots of female friends but I just couldn't find a girlfriend or even a one-night stand. Not even a single kiss for more than four years in the end. That is a long time for a human to be devoid of affection.

The depression I had felt after the break-up with Ariel had not gone away. Rather it had entrenched itself and more or less just became part of my personality. When I wasn't drunk, I wasn't a very nice person. A bit of a miserable cunt in fact. Unless I was stoned and then I was okay but at this stage of my life I was slowly but surely consuming less cannabis and drinking a lot more alcohol.

I was also doing a lot of coke and MDMA. However, I had a strict code of not drinking during the day or at least not before lunchtime except on very special occasions. This was soon to change but at that point, I still wanted to do fun things with my free time.

The Dude is from the San Francisco area and had an equal love of cannabis to mine but luckily he was not at all a big drinker. He could certainly drink with the best of them and had been a part of the Mariette program for many years.

In fact, The Dude was currently the Mate on Fabulous, a stunning Swan 80 and it was one of the coolest yachts I've ever been aboard. I never sailed on it but I spent a hell of a lot of time hanging out on it with The Dude in the summer months and I certainly smoked a hell of a lot of joints in the lazarette.

The yachts program was to do a handful of regattas each summer and that was all. A yacht that size must have at least two crew at all times despite there actually being very little to do. This might sound like a dream job but in fact, it meant that The Dude had to be around all the time but never actually had anything he needed to do. Well not much anyway.

That was where I came in. Basically, as entertainment and chief joint roller. We smoked a lot of weed together. A lot. Like really a lot. We were always running out. Everything we did required the consumption of a joint before, during and after. That's just how it was. Rock-climbing was no exception and some days we would end up so stoned at the crag that we could hardly stand up let alone climb.

This might sound ridiculously dangerous but as I said before cannabis actually gives you an enhanced sense of consequence and you tend to think things through more carefully before moving a muscle. What this means is that most stuff happens slowly and carefully and climbing up a cliff is no exception. We would set up a top rope system meaning that we had a rope secured to the very top of the cliff that we wanted to climb.

That way if one was to fall then they would only fall a very short way or even no drop at all depending on how close attention the belayer was paying. It was actually very safe as long as the ABC were followed and we never had even a remotely close call or incident.

Rock-climbing, while stoned out of your brain, is actually a very curious thing. When you stop for a rest, it feels like you are on another planet. You find yourself paying attention to the smallest details in the cliff face and not really thinking that much about the actual climbing. One time I was high up on a cliff, Le Tete du Chien, looking down over Monaco and there was this beetle on the hold I wanted to use.

There was no other hold but I couldn't bring myself to squash the beetle so I hung there and watched for a while until the beetle went into this sort of weird, crouched position. I thought it was about to meditate or something but instead, it squeezed out a turd. Yes, it seems they do do that...do do...do you?...Never mind, and then it just flew off.

I just hung there for a while and was like, 'Wow man. Like far out.'

All the while I was hanging 20 m above the ground but perfectly safe. What a trip.

For me and The Dude, our daily working lives revolved around doing stuff that was inherently dangerous and where a single mistake could cost you or your colleagues lives or limbs. As such it didn't seem at all out of the ordinary to be stoned out of our brains while rock-climbing somewhere in the mountains.

And mountains there were or are I should say. Within a 30-minute drive from Antibes, you can be right up in the hills and the proper mountains are not far behind. There is climbing everywhere and a fair few really well-developed crags.

We got to know some of the local crags really well and they became our regular evening spots. But at weekends we always wanted to explore further and we would often pick a new crag out of the guide and go check it out just for the sake of adventure. Often with a stinking hangover and always with lots of weed for company.

Many adventures were had this way and I'm going to tell you about one particular weekend that stands out for me and The Dude. In fact, this is just one of many that could have made it in this book. I will try to tell them all in due course but for now, we will have to settle for Monte Grosso and the "Brown girl in the ring".

So, gross means fat or big in French. The place we decided to go to on this day was called Monte Grosso. I guess because it was up behind Monaco and as such close to Italy. Anyway, it didn't really click to us that what this translated to was the fat or big mountain. I mean why would pay any attention to the name of the place? You have to remember that this was Bobby and The Dude, we are talking about.

We most certainly did not do anything conventionally nor did we like to make our lives easy. Does that sound like a familiar pattern? We tended to pay a lot more attention to the actual climbing routes at the place rather than reading the instructions about how to find the place.

The guidebook to this particular area was written way back in the day by a very old-school climber who thought that finding the crag was all part of the adventure. This guy had pioneered many of these crags so who can blame him. What this meant was that he liked to give rather vague descriptions of how to find the actual rock-climbing.

Remember that France is a big place and even just in this local area there is enough space for 100s of venues. We had maps and knew how to use them but we tended to just have a quick look at the description and go for it. Which usually worked.

On this day, we got to the car park around one-ish but we had not eaten. We had a packed lunch, of sorts, to share, a little water and our climbing gear. It was mid-summer and hot. Well over 30. A nice day for reclining by a pool or on a beach.

But no, me and The Dude were going to find Monte Grosso don't you know. There were several ways we could depart the car park but The Dude was sure he knew the way and set off along one of them claiming this was certain to be the one.

I really didn't want to be there that day. I was feeling really depressed about another girl I had met who had seemed interested but then not. All I wanted to do was drink and forget about it. All The Dude wanted to do was climb. One thing we shared in common was that we both wanted to smoke as much weed as humanly possible.

We had a J in the car when we arrived. Then we decided to go for a coffee in a nearby cafe and we had one outside after the coffee. Then back to the car park and this time, The Dude was sure it was a different path to leave the car park. The guidebook was consulted and was in fact discovered to have been left at the cafe.

So, we drove back to the cafe and got the guidebook and then back to the car park. By now, we had drunk more than half the water we had for the day and had not even left the carpark. This time The Dude announced that it was a third different path to leave the car park and at this point, I announced that he was a fucking idiot.

His face darkened and he growled, 'Well you're a fucking cunt.'

We glared fiercely at each other in the car park in the midday heat. But this was clearly no good so we decided to have another J and then it would come clear which way to go.

Some form of clarity arrived and we set off down the path or rather up the path. After a while of climbing up a hill, I was thinking that there should be some sign of a crag by now. There was not. We seemed to be coming to the top of a large, wooded area.

We couldn't really see much around us, thanks to the trees, but it was clear that there was no mountain above us. By now, it was getting towards three and we still hadn't had lunch. We had also lost any trace of a path and were in fact bushwhacking through the forest.

After a few more minutes like this, we came out into a sort of clearing and below us it dropped right away. We were on the top of the crag as it happened but we still didn't figure this out. It was hot. We were stoned and very hungry and very thirsty.

By now, we had about a quarter a bottle of water between us and were a long way from the car. Not that we had more in the car. But for now, that wasn't a concern. What was concerning was our lack of lunch so a decision was reached to stop and eat our packed lunch.

Lunch consisted of leftover pasta from the night before. A yummy Fusilli dish we both loved. The only problem was that we had forgotten to bring a fork. Being civilised Europeans, we couldn't conceive of eating it by hand and as such this presented a problem.

How to eat lunch? Eventually, I located some chopsticks in the bottom of my rucksack (no idea how or why they were there) and these were duly used for the slow and tedious consumption of lunch. A shared one at that as we had only one box and one set of chopsticks.

While The Dude ate, I skinned up. Naturally. We sat on top of Monte Grosso in the baking heat, smoking our joint and decided that the best thing to do was to forget about finding this crag and get a cold beer somewhere. At that point, that seemed about as close a thing to heaven as possible and I was now motivated to get moving for the first time that day.

In our wisdom, it didn't seem like the best thing to go back the way we'd come but rather to forge a new route down the side of this hill and then loop back around. Not a decision we were to look back on with a lot of cheer.

We ended up in a right pickle and at one point it really seemed like we would have to turn back and go back the way we'd come. By this time, that was a very long way. Eventually, we were spat out onto a path that seemed to be going the right way and were able to make some good progress in the right direction. However, storm clouds were gathering in the hills behind us as they do most days around those parts in the summer months.

I was walking briskly along the path looking up at the cloud but thinking about beer when something blue and about one m long shot across the path in front of me. It was a snake. It had shot across from on top of a big rock into a bush on the other side of the path. I was frozen just watching the bush for signs of movement when The Dude walked around the corner behind and nearly bumped into me.

'What's going on?' he causally enquired.

'Oh, nothing man,' I said as I didn't want to alarm him and stop us from being able to make our way along this path.

I wanted beer and beer meant going this way.

But right then the bush gave a significant rustle and I just screamed, 'SNAKKKKKEEEEEEEEE,' and sprinted headlong down the path towards the car.

Before we made it to the car, the heavens opened and by the time we arrived we were simultaneously soaking wet through and about the most dehydrated I have ever been in my life. This seemed wonderfully fitting yet we were way beyond the point of recognising the irony.

All I could think about was water. I've never since put myself in a situation where I will be away from drinking water for so long and it makes me quite scared of being in a situation where I would be.

Now you might be tempted to think that after a day like that, we would decide to take it easy the next day. But by now you have probably worked out that the Dude and I did not like to make things easy for ourselves. No, instead we liked to add as much adversity to any situation as we thought it could reasonably handle.

Once a couple of cold beers had been consumed everything seemed more in tune and back at The Dude's place that evening we cooked up a big curry, drank a 12-pack of beers and laughed and laughed about the day we had just had. That particular argument in the carpark went down in legend between us and our circle of friends for years after.

While we were chatting, The Dude's phone rang and it was our mutual mate Mush. Now I'm going to devote a whole chapter to Mush so I'm not going to talk too much about him here and now suffice to say that he was another top all-round legend of a man.

I feel blessed to have shared time with him. I would add that he also ranked as one of the biggest cainers I ever met all while successfully working as a superyacht captain. The last time I saw him he was chief on one of the biggest and coolest sailing yachts I've ever seen. Shout out Mush.

Anyway, Mush called and said he was in the Calanques for the weekend and we should come and join him tomorrow. The Calanques are a series of long inlets along the coast between Toulon and Marseille. It's one of the most beautiful places I've ever been. Massive stunning cliffs jut straight out of the

Mediterranean Sea and are home to a wide array of very serious and committing climbing.

Not the sort of climbing me and The Dude liked to do. In fact, we'd never been there together before. The Dude had been there a few times and was trying to sound like he knew the area well and yes well you might have guessed by now. A plan was hatched to head down there the next morning and find somewhere to bivvy for the night.

It was the middle of summer and it didn't get cold at night in those parts. We'd done several bivvys already that summer and they had gone okay. We just found a good spot in the wild and slept out in the open in our sleeping bags with Thermarests to lay on. It's an amazing thing to do but you don't wake up feeling refreshed or doing anything like climbing.

Anyway, the plan was established and the next morning we hit the road once The Dude had finished his inevitable faffing. If you are not familiar with the term or meaning of *faffing,* then it's hard to explain but it's a kind of disorganised procrastination before embarking on something. I know that's a bit vague but I'm sure every one of you knows someone who is a *faffer*.

They just can't get out the door without having to go back in five times for various things or to change things or for any old bloody reason. This can and usually did delay us departing for about an hour as The Dude was without question the biggest faffer I ever met. Bless his little cotton socks.

I would usually just end up sitting down again with my rucksack on my back all ready to walk out the door, while The Dude would go back and forth reorganising his bag and clothing or whatever it was. This was a pain in the ass at the time but a great reason to give him shit the rest of the time. So, it sort of balanced out really.

Let's recall that it was the middle of the summer and very busy in that part of France. We got about halfway to Marseille and hit traffic. Now, The Dude is one of those people who would rather drive for two hours around back streets or country lanes rather than sit in a queue for five minutes so it didn't come as a big surprise then when we found ourselves totally lost in deepest, darkest Marseille.

We took a shortcut which added another two hours to a two hour drive. Rather than taking us to where we wanted to go our shortcut had in fact delivered us right into the heart of the Marseille ghetto. I'm still not sure how that happened but we ended up sitting there, engine off, trying to work out from a map how to get from where we were to where we wanted to go.

Somehow we managed and eventually met up with Mush at Cassis which is a stunning little town at one end of the Calanques. It was much too late in the day to set out on one of the sea cliffs that the area was famous for so instead we went to look at another crag which was a short walk up a little valley just close to where we were.

In theory, it didn't seem like such a bad idea but in fact, the valley was in the full sun with no shade and there was no breeze at all. The short walk turned out to be more like an hour and by the time we arrived at the crag it was mid-afternoon so about as hot as it gets all day. All the routes were in full sun and we generally looked for climbing in the shade at this time of year.

One look at the crag told me that there was nothing I wanted to climb anyway so a group decision was reached not to climb there and to head back to the cars. During the return leg, I named that place the valley of fiery death and we didn't even take our rucksacks off to stop and consider climbing. What we did was hike for two hours in full sun.

By the time we got back, all I could think about was cold beer. Mush disappeared with his girlfriend and wasn't seen again on that trip. The Dude and I hadn't eaten since breakfast and had nowhere to stay and neither of us had much money either.

We drove to a local supermarket and stocked up on cheese, ham, bread and some salad stuff. Also, beer, obviously, a big box of Rose (as there would be no fridge for the beer) and Red Bull as a substitute for coffee in the morning.

The Dude had mentioned several times that he had found a cave on Google Earth and that he thought it would be a good place to bivvy. This didn't seem like such a bad option to me but first, we had to find it. We drove down into one of the valleys that make up the ends of the Calanques where we parked the car and proceeded to have another blazing row.

I lost my rag about the fact that we'd come all this way and spent a fair bit of money and not even had a chance to climb a bloody thing. Of course, this both was and wasn't The Dude's fault but he saw it more as being not his fault and we sat in the car and yelled at each other for a good few minutes.

Once we had both vented and felt better we set out to find the cave. We had to carry everything we would need for the night and the morning after. Not climbing gear as we knew that we would not be climbing up there. Or at least that's what we thought.

You see it turned out that The Dude's cave was right up high on the side of the valley and looking up at the hillside before me I started to get nervous. We couldn't even see the cave from the bottom because it was so steep but The Dude was convinced that he had seen a way up on Google Earth and set off enthusiastically picking his way up the steep slope.

I was wearing my rucksack which contained my sleeping bag, Thermarest, water, box of wine, Red Bull, beer, cheese, ham, bread and some clothes. It was full and very heavy. The box of wine had been balanced on the top by The Dude after I got the rucksack on my shoulders.

I was also in my standard Reef flip-flops. By now, it was getting dark and I quickly lost sight of The Dude as he scampered on up ahead. It came to a point where I was having to hold on with both hands and a big drop was opening up below and The Dude was shouting down that he was up and it was awesome.

Shortly after I could see I was actually going to have to make a few rock-climbing moves to get up a short steep section. There was no choice now and I was just soldiering on. As I was on the steepest bit I tried to move my foot up and lost grip on my flip-flop. It nearly fell off. I caught it with my toe and leg fully outstretched behind me.

For some reason at this moment, I became aware of a nightclub down in the village below that was blaring out, 'Brown girl in the ring la lala lala, there's a brown girl in the ring la lalaaa la la.'

This moment seemed to freeze and I was just stuck there with my flip-flop nearly falling off, hanging onto this cliff while listening to this music. The absurdity of the situation was somehow readily apparent and I couldn't help but laugh.

Eventually, I made it up and found The Dude who by now was making himself comfortable. We enjoyed a big fat joint, drank the warm beers and promptly fell fast asleep amongst the rocks and boulders at the mouth of this cave.

At some point, it was daylight and I was just lying there staring at the sky having quite a surreal experience. Coffee was what I needed but we didn't have any. What we did have was a Red Bull so I rolled a joint and opened a can and bashed them both right back. Even with all the caffeine, I went straight back to sleep for another couple of hours.

Later that morning we descended by a different, much gentler route but after looking at the various options for climbing around there we had to admit that it was all well outside of our skill level. In the end, I don't even remember what we did the next day.

I think we just went home. We didn't climb anything, I know that. It was a long enough trip back and The Dude and I had had more than enough of each for a couple of days.

All through that adventure with The Dude, I was so miserable because of a girlfriend situation or lack of one more to the point. Looking back I can see that I was having the time of my life. Or should have been. I'd give my left arm to go back there now and spend time in those places. Climbing or no climbing. I hope and plan to revisit France in the near future and generally most things that I want to come to pass one way or another so let's keep our fingers crossed for that.

For now, we are going to get better acquainted with Mush as our next adventure takes place high on a cliff face in the mountains of the Alpes Maritimes. Not one to miss as this was the first time I found myself in a very dangerous situation and actually had time to think about it.

15

The Mountain Adventure with Mush

It was inevitable that Mush would find his way into one of my stories. He already played a Cameo in the last one but now he's gonna take centre stage. Well no actually I shall take centre stage. Naturally. As it's my book and my story and my bloody ball…Alright then.

The fact is that Mush and I certainly got into our fair share of mischief together. Just like me, Mush had a taste for the party. A rather keen taste and just like me, he was usually one of those who was still up for more at the end of the night.

Unlike me, he somehow managed to balance this with being exceptionally good at his job and popular with everyone he knew. Back when I knew him he had a beautiful French girlfriend and a large house in a very expensive part of Antibes.

Mush and I didn't get along that well to start with. I was pretty loose at the point when I first met him. I seem to recall, The Dude had arranged for us to all go climbing together for the first time. Mush was to drive as he had a nice Audi SUV. Once we were under way I automatically started to roll a joint.

This was standard practice on any journey with The Dude but he suddenly started acting nervous and was like, 'Oh errrr, I'm not sure about that in here errrr…Mush, is it okay if Rob skins up?'

Now let's just remember that to my way of thinking I wouldn't generally get in a car with someone who would not allow me to skin up. So, this question came as something of a surprise. Equally surprising to Mush was the fact that there was some bloody scally rolling a joint in the back of his SUV.

A grudging agreement was received with strict instructions to smoke it out the window and I think we both decided that the other was going to be a problem at some stage. Well, we were both right but after a while, Mush warmed to me as he recognised my unlaying qualities and saw some potential. Both as a climbing partner and as a wingman for his naughtiness.

He also saw that I was a very strong climber and in fact much better than him or anyone else in our circle of friends. This was mainly due to the fact that I had started climbing at Anstey's Cove in my hometown of Torquay when I was just 15. The Dude, Mush and BigK had all started climbing much later in life and as such didn't have that built-in ability that I had. Also, I think it's fair to say that it's just something I'm good at.

However, only in one respect and that was the physical or sport side of it. Rock-climbing is a complex sport with many ways a person can engage with it. In the last chapter, I explained about how we would set up a rope to the top of the crag to make it totally safe. Well, this was only possible at certain venues and even then it still required one of us to lead climb up there in the first place.

In order for me to tell this story and for it to make sense, I must attempt to teach you my reader a little about this sport of rock-climbing. I'll try to be succinct with the technical stuff.

So generally, not always but generally, access paths will deliver a climbing party or team to the bottom of a climbing venue or crag. With the use of a guidebook, the climbers will be able to identify the various routes which have been cleaned and then equipped with protection in the form of expansion bolts drilled into the solid rock.

These routes are named and given a grade which corresponds to a universal code recognisable to anyone with the guidebook. So, in theory it's possible for a party of climbers to approach a venue that none have visited before and climb there with relative safety and security. In practice, however, there's usually a lot of messing around the first few times you visit a new venue.

Guidebooks are notoriously inaccurate. Some even deliberately give misleading information just to amuse the authors. One such was our guide to the Alpes Maritimes. An area with so much developed climbing that a person might visit a different venue every weekend for years.

Literally. And that's kind of what we did as we loved the adventure side of things just as much as the actual climbing. But I still need to tell you some more about the actual climbing.

Okay, so let's take a party of two climbers who arrive at a crag and want to climb a route. Once they have selected a route of appropriate difficulty then the team must first locate said route on the cliffs. This is usually done by first looking at the photo or drawing in the guidebook and then picking out the line of expansion bolts which are placed in regular intervals up the route.

One of the problems here is that cliffs are constantly changing (i.e. bits fall off them) whereas guidebooks remain static. This causes a lot of problems when visiting a crag for the first time as things will have often changed a fair bit since the guidebook was written.

The more remote the venue the more this is likely to be the case. Once in the mountains proper all bets are off because up there the cliffs are covered in ice and snow for half the year and the rate of change is much more rapid.

So once a route has been selected and located the team of two must split into leader and belayer. It is the role of the leader to climb the route first carrying the rope up with them as they go. The rope is tied to a safety harness, worn by the leader, which is designed to catch and hold a person in the event of a fall.

However, if the leader is carrying the rope with them but it is not attached to the cliff then there is nothing to stop the leader from hitting the ground in the event of a fall. To counteract this the leader places metal clips (karabiners) into the bolts which are placed at regular intervals up the route and clips the rope into them.

These are usually spaced every couple of metres, but this is where things get complicated. Where the protection bolts are placed is entirely at the discretion of the person who established the route in the first place. One of the big problems here is that there is absolutely no established system for this and it's all rather subjective.

Establishing new routes is something which is generally done by strong and experienced climbers. Accordingly, on the easier routes (the only ones we were able to climb), the protection bolts were often very few and far between. The thinking being that if the climbing is easy then you don't need protection.

Well, it might have been easy for the guy who did it first but for us, it was still very much on our limits and as such it was terrifying to have to climb a long way out above the last bolt.

Let me explain this better. The way it usually works is that the first bolt is placed around the point where the climbing starts to get tricky. On some routes, this is right away but on others, the harder climbing may not be until a long way further up. In that event, you often find that the first bolt will be a long way above the ground. This means that as the leader if you fall before you get to the first bolt you will fall to the ground.

I never took a ground fall but I witnessed a nasty one and that was as close as I wanted to get. So, it was a sad fact that very often it was the height of the first bolt that would dictate which route we were able to climb. Just as a side note for any actual climbers reading this. This was long before the days of clip sticks.

Usually, it would be possible to complete the route once the first bolt was clipped because after that there was much less chance of hitting the ground. In theory that is but in reality that still depended on a number of factors.

Once the first bolt is clipped the leader may take a rest if they want. This is achieved by the belayer taking the rope in tight so that they use their weight as a counterweight and the leader is able to sit in their harness with no weight on their hands or feet. Once the leader is ready to climb the belayer feeds out rope or gives them slack and they can progress up the cliff.

However, once the leader moves above that last point of protection they are once again in a situation where they are going to fall down the cliff if they lose grip or slip off. Now that they have that one point of protection they will only be able to fall until the rope comes tight again.

If they are two m above the last bolt, then they will fall four m plus the slack which is usually about half again. So even though the last bolt is only two m below the leader they will still fall around six m in total. This varies a lot depending on a number of factors but in general, this is a good guideline.

As I was saying before, the placement of these bolts up any route is entirely at the discretion of the person who established the route in the first place. The usual protocol is to put a bolt every couple of metres or below any particularly hard moves. But this is really subjective and the reality is very different. Especially on older routes and even more so at more remote venues.

It's not unusual to find situations where you would hit the ground from very high up if you were to fall. Even after clipping lots of bolts. If the actual climbing is relatively easy (or was during the first ascent), the original climber would often not see any need for protection and you end up with a long section of exposed climbing.

For a person new to that venue and who is not as strong in the first place, a long-exposed section of rock like this can be terrifying. Sometimes even enough to have to admit defeat and come back down without completing the route. The ultimate failure.

I hope this isn't too boring or technical. It is important to be able to understand the situation I was to end up in.

Once the lead climber is at the top then everyone can relax and it's all good fun after that. But up until that point, every climbing day had a very serious edge to it as there was always going to be some danger to navigate for one of us at least. As the best climber by far, it usually fell to me to make this first lead ascent. There was only one problem with this. Despite being a very talented climber, I was useless at leading. Mainly due to my anxiety.

At my local crag in Torquay, where I had done all my early climbing, we had access to the top of the crag via a path. This meant that you could set up top ropes without the need for lead climbing. Accordingly, the vast bulk of the climbing I did before France was on top rope.

I did lead a few routes including a couple of hard ones but I practised them endlessly on top rope first and only actually climbed them once on lead. That's all well and good but falling off is as much a part of sport climbing as the climbing itself and without having learnt how to fall I had a big gap in my climbing repertoire.

So, the moment I found myself on lead and with any kind of fall potential I got really scared. I was still usually able to make it to the top but not always. Mush, however, was a very confident leader. Much more so than me in fact.

Although I was by far the better climber in terms of skill and strength, Mush had much more confidence and would push himself up into situations where I would not go. This made us a great climbing team as we were able to feed off each other's strengths.

So, okay then I think I'm ready to get to the story now. All right, all right that's enough now. I did warn you there would be some tangential manoeuvres.

It was during the summer while I was living in my apartment in the old town of Antibes. As was often the case, I was out of work again due to the time of year. By now, I had settled into a fairly laid-back existence, freelancing as a painter/carpenter on the yachts, doing a variety of shore-based joinery work and also working for an exhibition company in Cannes.

One way or another I was making ends meet but it was a problem in the peak summer months as work in the first two fields would dry up. There was always the odd exhibition going on but I hated that work and only did it when I needed to.

One day Mush called me up and asked if I wanted to join him for an expedition to check out some canyoning he wanted to do at a later date with some other friends. The start of this canyon he wanted to look at was a very long way up in the mountains and required a 4x4 to get to. Mush had a big 4x4, so this seemed like a cool adventure and I was happy to accompany him in his explorations.

He said to bring my climbing gear as well as there was a venue on the way back that we could stop and check out if we wanted. It was a gorgeous day and we stopped to pick up supplies for lunch in a village along the route. This was one of my favourite things about these trips. We would never usually plan where to go to get lunch.

We just knew that there would be nice shops in most of the villages we would pass through and we would be able to get ham, sausage, cheese, pate, bread of all sorts and sometimes even pies and who knows what else. It was all part of the fun of the adventure. Not one single of these shops was part of a chain or had a brand name. They were all just local village shops selling local produce. God bless France.

By now, I'd got pretty good at organising picnics that worked well in high temperatures. You need to pick the right cheese for one thing and certain foods like chocolate are right out while other things like pate seem better when warm. We always ate like kings when we went on adventures. It was a big part of the whole experience for us.

We found the start of the canyon without too much trouble and stopped on top of the mountain for lunch. Happy daze. However, that was essentially all we came up there to do and right after lunch, we headed back down. For Mush, a day out like this isn't complete until it has involved some kind of adrenaline buzz.

To be honest I would have been quite happy to just find a bar and have a couple of cold beers. But after an hour or so Mush pulled over and announced that we were at the point he thought should be the access path to this crag.

We organised our rucksacks and set off into the wilderness. We were still a long way up in the mountains and neither of us had much experience of climbing in this kind of location. However, this did not deter us and we made our way to the foot of the very tall crag. Mush showed me the route in the guidebook and it actually looked okay.

However, this was to be a multi-pitch climb and I had only done one of these previously in all my years of climbing. The big difference is that when the leader gets to the top of the climb they do not descend to the bottom. Instead, they make it safe up there and then they belay the other person who climbs up to join them at the top.

The general thing is to then continue climbing until the top of the cliff is reached. This may involve repeating this process many times over in a reverse *yo-yo*-like manner.

This route was only two pitches and the first was more difficult so Mush said he would go first and then belay me up on top rope. Once I reached the belay it would be my option to lead the second pitch if I wanted to.

This all sounded okay as both pitches were well within my usual climbing grade and so Mush set off and made short work of the first pitch. He organised his belay and then called me up. The climbing was fun and I was quickly able to join him at the hanging stance.

So, at this point, we are both sitting in our harnesses suspended about 30 m up a cliff face. We knew that the second pitch went off to the left around a bulge and then out of sight. It wouldn't be possible to see the rest of the line until the leader climbed around the initial bulge.

Mush asked if I wanted to lead and I decided to try and impress him a bit and said I'd give it a go. He was, in fact, duly impressed and we got ourselves ready for me to start leading the second pitch.

Wow. Recalling this vividly is making me so nervous that it's actually made my palms sweat. I guess I'd better get on with it but I'm nervous now.

A couple of metres after the belay was a solid-looking bolt. Let's remember that we are not at one of the coastal venues where everything is super well-maintained. Instead, we are high in the mountains where it's possible another person has not been for years.

This means a bunch of things but one of them is that you cannot always trust the protection placed by the original climber. It may be so old or damaged that it's no longer safe.

I made a couple of easy moves to this bolt and clipped it which gave me some added confidence. Just remember that I am starting out at the bottom of a new pitch but I am not on the ground. I am already 30 m up so there is a much greater feeling of exposure and fear. Moving around the bulge I reached a peg that we could see from the belay but that was the last point of protection visible.

I was working on trust that there would be more bolts once I got over the bulge. Pegs, unlike bolts, are not actually fixed to the rock through a mechanical action like expansion but rather hammered into cracks and held in place by friction alone.

A brand new, well-placed, peg is a perfectly acceptable form of protection. But that's if you placed it yourself and its brand new. In most cases, you have no idea who placed it or when and as such have no idea how likely it is to actually hold you in the event of a fall. The general rule of thumb when encountering pegs is to clip them but don't fall onto them.

I clipped the peg and was now able to reach up and look over the bulge and up the slab above it. What I saw was a quite blank-looking slab with some shelves but no bolts. Hmmm. Without the security of knowing where my next bolt was, I didn't feel confident enough to keep climbing so I decided to take a rest and ease my weight gently onto the peg. This was done by asking Mush to take the rope tight.

As he did so I watched the peg closely for signs of movement as I would now be trusting my weight to it. It seemed okay but then Mush called up to ask how it was looking. I replied that I couldn't see the next bolt but that this peg looked okay. As I said that I sort of bounced my weight on it to test this theory some more. It moved a little. Not a lot but a little and a little was enough to tell me that it was not at all solid and would very likely come out in the event of a fall. Fuck.

Now what I should have done at this point was to climb down and ask Mush if he wanted the lead. But for a change, I manned up and decided that I would just go for it and hope for the best. *There must be another bolt up there somewhere after all*, I thought.

I informed Mush of my intention and set off. The first couple of moves to get over the bulge were quite hard and as soon as I was up I knew that I would not be able to downclimb. I now also could not see or hear Mush. Communication was through the rope alone. Fuck.

Downclimbing is your first means of escape in the event that you cannot continue upwards. But climbing down is actually harder than climbing up. Believe it or not. It's just simple human physics. So now I was a bit fucked really. Especially as I still couldn't see the next bolt. However, I was standing on a ledge and I didn't need my hands except for balance so I was not in immediate danger of falling.

Looking around I was finally able to locate the next bolt and it was about three metres to my right. Well out of reach and the rock between me and it was blank. There was no way I could get to it and clip from here. What this meant was that I was off-route.

I had somehow gone the wrong way and was now not actually on any established route and as such who knows how hard it might be. Plus, it meant I couldn't clip the bolt and as such my last point of protection was the peg which was wobbly and a long way below me. Double Fuck.

This wasn't good. A quick assessment of my situation told me that even if the peg did hold I was going to fall a very long way before the rope would catch me. Long enough to mean that the rope or other equipment might fail. I didn't really stop and consider this in detail though.

I knew I was in a really bad spot. Or potentially bad at least. This was the first time in my life that I had found myself in a situation like this where I had the chance to stop and think and be aware of what was happening.

Fortunately, I didn't panic. What I did instead was have a little chat with myself. I used reason and logic as my tools to convince myself that I could get myself out of this situation. This might have been the first time I had to do that but it's certainly not been the last.

I told myself that I was a good climber and that I knew that I could get up this slab ahead of me. It seemed reasonable that if I could get up this slab then I would be able to find more protection further up but if not there would be a safer place to rest and make another plan at least.

So, I just engaged beast mode and went for it. The climbing was actually quite easy and I quickly found myself at the bottom of a chimney corner thingy. And there was a bolt. Thank God. Now I was clipped in and all I wanted to do was get to the top ASAP so I dashed up the corner with no issues.

This led me onto another ledge and there before me was another slab. Shorter than the previous but also quite blank-looking. I didn't care. There were only two bolts on the whole slab but I just flew up it without even caring as by now the adrenaline was in full effect.

Halfway up this slab, I found a snakeskin attached to the rock. It was about one meter long and still very intact and whole. The sun had cooked it onto the rock after its owner had shed it. After my recent experience with a snake, you might think this would have added to my woes but in my current state of mind, I didn't even notice it and just charged past to the top and safety.

When Mush joined me at the top, he was wide-eyed.

He wasn't a man who gives compliments at all but he gave me a wry smile and said, 'Nice lead, Mate.'

All I wanted by now was a spliff and a beer but we were still on top of the mountain and had to make two rappels just to make it back to the base of the cliff and then a one-hour hike back to the car.

Thanks to the adrenaline I was buzzing my tits off the whole rest of the day. Back in Antibes Mush invited me back to his place and then a load of our mutual friends turned up for a dinner party. What a day. WHAT a day. In difficult times since then, I've drawn on that experience.

I've found myself saying, 'C'mon, Mate, you can do this. You know you can do this. Just pull yourself together and you can get up there.'

I feel deeply blessed to have had an experience like this that taught me so much about myself and about rock-climbing in the mountains. Thanks for sharing that with me Mush.

From here on in, my vortex of chaos is going to be taking centre stage a lot more. You might be thinking that it's been quite prevalent already but let me tell you that so far it's just been taking notes. I was about to meet Amber who was without a shadow of doubt, the single worst thing that ever happened to me. We met at a point where I was wobbling but still had a good community around me.

Well, she helped me make sure that wasn't to last much longer. I would also soon stop using cannabis completely and have a full five-year break. In those five years, my life went from a volatile mess to a catastrophic disaster. Stick around. It's gonna make good reading trust me. I always managed to keep things interesting wherever I was and whatever I was doing so there was never a dull moment. In the words of the great man himself. We continue.

16

X-Mas Eve Busted on the Beach

It was inevitable that it would happen sooner or later. Considering my love of naughtiness, all that's surprising is that it didn't happen until so much later in my life. I was 31 by now and had been living in Antibes for a few years. I had a good network of local friends and felt like part of a community.

It always seemed interesting to me that I was born and raised in a part of the UK known as the English Riviera and then by complete chance I moved to the original French Riviera and ended up spending well over a decade based there. At the point of this story, I had spent more of my adult life living in France than I had in England and I really thought of France as my home and the UK as an inconvenience that I had to deal with periodically.

My relationship with my family had reached rock bottom by then. It had never been good in the first place. I fell out with my mother at around the point I reached puberty and we never got on again after that. My father just went to work and stayed out of everything at home. I had one older sister who was the achiever and the all-time golden balls in the eyes of my parents.

Although in many ways I was still living the dream, little by little things were going downhill. My response, as always, was to consume more things that changed the way I felt to a positive state of mind. Essentially self-medication which is what I'd been doing with cannabis since I discovered it in my mid-teens. Gradually this was becoming less cannabis and more alcohol but I wasn't to recognise that for a good while yet.

Unfortunately, I had also failed, in any respect, to find anything even approaching a girlfriend. I honestly couldn't get past hello. I would get plenty of smiles from girls but the moment I opened my mouth they ran a mile. Without fail.

My conclusion was that the opposite sex just isn't interested in me and my response was just to stop paying any interest in them. I had tons of beautiful female friends who all used to enjoy my company because they knew I wouldn't hit on them.

Now at this point, and quite possibly long before you'd be forgiven for thinking that perhaps I'm gay and although in later years I did open my mind to this possibility, at that point I was deeply against such an idea. The fact is that I do find men attractive but not in a sexual way and that's just how it is for me.

I'm quite sure that if I had grown up in a sexually liberated community then I would see this differently. However, I've never seen much merit in speculating about hypotheticals so perhaps I should just get on with the story. What's that? That would be a first did you say?

Considering my relationship with my mother in later years it seems ironic that she always said I'd end up a beach bum and for a good few years she was right. During the years I lived in Antibes the vast majority of every summer was spent on the local beach.

Antibes has a few beaches as it has a long stretch of coastline much like my hometown of Torquay. Actually, one of a number of similarities between my hometown and Antibes.

The beach closest to the old town, where I lived was not really the most glamorous of those to be fair. It was affectionately known as the toilet bowl by the local yachty community as it had a breakwater which created a safe area for swimming but which stopped any natural circulation of the water. I rarely swam there. I hated the water as by now I was usually drunk and as such just not drawn to being in it.

I say I was usually drunk. Let me be clear about that. What I mean is that I would usually open my first beer around 12:00 if I was not working or climbing. Usually, the same if I was working as we would always have a beer or two with lunch. But never ever when we were climbing. Never until after the day was finished. That was something that never changed.

But on days when I was doing neither I tended to have my first beer around noon and then just steadily drink beer for the rest of the day and night. Usually Heineken. Sometimes I would drink them fast and sometimes I would drink them slow. But wherever I was and whatever I was doing, except climbing, there was beer involved somewhere at some point.

In the first summer I spent in Antibes, I was working with John but by the second summer, I was freelancing and work became scarce by the time July rolled around. As such I found myself spending more and more time at the toilet bowl. The toilet bowl is actually a place I hold very dear to my heart. I spent many happy hours on that beach doing things I loved in the company of good people whose company I really enjoyed.

All in a place, the rich and famous come for holidays. Literally anchored right in front of the beach would be superyachts on charter that could be anywhere in the world but their clients choose to have them there. It wasn't a coincidence that I found myself in this place you know.

The toilet bowl offered a number of significant advantages for someone of my disposition. There was only one way in and out of the whole beach and that was by a narrow gateway that was through the old town wall defences. What this meant was that it was a relatively safe place to smoke weed without the fear of being spotted and busted by the police.

By this stage, the police in France were already taking a fairly liberal attitude towards cannabis use but it was still illegal and had to be policed. As such the possibility always existed that if you found yourself in the wrong place at the wrong time you could end up in trouble.

I'll give you an example. A group of my friends had very nearly been busted on the way back from a day snowboarding in the mountains. Periodically the French police will set up a roadblock on a busy stretch of road and test for documents, alcohol and drugs. Bad news for about 50% of the cars on the road leaving a ski station at the end of the day.

The group were all drunk, yes even the driver had had a few as it was actually quite normal back then. Also, a big joint was being smoked in the car at the time they realised what was going on. The way they set the roadblocks up, it's impossible to escape once you are in the queue and my friends hadn't noticed why there was a queue until…The windows rolled down to find a bunch of big policemen who wanted to see their passports and have a look inside. Whoops.

Somehow they talked their way out of it but only because they were not French and the police couldn't be bothered to deal with the hassle of processing a foreigner. This was to save my bacon a few times but not in the end.

So where was I? Yes, the toilet bowl. With the limited access, the toilet bowl was quite a safe place to smoke because the police very rarely came in there looking for trouble and when they did they always went to the other side of the beach where we didn't often go.

When they did do that, it was always easy to see them coming because we would sit a long way down the other end and there was only one way they could approach. As it was a sandy beach this gave the added advantage that you could hide anything incriminating in the sand before the police would arrive.

Second advantage was that there was a kiosk selling everything a person might need for a day on the beach. Cold beer obviously but also chips, fries, burgers etc. The food was shit but in worst-case scenarios, it made do and the two ladies who ran the place became like family to us and us to them.

Third advantage was that around 4–5 pm, space would start to clear as the shade line from the wall behind moved down the beach. I usually chose to sit in the shade anyway because it was super-hot in the full sun but we needed the space for frisbee. Frisbee always has been and always will be one of my favourite things in the world. I simply love to throw a disc around with a group of friends.

If the location is stunning and there is beer and weed involved, then all the better. As such the moment space was available the disc came out and stayed out for the rest of the night. The beach was floodlit until 11:00 pm when it was closed and we would be kicked out by the town security people which was how many nights ended. With the floodlights, it was possible to play frisbee all the way until 11:00 pm and we often did.

The final advantage and one I possibly miss the most was the sheer abundance of beautiful women with very little on. Please don't think I mean this in a pervy way but I'm in no way ashamed to admit that I am a massive fan of the female form. The male also but much more specifically the female form. I can very happily spend all day admiring beautiful women with very little on.

It's just not something I grow tired of. It has to be said that the south of France is not a bad place to be for someone of that inclination and I was not afraid to indulge my fascination in a location like that.

I was often the first person to arrive on the beach (you now know why) but I had a big group of friends who all knew where to find me and little by little more people would turn up until there would usually be anywhere from 5–15 people. Some would play frisbee and some would sit around in a circle enjoying wine, beer, joints and many laughs. Those playing frisbee would rotate with those sitting down and so we passed our summers.

This would happen literally every evening for the entirety of July and August. Weekdays or weekends made no difference. Every night we'd be there and everyone knew it. Although I was desperately lonely, these were undoubtedly some of the best days of my life to date.

All good things, as well as bad, must come to an end and this seems like a nice spot to share with you one of my favourite bits of wisdom. One that I discovered around this time while watching the movie "24 Hour Party People". A film I thoroughly recommend to anyone who's enjoying this book.

The passage goes like this.

It's my belief that history is a wheel. 'Inconstancy is my very essence,' says the wheel.

Rise up on my spokes if you like but don't complain when you're cast back down into the depths.

Good times pass away, but then so do the bad.

Mutability is our tragedy, but it's also our hope.

The worst of times, like the best, are always passing away.

It's got me through a few hard times that one has. Take it and use it as a tool of defence against that feeling of helplessness that you are stuck in a situation that won't change. It's a big part of our brainwashing to think that things should always remain the same. We have this normality myth where everything is just right and has always been just so. We all crave this. It's comfortable and reassuring to think that things will be okay if they are just normal.

It's one of the biggest lies of our whole paradigm. There is no such thing as normal. Nothing stays the same for even one millisecond. By the very laws of physics that hold our entire society together, we are all in a constant state of flux. Everything is changing all the time all around us. Nothing is constant.

Normality is a myth designed to distract and confuse. One thing this applies to more than anything is nature and the world around us. In nature, the only thing which is constant is change. And that's a purely scientific fact.

'Surf the wave of change, get in the barrel and ride it to its conclusion.

Miss that wave and you will be left wallowing in the shallows of yesterday.'

That one's my own.

When the first weekend of September arrives, all the madness of August just stops dead like nothing I've ever known elsewhere. One day the town is in full swing and the next it's over and that's that.

The fact is that the weather changes rapidly as well and although autumn became my favourite time of year it does cool down a lot and also the daylight quickly starts to fade meaning that by October it's pretty much winter living again and the beach life is a thing of the past.

Winter living in France was great but it also meant work and an end to beach life. Around this time, I started working for PKW Yacht Joinery which had contracts on a variety of large super yachts. Some really big yachts actually.

Some of the contracts were extensive and took weeks and some took just a few hours but PKW had a very professional setup which was the only way into these big yachts. To be clear, the smallest I worked on with PKW was 70 m and the biggest 105 m.

I worked with PKW all through that next winter and we spent a lot of time on the International Quay in Antibes. To get to that section of the port one had to pass right by the entrance to the toilet bowl. As such I would sometimes find myself on the beach having lunch.

I actually remember the specific day and you'll see why because it was the 23rd December. It was my last day of work with PKW before we had a break over Christmas. I'd gone down to the toilet bowl for lunch as it was still a popular spot in the winter.

The weather was warm and sunny even in December and it wasn't unusual to see people sunbathing in bikinis or speedos. But no, that's not why I was having lunch there. Well, not the main reason anyway.

Well alright, it was kind of a big reason but look…Anyway, the beach wasn't exactly busy but it was certainly in use and I had taken a spot sitting by the wall to the right of the gate. As I was sitting there eating my baguette I watched as a bunch of police men and women came in and split up, heading the other way to the left side of the beach.

I knew what they were doing right away. They were looking for people smoking weed. It was a popular spot to do so. One reason we did not do so was because it was known by the police, and we had seen them come and search for people in this same way a few times before.

Their routine was to spy from the top of the wall above and find someone committing the crime of smoking cannabis. Another team would then come down the beach cutting off any means of escape and the bust was made. Well done guys. What a brave and important defence of society.

On this occasion, they found a victim. A couple were sitting down by the wall enjoying a spliff and as I watched they got busted. I was really pissed off because the poor people were not harming anyone and as far as I was concerned this was all a stupid waste of police time and an attack on civil liberty.

However, at that moment, it occurred to me that I still had a small piece of hashish in with my rolling tobacco. I used to smoke cigarettes at work when I couldn't smoke a joint and I often used to carry around a little bit of hashish so I could roll a joint if the opportunity arose. Always the opportunist me.

Although the police were a long way over the other side of the beach, it still occurred to me that they might decide to come down this way as well and I thought I better ditch the bit of hashish. Could I find it? Could I fuck. I looked and looked and in the end, the police had left the beach and I gave up looking thinking it must have been lost.

That evening my friend Nicole got in touch asking if I wanted to meet up with her the next day and have a drink and a smoke on the beach. Nicole was hot and thinking about splitting up with her boyfriend…Or so she told me.

We had been friends for about six months by now and I was also helping her get cannabis as I actually had better connections than her in the local area. She was originally from Nantes and had moved to Nice, where she lived, around 10 years before.

I fancied the pants off her but I was not the kind to mess around with someone else's girlfriend…Unless, they made it very clear they wanted me too that is. Nicole made it clear she fancied me but just not clear enough to get me to make any move so we just had this flirty thing going on which we both enjoyed and was all good fun really. I've since come to understand that this is quite typical behaviour of naughty French girls.

So, the plan was made to meet up in Antibes old town and get some supplies then head down to the beach for the afternoon. Don't ask me why but for some reason we headed to the exact same spot where I had seen the other couple being busted the very day before.

Maybe in my mind, I thought if they were there the day before then surely they wouldn't come again the next day. To be honest I don't think I even thought about it. Probably because I was thinking more about the contents of Nicole's knickers than anything else.

It was a gorgeous day. Warm and sunny. We were sitting in the full sun just soaking it up. We both had a couple of big cans of Heineken and were now tucking into our second joint when I looked over and walking down the beach towards us, looking right at me, was a policeman.

I had a joint in my hand so I just thrust it deep into the sand right away. The policeman yelled and came running over and then I looked up and saw that there were a couple of them on the wall above us. It was a bust.

The policeman saw my packet of rolling tobacco sitting on my towel and pointing saying, 'Let's have a look in there then.'

I smiled knowing there was nothing incriminating in there.

However, he opened the bag and without even looking just pulled out the lump of hashish and grinned saying, 'Well now. What have we here then?'

I was incredulous. I couldn't find that thing for the life of me the day before but now…Fuck.

He told me to stand up and I just decided to be honest and said, 'Well as you've got me I might as well just give you these.'

I pulled out my box of weed which had about half an ounce in it but I had also brought down another half for Nicole. So, I had a total of one ounce on me which, if you don't know about weed, is a lot to be carrying around. I just handed them both over and their eyes lit up. Now all the police, about five of them, were elated. They had achieved their mission for the day and could go home and start to celebrate Christmas.

But first, we had to take a trip to the station and get me processed. They didn't even search Nicole and although she did her best to convince them to just let me go they were adamant that because of the large amount of weed I had on me, they needed to take me to the station and ask some more questions.

So, I was led off the beach by the police on Christmas Eve after spending two years smoking weed down there every night in the summer. It already seemed ironic to me even back then.

All the way down to the station I was chatting with the police, in a very friendly way, but telling them that what they were doing was immoral because I wasn't hurting anyone. They agreed but said they had a job to do.

Down at the station, they left me sitting in a corridor for an age but after some time I was led into a smallish room with a desk in the middle and a middle-aged man sitting at it. He didn't look at me and I just sat down opposite him. On his desk was my weed in its special box I used for storing it. Also, my grinder which was used to crush the weed up. The room was decorated in a way I'd never seen before or after.

He had shelves and cabinets containing every kind of street weapon, drug consumption device or basically anything to do with street crime. It was his memorial of years of policing the streets of Antibes and he had been collecting all this stuff for a long time.

I was just sitting there staring at all this stuff until, after a while, I realised he was looking at me and grinning.

I didn't even bother trying to speak French and asked him, 'What is all this stuff?'

He grinned more and said, 'It's my job.'

I didn't reply but thought, *Fair enough* and a level of respect was established. He was now looking at my weed. He took it out and weighed it all together and it was just under an ounce.

'Where did you get it?'

It was a question I had been expecting and the answer was long previously prepared.

'Off some Arab guy in Nice town centre,' it was a reply we both knew was a lie but we both knew it was a legitimate answer as it was a place everyone knew one might obtain anything they might desire.

As such he couldn't dispute it and wrote my answer down on his form. That was the only question he asked me.

Then there was a pause and he seemed to be writing some other stuff down and looking through some other documents and then after a while I was just sitting there looking at my weed and my box and my grinder.

Our eyes met as I looked up from my things and without thinking about it I asked, 'Can I have my box back?'

He looked at me and simply nodded.

'Can I have my grinder back?'

Again, he nodded.

'Can I have my weed? It is Christmas after all.'

He grinned more and said, 'This time you're just getting a caution,' and he slid a document over the table.

'Next time there will be trouble. Clear?'

'Crystal.'

'Off you go then and Bon Noel.'

I never even found out his name but what a top bloke.

I wandered back through town and it was getting dark by now. I had a day snowboarding planned for Christmas day and by now my thoughts were turning to that. I called Nicole and informed her all was well and to be honest I didn't even give the remotest damn about what had happened.

Even the fact I'd lost an oz of weed didn't bother me too much because I had plenty more at home. The thing that stuck in my mind the most was how I couldn't find the lump of hash the day before and then it was right there for the policeman the next day. Things have a funny way of going like that.

Next up we are heading north to the Bordeaux region of France but the story begins mid-Atlantic on the infamous motor vessel Ramu. This is actually one of my favourite and most retold stories so I can't wait to get into it. See you there.

17

Lost in Deepest Darkest France

Okay, so this time we are going to jump forward a few years but then go back a few months in order to try and give some picture as to how disjointed my life had become by this stage. It's also time for Amber to enter the story.

It's worth pointing out that in recent years, with the help of hindsight, I've come to think of Amber as the worst mistake I ever made. The problem was that I didn't just make it once. I made it five times over a period of five years. I just couldn't stop going back for more.

As is usually the case in situations like this there was a good reason I kept going back for more. Well, it wasn't a good reason exactly. But we'll come back to that later. Five years is a long time to be banging your head against a wall and by the end of it, all I had left was a shattered lump of a neck.

But Amber's role in this particular story is only a very minor one. Although she was my girlfriend at this point, loosely speaking that is, during the story, we were actually many miles apart.

But we start out in the Caribbean Sea. Not a usual place to start you might think and you would be right. The reason I'm going to start out here is that it's where the pattern once again moved into its negative cycle for Amber and I. The pattern went like this. After some time, apart Amber and I would forget the horror and start to miss each other.

Next, we would get back together, take loads of drugs and have a wild party for a while. This would last either days, weeks or months. But never more than a few months. Then at some point, Amber would become displeased with me. Usually because she would try and force me to do something I didn't want to do and I would refuse. Her response to this was always to decide that she didn't want to have sex with me anymore.

At this point, maybe I should point out that a large part of the reason I was with Amber was because I liked having sex with her. A lot of the time we were not having sex she was a right royal pain in the arse. However, when the sex was flowing I could tolerate the bullshit enough to get by for a while. So, when she cut it off it didn't go down well.

The first problem would be that I would sulk. Which did not go down well with her. Then I would drink more each night and there on in we would enter a cycle of starting to hate each other. This would escalate until Amber would call it off at some point down the line.

This exact pattern happened five times over five years and by the end of it, my heart was so torn to pieces that it was nothing more than a tatty rag. You see, just like with Ariel, I really loved Amber. In reality, there wasn't much to love about her, except her looks, but I was so lonely that I was just blind to any sign of sense or reason.

My friends all tried to tell me to leave her alone. Unfortunately, I'm not friends with any of those people now and I don't blame them frankly. If I was to find myself in a friendship with someone who kept going back and willingly hurting themselves, then I would have to walk away at some point as well.

I'm sorry this is all a bit miserable. The story won't be, I assure you but it's important for me to talk about this stage of my life as it really was. By now, the dream was finished and the nightmare was in full swing. That wasn't to make it any less interesting though. Oh no.

Not by a long way in fact it just keeps getting spicier from here on in. And being spicy it was far from comfortable for me at the time. My vortex of chaos was now cooking up a big pot of stinking hot curry and was about to dump it in my lap.

Amber and I had both been living/working/job hunting on the Caribbean Island of St Martin during a winter in the late noughties. The time I spent on that island during this period could be a book all of its own. It was truly one of the most hedonistic periods of my life and I shall attempt to give you some insight.

Since I first tried it when I was 18 I had always been rather partial to cocaine. If you've not tried it, please don't be judgemental. The simple honest truth of the matter is that there is very little difference between cocaine and coffee. Now wait a minute, just hear me out now. In a nutshell, both things perk you up, give you motivation, energy and confidence. Coffee seems quite popular these days, wouldn't you say?

Even if you don't like it yourself you can't help but notice the abundance of cafes everywhere you go. Energy drinks as well. So, whether you want to admit it or not, if you like coffee then you would like cocaine as well. If there were a legal market for it in the same way that there is for alcohol and tobacco, then you would no doubt use it in much the same way you use coffee or other stimulants.

This whole system we have of splitting substances up according to a series of rules made by people no different to you and I is just utterly absurd. But I'm not going to go into a long one about that just now.

Let's just settle on the fact that Amber and I had been doing a lot of coke while we were in St Martin together. Being so close to South America, the home of the coca plant, the coke was a lot purer and way cheaper. We indulged accordingly and had one hell of a good time. I mean we really got stuck in and indulged our fantasies together.

I'm just going to make one more point about illegal drugs here and that is to say that out of all the times I took illegal drugs, on 99% of those occasions I had one hell of a good time. No dramas, no issues, no problems. Just good fun. Whereas with alcohol, a legal drug, well I'm sure I don't need to explain to you the amount of trouble that gets involved with the consumption of alcohol.

A lot is a fair thing to say. For me and for a lot of other people. Do me a favour and read that last paragraph again. Then, have a good think about what I've said.

Our society needs to adjust its attitude to substance legality and it needs to happen soon. Adult humans should have the right to choose for themselves what they consume. No government has the right to dictate to us what we may or may not put into our own bodies. If we hadn't grown up with prohibition, then we would all see it as the farce it truly is rather than just accepting it as a way of life. I for one do not accept it and nor should you.

During that winter that we spent in St Martin Amber got the job as the cook on the infamous motor vessel Ramu. Ramu was well known as a very unconventional yacht and I can assure you that everything about my time on Ramu was in every way unconventional. So being a somewhat unconventional kind of person this suited me quite well.

Amber had been off for a two-week charter with Ramu while I stayed in St Martin and worked on a big motor yacht doing some varnishing work. We were both earning really good money and spending very little of it. At the end of the charter, it was agreed that I would join Ramu as deck crew for the Atlantic crossing back to Malta where the yacht was scheduled for a yard period.

To me, this was a perfect scenario as I had always wanted to be a part of the Ramu thing and it meant that Amber and I would share a cabin for the crossing. I was about to have my cake and eat it. *Or so*, I thought.

We had the chance to spend a weekend together before the crossing so we booked a hotel, bought loads of coke and pills and just snorted, swallowed, drank and fucked all weekend. It was a lot of fun. However, an undeniable law of the universe is "that which goes up must come down". Pure cocaine used in moderate quantities has next to zero side effects.

As you increase the amount and reduce the purity the side effects start and take the form of the "come down". This is much like a hangover but takes quite a different form. Both leave you feeling utterly wretched but in quite different ways somehow. If you add large quantities of alcohol and MDMA to the cocktail, then you are in for one hell of a rough ride for a good few days after a prolonged session.

You could certainly say that our session was prolonged. We went at it hard for the whole weekend. We hardly slept. We certainly did not sober up. On Monday morning when we were supposed to be on the dock to meet the captain and get a ride out to the boat, we were still in the hotel room, high as kites and still having sex. Not an ideal start.

Captains generally don't like being left waiting on the dock. Fortunately, this particular captain was a very easy-going guy. Shout out Raffa, one of the best men I ever sailed with. He had waited a while and then, with some idea where we were, he had left the dock and returned to his yacht. Raffa was due to leave for an Atlantic crossing that day and couldn't lose his cook so he had no choice but to wait for us to call and then send a crew member in to get us.

I think it's fair to say it's not the best way to arrive at a new job but he did forgive me and we ended up getting on really well for the crossing. Me and Raffa might have got on well for the crossing but that morning in St Martin something happened between Amber and I that was to have a knock-on effect for months after and was in fact the beginning of the end for that period of our relationship.

The pattern was in full swing again. I pissed her off so badly that she stopped wanting to have sex with me again for the first week of the crossing.

I mentioned that Ramu is err, unconventional shall we say. Well only in certain respects. One thing that remained standard was that she was a dry ship once off the dock. Once at sea, there was no drinking or drugs although weed was fine on Ramu. One of the reasons I had always wanted to work on board.

So, the moment we had joined the boat we had both been going cold turkey. This seriously fucks with your head. Really badly and it makes you think all sorts of nonsense. In some ways, an Atlantic crossing is the perfect place to do it because you are totally removed from the normal world and all the normal things that might present a problem. However, Amber and I had to share a cabin as well as cook and eat together all day every day.

Actually, as crossings go it really wasn't that bad and apart from the fact that Amber didn't want to have sex with me we had a great time. We got really into cooking all sorts of yummy food and Raffa asked me to make a DJ mix for him which became a big project and something I am still proud of today.

The lack of sex remained a problem until Amber got her cycle and got horny again. After that things started to get better between us as they hadn't really been that bad in the first place. By the time we got to Malta Amber and I were actually getting on a lot better. However, there was about to arrive a serious spanner in the works and yes well actually there was about to arrive a serious spanner on board.

His name was Pablo and he ranks in my top five all-time cunts list. We hated each other from the moment we laid eyes on each other. The problem was that he was there to be the relief captain while Raffa took a two-month break. This was bad news for me. What was worse news was the fact that Pablo had immediately taken a shine to Amber.

Within one week of Raffa leaving and Pablo arriving, I was fired. Not fired exactly but I was told I was no longer needed because the owner wanted an old crew member back. It was a bullshit story and I was told this by the other crew who I had earned the respect of by this point. Pablo just wanted me gone. To be fair I wanted to go. The second Raffa was gone and Pablo was in charge the whole vibe on board had changed. As is the way with boats and their captains.

I flew out of Malta the day after my 33rd birthday. I actually had no idea how much money I had in my bank as I was too scared to find out. This was pre-internet banking. We had the internet but banking wasn't as easy to do as it is now. I needed to actually go to one of my banks and put my card in or call them which always meant loads of security questions and it was all just too much hassle. Instead, I just hoped for the best and worried a lot. And drank more.

Before leaving, I had called Nicole and begged her to let me stay at her place for a few nights while I was working out what to do next. She grudgingly agreed but she lived with her boyfriend and they were going through another difficult patch. It seemed as though it was always the case but the fact was she just really didn't want me there and I can't say I blame her.

What happened next is what always happened in these situations. I pulled my finger out and found a job. Although this time I did not pick well. Or more to the point it was time for some karma to catch up with me. Look out, Bobby. Incoming.

I saw an advert on a local website for a construction company looking for carpenters for a project in the Bordeaux region of France. I called the number and spoke to Brian who was actually an East Coast American but was now doing construction, of sorts, in France. Brian, curiously enough, ranks as number two on my all-time cunts list.

However, we got on well enough on the phone and he informed me that the project was to rebuild the roof of an old barn. There would be a team of four of us, plus Brian, for one week. Brian had organised accommodation nearby and would drive us to and fro each day. In theory, this all seemed okay and I agreed to go along.

The plan was for me to get the early train to somewhere near Marseille where Brian and his team were currently based. We would then meet up and all drive together up to the main project near Bordeaux. If you don't know France, the Bordeaux region of France is quite a big place. It's a pretty wide-open county with nothing but massive, flat, empty fields. Well, some empty and some being farmed but most of it just looked empty to me.

To try and give it some context the drive from our accommodation to the actual farm was about 30 minutes and was all along straight roads and driven at well over 100 mph by Brian as he was a rally driver (or so he told us) and thought it was funny to scare the shit out of us. He nearly killed us all several times.

So, if it took 30 minutes at that speed and the two places were supposed to be close then I think you get what I mean. Big, wide, flat open fields and not much else. The odd farm and little town. But first, we had to get there.

I got really drunk (on my own) at Nicole's the night before leaving and was really hungover the next morning at 4:00 am trying to get my shit together to get to the train. For some reason, I stole a packet of cigarettes from Nicole's boyfriend. He had a whole carton on the side and I wanted something to smoke. I just took a packet thinking he wouldn't notice. What a twat I was.

I made it to the train okay but was feeling worse and worse all the way as I sobered up. The moment I met Brian in person I knew he was a cunt and was going to be a problem. However, now I was there I didn't have much choice but to continue as I had now spent my own money on the train ticket. So, I was kind of committed to getting paid at the end or I had already made a loss.

On the drive up to Bordeaux, Brian went on and on about how he was an ex-marine and a rally driver and such an all-round hero. I sat there thinking, *Oh fuck what have I got myself into here?*

It's a long drive, about six hours and by the time we got there, I hated his guts already but had formed a pretty good view of the other guys. We had Tommy, the English foreman, a short fat Jordie in his early 50s and two lads in their early 20s. One Scottish, Jock, and another, Paul, from somewhere else in the north of England. They were all legends. Really good blokes and we bonded together into a tight unit for the duration of this job.

Brian, on the other hand, was going from bad to worse. When we arrived, he announced that he was not paying for our food. To me, this was unthinkable as it was his responsibility to feed us in such a situation. He dug his heels in and just refused. My response was to get all the other guys together and make them a deal that if we all chucked a little money in together then I would cook us all a decent meal every night after work.

As long as they all did all the cleaning up after. This excluded Brian obviously but worked like a dream for the rest of us and was a solution to dinner but not, however, to lunch. We needed to be able to eat a meal during the working day as well. But Brian thought that we should be like marines and didn't need to eat and should just work all day with no food.

Like 10 hours day straight through with no meal break. Again, I dug my heels in and we fought bitterly. This battle was to run over the course of the whole job.

Before we could build the new roof, we had to get the old one off. Tommy was the only one with any roofing experience between the lot of us. And he was not a roofer but had just done a bit a long time ago. Tommy was a bricklayer by trade. Paul was a welder, Jock was a labourer, Brian was a cunt and I was a trainee shipwright who in reality didn't have the first clue about how to dismantle or build a roof.

None of us did. Literally. Brian had this vague idea, how he thought the whole thing might go but in reality he had never done this work before and had no idea how to do any of it. Basically, he was trying to make it up as he went.

The moment we arrived I got nervous because this roof was high and we had no scaffolding. We had a couple of ladders but only one which was going to be long enough to even get us to the roof. This roof was high up. It was a big barn. I would estimate around 30 x 20 m.

The roof started at about a height of 10 m and at its top point must have been well over 15 m of the ground. I just stood there looking at it thinking FUCK. We are going to have to go up there and take that apart with no safety equipment and no scaffolding.

Brian's solution to this was to hire a mobile lifting platform, or cherry picker, for the first two days only. He was sure we only needed two days to get the old roof off and that after that we would be able to build the new roof with only ladders to access the bottom corner.

The first day we arrived it was looking grey and the mood was grim. What didn't help was that the rental company was supposed to be delivering our cherry picker that morning but that morning was part of day one and Brian had only allowed for two days.

The cherry picker arrived around noon so we had already lost half a day before it even turned up. Beyond giving us a cherry picker, Brian didn't actually have any more plans as to how to get the old roof off. He figured that it was up to us to work that out.

We managed okay to start with but it was really hard work and very time-consuming as it took us a while to work out a system for getting the old roof off and down to the ground. By the end of day one, we had only made a tiny dent in the old roof and we were all totally exhausted after working well past dark with no lights. Brian was livid that we had made so little progress and thought that talking to us like some sort of drill sergeant was going to be the solution.

I was having none of this. I am no kind of hard man but I wasn't going to take shit from this guy. By now, I had developed something of a razor-sharp tongue. Years of working around salty old sea dogs and hard-arsed English tradesmen had given me a resilience to being given shit and an acute ability to give it back.

Sometimes in a way that couldn't be taken as an actual direct insult. I was skilled at it and used it as a weapon. With hindsight, I can see that all it really does is wind people up and all that does is make them a bigger problem.

The next day it was pouring with rain and things got spicy. The previous night I had gotten really drunk on cheap wine and the next morning I had a stinking hangover. Not fab when combined with pouring rain and working at heights with no safety equipment.

Brian was expecting us to have the whole roof off by the end of the day as the cherry picker needed to be returned to the rental people the next morning. We knew this was simply not going to happen. We also had no lunch again.

The day before we had somehow managed to get through but mainly because we spent a lot of the morning doing nothing and waiting for the hire equipment. Now we were in full work mode and needed calories. Add to that the fact that it was cold and pouring with rain and blowing a gale.

That morning the idea of going back up onto that roof was about as close to a kind of living nightmare as I've ever experienced. However, I did what I've always done in hard situations like this. I knuckled down, pulled my finger out and got the job done. I worked out a good system for getting the old roof off and cracked on full pelt. At lunch time, I told the others to stop. Brian saw me.

I didn't care. I told him why myself straight to his face. We were not working another full day without lunch and either he went and sorted something out for us or we were not lifting another finger. The barn was owned by an English couple who were in the process of converting the farmhouse next to it. They were also living in the farmhouse but had a caravan outside and we had that to use as our crew hut.

We all went and sat in there and refused to work until we were fed. In the end, the owners were so desperate to see work progress that they cooked egg and bacon sandwiches for us. It wasn't much in the way of calories but it was enough to get us moving again and by dark, we had 90% of the roof off.

That evening went much the same as the last. Brian tried to act the big boss man and I got drunk and told him to go fuck himself. At that stage, he needed me to get the job done. What I was failing to see was that the moment the job was complete he would have no use for me but I would need him to pay me. My whole reason for being there was only to be paid after all. Or was it?

Looking back, I can see that I was actually far more concerned about my relationship with Amber than I was about anything that was happening in my own present reality. One big reason for that was that Pablo had the hots for Amber and that was a big part of why he wanted me out of the way.

So, it didn't come as a big surprise to me when Amber informed me the next day that Pablo had come into her cabin the previous night and declared that they should have sex. She had politely declined without incident but it was clear that unless she did what he wanted her time on board would also be short.

Amber seemed to think that because Raffa had hired her that Pablo could not fire her which was of course complete nonsense. I was trying to tell her that all along but she wouldn't listen and kept saying that Pablo wouldn't fire her because Raffa wouldn't let him. He fired her. She left the boat about one week later. But that's another story.

For now, I'm stuck in deepest darkest France doing battle with Brian. Again, the next day we fought over lunch and again we ended up downing tools. This time we eventually convinced Brian to go and get us a McDonald's as there was one a 30-minute drive away. He was gone for nearly two hours in the end and it was past 15:00 by the time we got any food.

We'd started before 08:00 am. It wasn't like we could just walk to the local shop and get our own. We were literally in the middle of bum fuck nowhere. Brian knew this. We knew this. Somehow work progressed. The cherry picker went back and we ended up working up on the roof building the new one in some of the most dangerous working conditions I've ever endured. Ironic considering all the stuff I'd already done on yachts.

The last day I was literally shitting myself before starting. The day before Tommy had nearly fallen to a serious injury or even death right in front of me. It was only because of a very quick action on his part that stopped him from falling through and down a long way.

It could happen to any one of us if we were not super careful and it was terrifying because we had to do hard work which was tiring and required balance and skill. All with zero safety equipment and a long fall as a result of the slightest mistake.

It was emotionally exhausting and when I got back to the ground at the end of the final day I actually got down on the ground and kissed it because I was so happy to still be alive. Literally. By now, Brian and I hardly spoke unless we needed to and we avoided that. But it had always been the agreement that he would drive me to the train station and buy my ticket home at the end of the job. The full wages would be paid once I sent him an invoice as was standard.

By now, I was seriously out of pocket. I'd paid for a train fare and all my food for the week without getting a penny back. Every time I used my card I was shitting myself that it wouldn't work. That was my only way of finding out I had no money.

After completing the project, Brian decided to celebrate and took the two lads off with him to a local nightclub. Tommy and I stayed at the cabin and I, yes you guessed it, got drunk. Really drunk. I'd reached a point where the only time I felt good was when I was drunk. So, when I started drinking I didn't want to stop. Especially if I didn't have to work the next day. So, I stayed up late downing beers and then finishing the wine.

I got some sleep and in the morning Brian was home but I hadn't seen him and no plan had been made to get me to the train station. I wanted to get there as early as possible as I knew it was a long train ride back and I wanted to get home ASAP. Not that I had a home to go to but I wanted to get back to Antibes as I did at least know people there.

I figured I would call Nicole at some point that day and she'd be cool to give me a sofa again for a few days. But I had to get there first and I was still halfway across France.

By 07:00 am, there was no sign of Brian and I started getting angry. I started shouting and banging on the door to his room but he locked it and just ignored me. I knew he wasn't sleeping through the racket I was making so it was clear he was just lying there ignoring me. I got my main weapon out. That being my tongue.

I threatened to report him to the French authorities and get him banned from working in France ever again. This got his attention and he came storming out of the cabin and marched right up into my face.

I was standing in the middle of the lounge where Tommy had been sleeping on the sofa. He was now sitting there wide awake and watching. Brian came right at me. He marched right up to me and came eyeball to eyeball with me. To my credit, I didn't flinch or move a muscle. I just stood there and stared right back at him.

I knew that he wasn't going to touch me and I was safe from physical attack. It was a very quick, cool and calm calculation made by a part of my brain that takes over in critical situations. I knew he was an ex-marine. He hadn't been making that up. I knew he could kill me in a second if he wanted to. But I also knew that he was an American in France.

As such he could be deported for the slightest crime and never allowed back in. I knew this having worked alongside other Americans. As non-Europeans, they are in a different boat altogether in the eyes of the French police. So, I just stood there and we had a staring match which I won.

After maybe a minute, he turned away, took a few paces and then turned back to say, 'You've been a problem since you arrived here. You're fired. Now, fuck off.'

He walked back into his room and shut the door and I never saw him again. I just stood there. Tommy was staring at me. I looked at him and said nothing for a minute.

Then I walked over and held out my hand and said, 'So long mate. Look after yourself.'

We shook hands warmly. He was a good man and we had grown fond of each other in that short space of time. My rucksack was on the floor next to me so I put it on my shoulders and walked out of the cabin without another word.

So, let's just do a quick recap for those at the back. I was somewhere in deepest darkest France. I don't have any memory of the actual name of that village. It was somewhere in the Bordeaux region as far as I know. At that point, I might as well have been on the moon because I really had no idea which way to go to get home. Not that I had a home to go to but we'll get to that.

It was early on a Sunday morning. I had no idea how much available cash I had but I was sure it was not much. I had no idea if it was going to be enough to get a train ticket to Antibes. Even if I knew where the nearest train station was. Which I didn't. I had literally no idea where I was or which way to go.

Does this sound familiar by now? I'm also still drunk from the night before (again familiar?) and utterly physically and emotionally exhausted after the week of work I had just had.

Add to this the fact that I didn't really speak French all that well. In that part of France, English is not as widely spoken as it is in the south where I lived. Down there everyone spoke English and it was as common as French. But up in the sticks you had a 50/50 chance of getting an English speaker at best.

Considering all of this you'd be forgiven for thinking that I might be a little down in my spirits but in fact, that wasn't the case at all. For one thing, I was still drunk and as such didn't really care about anything. For another thing, I was just massively relieved to be leaving and out of that nightmarish situation. Even without a train ticket.

So, I found myself walking down a country lane with a big rucksack early one Sunday morning, still pissed as a fart from the night before. I sort of knew the way around the immediate vicinity by now and it seemed best to head to a big roundabout that we had passed each day and start hitchhiking from there.

As a student, I had actually done a fair bit of hitchhiking and had always been good at it. I knew that out in the country, it was still quite normal and quite honestly at that point it was that or walk. I knew that whichever direction I wanted to go it was a long way to the nearest town and by long way I mean I knew it would take most of the morning. I needed to get to a train station ASAP so I planted myself at the first roundabout and started waiting.

The problem was that it was still early. Maybe 08:00 am by now and there was very little traffic out and about. What traffic there was not the sort of people who were likely to stop for me. It was mostly old couples and I stood there for the better part of an hour without getting any interest. Only a handful of cars even passed.

Eventually, I thought fuck it and decided to set off down the road in the direction of a big-sounding town that was signposted. It was shortly after as I was walking down the road that I had something curious happen.

This was long before the days when phones had video cameras, but I thought to myself, *How cool it would be right now in this totally fucked up situation to have a little video camera in my pocket that I could pull out and record a short clip about what was happening.* At that point in time, social media was still in its infancy and what I just described wasn't to actually become an available reality until years later.

Yet at that moment as I was walking down that road in the middle of bum fuck nowhere, I saw how funny my situation was and I thought how good it would be to record it for other people's appreciation at a later date. I guess it's a good job that I have a good memory instead.

I didn't make it far down that road before I saw a car coming and so stuck out my thumb. This time they stopped but as I went to the car I saw that it said taxi on the side. The window rolled down and a woman in her 40s started speaking French which I somehow understood and was able to reply. She informed me she was a taxi service and where did I want to go. I informed her that I wanted to go to the nearest train station.

She informed me that it would cost 50 Euro to which I said, 'Oh no. Sorry, I can't afford that I will have to keep walking.'

She replied, 'Oh okay don't worry. In that case, just get in and I'll take you for free.'

I was elated. Just like that 50% of my dilemma had been resolved. I was no longer lost and now all I needed to do was get a ticket and I was home again. But would my card work? She dropped me at the nearest Gare SNCF and I requested a ticket to Antibes. I don't think I've ever been so nervous to see if a payment will go through. It did.

I nearly broke down when the machine worked and my ticket came out. The only problem was that the next train was not in fact until 18:00 and it was still only just coming to 10:00. I had eight hours to wait.

As soon as I had fixed my immediate concerns one thing came very clearly to mind. Beer. To my way of thinking back then the sensible thing in a situation like this was to find the nearest Bar Tabac and have a beer as I was a bag of nerves and feeling the hangover start to creep in.

The station was a bit out of the town itself so I had to walk for maybe 10 minutes before I was coming into the town. There, sure enough, was a Bar Tabac. You can't go far in France without seeing one and they usually serve beer on tap. This one was tiny but open and indeed served beer on tap.

The first demi went down like a dream and the second was about halfway down when exhaustion kicked in. The adrenaline which had been keeping me going since I left the cabin was now gone. I suddenly felt very tired and all I could think about was laying down somewhere dark and sleeping for a while.

During the first beer I had called Nicole and she had said it was fine for me to stay again when I got back. I had left a couple of bags there as well so I needed to pick them up at least.

So now I was going home and I had a place to stay. When I got there, I could finally fully relax. Only I still had to actually get there. Which still meant a long wait as it was only 11:00 am by now.

I decided that the best thing to do was to find a hotel and see if they would rent me a room for half the day or something. Yes, this was a ridiculous notion but I was drunk and I couldn't think straight. All I wanted was to lie down and go to sleep. The lady who worked in the Tabac told me there was a hotel on the road out of town so I headed back down the road I had come in on and then took what I thought to be the turning for the road out of town.

After walking up this for about 15 minutes, the town was thinning out and there was no sign of a hotel. I saw an approaching car and decided to thumb it down and ask for advice. The guy stopped. He was middle-aged and didn't speak a word of English but I managed to explain my situation a little and got it across that I wanted to find a hotel.

Let's bear in mind that this is not a tourist region of France, people don't come here on holiday. As such hotels are not as common as I expected and as they are in other parts of France. However, the guy said he knew a hotel and he could take me there if I wanted.

Deeply relieved, I accepted his offer and jumped in. We set off and after about 10 minutes of driving down a straight road, we had left the town way behind and were now once again in the middle of nowhere. I didn't panic but just decided to see where I ended up. After a 30-minute drive, we arrived in another small town and pulled up outside a very shabby-looking building right in the middle of town.

'Here we are,' he announced.

I got out and looked at the building. It was half falling down and there was a sign hanging in the dirty window. The sign was half hanging on its side, so it was hard to read but it said Ferme. Closed.

I looked at the guy who looked at me and I said, 'Thanks.'

He said, 'No problem,' and drove off.

Standing there for about five minutes or so I just didn't know what to think or do. What usually happens in this case is that my need for alcohol kicks in and I decided that the sensible thing to do would be to find the local Bar Tabac and have a beer. The Bar Tabac was in fact just around the corner and as I walked in I was greeted by a sight I've never seen anywhere before or since.

It was really very close to the Star Wars bar if you know what I mean and the place was pumping. Rammed full of people of all sorts of shapes and sizes but also some of the most deformed and inbred people I have ever seen in my life.

Everyone was drinking hard and smoking hard and many were playing the lotto thing they have in Bar Tabac as well. A kind of gambling. To me, in my current state, this seemed perfect and I strolled up to the bar, or rather pushed my way to the bar, and ordered a beer.

Drinking my beer at a table I just marvelled at the crazy twists and turns my life takes but within about 10 minutes of my arriving the place completely emptied out. It was now 12:00 and this was clearly time for everyone to head off to have their Sunday lunches. Before I'd finished my first beer, I was alone in there. What a trip. The place had been pumping just 15 minutes before.

Well, I finished my beer and decided that I better hitchhike back to the town where the train station was. This time it was easy as by now everyone was out and about and many of the drivers had had a few beers at least. As such I quickly found a nice chap to take me back and we both chatted happily all the way there. By now, my French was getting way better than ever before.

Like on another level. I could just jabber away like I was fluent and could also understand most of what he said. Which was unusual as that was normally the thing I found hardest. Curiously I've never again been able to come close to that level of French speaking.

Back in the town I spent the last of my cash on a plat du jour and staggered to the train station. It was still only 15:00. Another three hours to wait so I just pulled my clothes out on the floor and did the best I could to make a bed with them. The journey home was uneventful but when I got to Nice I got a shock.

Nicole wouldn't answer my calls and instead just sent me a single text saying that my bag was in the hallway downstairs and if I told her when I was there she would unlock the door but I was not to come up as she didn't want to see me or speak to me.

I was really confused because she had been fine just the day before but considering that I stole a packet of cigarettes from her boyfriend it's hardly surprising. The double whammy came when I discovered that the train fare had taken the very last of my money. I had less than 10 euros to my name. Just enough for a ticket to Antibes.

What happens next is another story but I can tell you that I did find a place to stay and I found more work and Amber came back and it all ended horribly ever after. I mean it really turns bad from here on in. Keep reading. Don't worry, it's not gonna get boring at all.

Only for me, I was about to find out what happens when you think you can behave however you want and get away with it. The fact is that it will always come back around. Karma will always come back and bite you on the ass. Always.

18

A Tight Spot in Antibes

The more I think about how to tell this next story, the more I think I might as well just pick up where I left off in the last chapter. You see, the events of the next six months were to have an impact on my life that is still with me now. What I mean by that is that it was during this next period that I made the decision to stop using cannabis and just like that I completely cut it out of my life for five years.

At that point, in time I still had a good network of friends in the Côte d'Azur area and a reasonably sound professional reputation in the super yacht industry. It was no secret that I liked the party but everyone also knew I was a grafter and would always show up for work and get the job done, no matter what had gone down the night before.

However, I was on a seriously bad downward spiral and it's hard to think that anything or anyone could have stopped or even slowed it down by then. People did try. People who are now not my friends. That hurts but I don't blame them. We have to move on and do what we believe is right for ourselves.

By now, I was in my mid-30s and really should have been showing some sign that I was growing up and becoming a man. I was not though. Not in any way. In fact, I was regressing in many ways. All I really wanted was two things. Number one I wanted to be loved and number two I wanted to get drunk because when I was drunk I didn't care that no one loved me.

The only thing I had ever really wanted was to find a good woman who would love me and want to share my life. But as is the way with most things, the more I wanted it and the harder I tried to find it the more elusive it became.

This was the state that Amber had found me in and her eyes must have lit up when she worked out just how vulnerable I was. I became her emotional plaything for the next five years. For a long time after we split up, she would still keep me in my box until she wanted to get me out and play with me. Then she would get in touch, flirt and play until she was bored again whereupon…yes back in my box. Until the next time.

If this pattern of behaviour sounds familiar to you and perhaps you or someone you know and care about is going through something like this, then I have some advice for you. It's a very simple bit of advice. It was handed to me over the counter with my coffee by an amazing woman I knew briefly in Exeter.

I don't recall her name but the advice was simply this, 'Some things are just toxic.'

I don't believe it was a reference to Britney.

It was those words that kept ringing in my ears until years later, when I was finally able to shut that door. The other large part of what helped me shut that door was the acceptance of the fact that I was a very poor judge of character. I probably still am to be fair.

I tended to look for what I wanted to see in people. Not what was actually there. Accepting that and owning the errors as my own and not something inflicted upon me was instrumental in helping me let it all go. So, before I go into full Yoda mode again.

'Hmmmmmmm, if in three thousand years, still chasing stupid bitch you are, sorry you will be, yes yes…hmmmmmmmmm.'

Let's get back to the story. Things weren't looking to fabby do when I turned up in Nice. I had no money and nowhere to stay. I wasn't that worried though because I did know a lot of people in Antibes and I was sure that I'd work something out when I got there. That was my usual tactic with most things, to be honest. Work it out when you get there. It usually worked.

So, I did what I always used to do back in those days and I went to the Blue Lady pub for a chat with the owners who were still friends after many years of knowing me. Errrr perhaps acquaintances is a more appropriate word than friends.

Alas, they were not the sort of people I could ask for a place to stay but they were certainly pleased to see me and welcomed me into the bar and that was all I really needed.

You see the Blue Lady pub was and is still a centre point for business revolving around the local superyacht industry. Many of the captains and crews had breakfast, coffee, lunch and late-night drinks all at the Blue Lady in one day. Whenever I needed work I would just have to spend a little time in the Blue Lady drinking coffee in the day and beer at night and chatting with the many people I knew who would pass through on a daily basis.

It never took long to find work or anything else I needed. On this occasion, I certainly needed work but before that, I needed a place to stay. This had never been an issue in the past as I had had my apartment. However, I had moved out of there a while back by this point.

Now I was somewhat up shit creek without the proverbial paddle but somehow my karma was good and I found a place to stay and shortly after I also found work.

Ramu arrived back in Antibes about two weeks later. She never actually docked as that was too expensive and instead, they always anchored just outside the port. Actually, right in front of the toilet bowl beach where I had sat looking at it for years before. Pablo fired Amber the day after they got back to Antibes and she was utterly distraught.

We now entered into a very difficult phase of our relationship. By now, Amber had decided that she was sick of me again but for the time being it was convenient to stick around and make what use of me she could. At least until such a point as it would become more convenient to move on again. Which is basically exactly what happened later that summer.

Now you might be tempted to ask why I didn't just kick her into touch if things were as bad as I'm making them out to be. The fact is that I was still hopelessly in love with her. To be fair there was actually far more than just sex to our relationship and that was what I found so hard to let go each time things went wrong.

I loved the way she looked but I also really loved the way she talked and even sometimes I was interested in the things she talked about. She was a fantastic cook and I loved her food and her whole attitude to nutrition. She loved my music, my body and my cock…cock…cocky sense of humour (yes that's right) but mainly she loved going rock-climbing with me and I also really enjoyed doing that with her.

I had introduced her to the sport shortly after we met and it was one of the things that really brought us together and that we shared a mutual love for. As soon as she tried it she loved it and to me, this was the icing on the cake. I already thought she was the best thing since sliced bread but when she fell in love with climbing it was clear to me that she was my soulmate and I wanted her more than anyone I'd ever met before.

We did share some amazing climbing adventures together and I have happy memories of those times. But the fact is that there was always drama either recently before or close behind any of those nice trips.

That summer in Antibes we managed to get out climbing a lot. Even when we were really short of money all we needed was enough fuel for Ambers's wicked little Honda Civic and we could get out of town and into somewhere stunningly beautiful where we could spend all day doing something we both loved. At no expense other than the fuel to get there.

We did this a lot but by this stage, Amber had no interest in me sexually. When she wouldn't have sex with me after a really nice day out, I just couldn't understand it or deal with it in any way except to get really drunk. Once really drunk I would get surly and sulky and she would usually go to bed alone and I'd stay up drinking till late.

As such the next day I would be really hungover and my anxiety would be going through the roof that she was going to leave me again. And so we would start another day.

So, you see there was a lot to love about the life we were living together that summer. But at the same time, there was the issue of no sex and that was building a strong sense of resentment in me against her. This meant that I stopped doing nice things for her. I figured that if she wasn't giving me what I wanted then I wouldn't give her what she wanted.

The fact of the matter was that I had no clue on earth what she really wanted. If I did, then I would have probably just walked out the door there and then. But I was blinded by love and desperate to try and make things better with her and we went round and round in this cycle the whole summer.

Shortly after Amber got fired from Ramu we had rented an apartment together in the dead centre of the old town of Antibes. It was a place she had rented in the past with an ex-boyfriend. An ex-boyfriend who had also been a friend of mine and there was a lot of history in this apartment.

I hated this apartment for a great many reasons. Not just the history but a whole bunch of things about the place just did my head in on a daily basis. But Amber loved this place and would go and on about how much she adored it. We fought often that summer.

I picked up work doing a painting project in the engine room of a large super yacht that had a ridiculous budget. The money they paid me to do a spot of painting in places no one would ever see was just insane. I was on a fat day rate and the work went on for four weeks. All through July I think it was. So come the start of August I was cashed up again.

Now Amber had got work on a busy charter yacht and so she was gone as well. This was good. We both had an income again and some space. This should have been the perfect time for things to get better again for Amber and I. But no. It wasn't to be.

After a couple of weeks working on her new yacht, she came home for the weekend. The yacht was berthed in Monaco so I drove the Civic up to collect her after she finished work on Friday afternoon. We had already made a plan to go climbing together up at La Turbie which was one of our favourite locations and very near Monaco port.

We had a good climb that evening and made it back to the car well after dark. Back at the apartment that evening the conversation turned to where things were going for us and she broke the news that she wanted to split up. I strongly suspected (and was right) that she was already fucking one of the crew on her new boat and when she told me we were breaking up again (this was the fourth time) I just lost it and started drinking the beers really fast.

We did have some weed but I wasn't that bothered about weed by now. Amber still loved weed though and we always had some around. I was still smoking it here and there in the day but usually by the evening when I got drunk, which was every night, I would stop with the joints because combined with the beer it messed me up too much and slowed down my drinking.

Amber had never planned to stay at the apartment that night and once her work was done she was gone again. It felt to me like my whole world had collapsed and all I wanted now was to not feel anything. Oblivion was my only desire.

By now, I had discovered Xanax and I had become quite partial to crushing one up and snorting it. This would knock me out for four to six hours generally when combined with a lot of beer. And so, for the next week I basically just drank and snorted Xanax in an attempt to hide from what had just happened.

There was a pizza restaurant very near and that became my source of food as I was quite well off for cash now and didn't care how much I was spending on anything. I didn't go anywhere or do anything. I just sat in the apartment and drank beer and did Xanax.

The Dude was in town and stopped by to see how I was doing. He was so disgusted with the state he found me in that he just gave me a load of verbal abuse and left again. I thought of him as my best friend at that point. He just walked away and left me in my pit without doing anything other than shouting at me. It didn't help. I felt like I had now lost my best friend as well. I drank more and at some point approaching the next weekend I went over the edge.

What I mean by that is that I started drinking spirits and for me, that was always the point at which things would go from bad to much worse.

Amber had been in touch by text periodically saying that she was concerned about the state of the apartment and didn't want me trashing it. I told her to go fuck herself. It didn't come as a big surprise then when she announced she was coming back on Saturday night to check up on things. By now, I had been drunk for more than a week without sobering up.

For the bulk of that time, I had only been drinking beer so I was not in the worst of states. Still, I must have been quite a mess I can assure you. I also bought a small bottle of rum the night before which had run out and I had got another, which was going down nicely, when Amber arrived.

It was early evening but already dark when she showed up. The conversation started badly and got worse with every exchange. She was saying that she wanted me out. That it was her apartment and I had to get out. As you might imagine this didn't go down too well and I decided that in fact it was her who was leaving and if she didn't want to go then I was going to help her on her way.

It was a small studio apartment with just one room and a narrow corridor to the main door which led out onto the hallway stairwell. The apartment was on the first floor and being old town it was an open stairwell with no elevator.

I started trying to push Amber towards the door but although she was a fair bit smaller than me she's also a fierce redhead and fought back making it difficult for me to move her in the direction I wanted. At some point, we ended up with me pinning her against the wall with my elbow against her neck. Clearly not a nice thing to do to anyone in any event.

I suddenly had a moment of realisation of what was going on and just dropped my arms and turned away from her in horror at what was happening. Amber seized the opportunity to take a large wine glass from the table and smashed it over my head. This knocked me to the floor and I lost consciousness for a short while.

Amber had started screaming at me the moment I tried to get her out and we had both made quite a bit of noise which had echoed out the window and been heard by both neighbours and local shopkeepers. After smashing the glass over my head, she ran upstairs to where the landlady had her own apartment and informed her that I had attacked her and asked her to call the police. Amber then ran off and was never seen again that night.

I came too covered in my own blood standing on my own in the middle of the apartment. Around me was a scene of devastation. Broken glass and bottles and stuff knocked around everywhere. At that exact moment, I had no idea what had happened.

All I knew was that there was a lot of blood around and that Amber was not there. I was concerned about her and just wanted to know where she was so I ran out of the door and there to my left was standing a big policeman while right in front of me, just reaching the top step of the stairway, was another one just as big.

Without saying a word, the one to my left grabbed me and without thinking I reacted by lifting both legs up and kicking the other policeman who was coming up the stairs. He fell backwards down the stairs a short way which didn't seem to go down very well with either of them. I was very roughly cuffed and thrown in the back of the meat wagon.

The way they cuffed me cut off the circulation to the side of my left thumb and I lost feeling to that part of my hand for about a year after that. To be clear, I don't blame them at all. I had just assaulted a police officer and deserved everything I got. I think they went quite easy on me considering.

The next thing I recall I was in a cell. Now, if you've never sobered or woken up in a cell then I can tell you that it's not a good feeling. If you add to that the fact that I was covered in my own blood and slowly starting to sober up after a solid week of drinking, then things start to get grim.

However, when I first woke up I was still drunk and didn't really know what was going on. I tried sleeping some more but after a while I was awake and there was nothing to do but just sit there and try to work out what was going on.

I was wearing nothing but a pair of board shorts. Literally nothing other than shorts. It was the middle of summer and hot. I often didn't wear much more than that. The one side pocket of the boardies was empty. Although it wasn't my immediate concern, it did register somewhere in my brain that this was going to present a problem at some stage in the near future.

I also didn't have footwear as it was the middle of summer and the only thing that went near my feet was my reef sandals. I'd not been wearing them when I had kicked the officer and to my surprise, they didn't think to grab my sandals for me when we left. How inconsiderate of them.

Of course, I wouldn't be left in a cell with anything in my pockets anyway but what I didn't know was that I had been arrested and brought to the station exactly as they found me when I walked out of the apartment. As such I had no phone, no wallet and no door keys. Nought out of three. Here's that merry word again which is becoming quite familiar in these stories…Fuck.

At this point, I was more concerned about the solid metal bars that were stopping me from leaving my current space. At some point, I started rattling them and wailing and a big burly policeman came and growled at me to shut up. I shut up. A bit later a doctor came in and cleaned me up. I hadn't even noticed the fact that I had a big gash on the back of my head. I still have the scar…On the back of my head.

Amber was to later claim that I had tried to strangle her and she had acted in self-defence. If that was true, then how did I get the scar on the back of my head and why did she have no bruising anywhere. I had to have been facing away from her at the point of the blow for the injury to have occurred where it did. But anyway. We'll come back to that later.

The doctor cleaned me up and then left without saying a single word to me. By now, I was really starting to feel the effects of sobering up after a week of being drunk. I'm sure that most people reading this have never spent a whole week drunk. In fact, I'm sure that the majority of you will have never even spent more than one day under the effects of alcohol. At the very most. What's that? No? Are a few of you fidgeting and looking sheepish right now? Wink, wink.

The moment you pass out and wake again still drunk, then drink again straight away you enter a new realm of alcoholic inebriation. It's different because now it's morning (or the next day at least) and the whole situation has changed to one where alcohol would not normally be a part. It's hard to describe but you sort of enter a dreamland where everything seems wrong but it's happening anyway so the only thing to do is keep drinking and roll with it.

I think it's fair to say that every addict engages with their addiction differently. Some alcoholics are able to function normally while under quite large doses. They drink heavily in the morning before going to work and are able to carry on their job without any of their colleagues knowing. They will usually be "topping up", here and there, through the day but at no point will they appear drunk as such.

During this stage of my life all my work involved using tools and many of them with sharp edges. Drinking before this kind of work was a really bad idea and even John would not drink before working (except very occasionally on Saturdays).

As such I had a golden rule that I simply did not drink in the morning before work. Somehow it seemed okay to have a pint (or even sometimes two) at lunch and then go back to work but I would never drink in the morning before starting the day.

Alcohol, heroin, coke, ketamine, gambling, sex, danger, violence, gaming, porn, or whatever it is. Addiction is all the same. In fact, I think this is a good point to have a chat about addiction and my understanding of it because the level of misunderstanding in our society today is still mind-blowing.

If you were to ask a cross section of the public in the UK what does addiction mean, then they would nearly all tell you that it involves "things" which are "addictive". People do too much of these "addictive things" and get addicted to the thing. This is complete nonsense and a big part of the problem we have in our society today.

Misunderstanding and fear as a result of miseducation and ignorance.

I can speak as someone who has suffered from addiction his whole life and on the one hand beaten it while on the other learnt to live with it. So please allow me to explain to you what my understanding of addiction is.

At some point in their life, every person will suffer some sort of emotional trauma. It's not a question of if but when. For every single one of us without exception. For some of us, this emotional trauma is very minor and never really becomes a problem as such.

But for most of us at some point in our lives, sooner or later we find ourselves feeling really down. If this negative feeling persists and gets worse, then this puts the person under an increasing level of emotional strain. If we are able to remove the source of stress, then for most people their level of emotional trauma will go back down again until they feel okay.

But for many people, it's the opposite. As one problem gets worse it usually triggers another, which triggers another and this all becomes like a vicious circle. This escalates until the person's life is very quickly spiralling out of control. This is generally where family and friends have to come in and if the person is blessed with good karma then they will have a support network around them to help them through this.

However, for a lot of people what happens is that the problems spread into their friends and family and then things get even worse. Now, the friends and family become part of the problem. If the person's life gets so bad that they alienate all their family and friends, then they are in big trouble.

Now if you are able, for a short while, to allow the person to forget about all this emotional pain then the person will be much relieved. Whatever it was, that made the emotional pain go away will suddenly become highly desirable. If it is as simple as drinking something, snorting something, injecting something, fucking someone, punching someone or (the list goes on) the person is immediately going to want more. Much more.

People seek their addiction because it offers relief from emotional pain. NOT because they want the subject of the addiction itself.

That subject is simply a means to an end.

The worse the emotional pain the more the need for an escape from it.

The more complete an escape the subject offers the more powerful the addiction will be.

Does that make sense? I hope so because I don't think it could be put any more clearly. A simple example is heroin. Supposedly (I've never taken it) one of the most addictive things out there. Why? Because a small dose knocks you out completely and you are in oblivion. If you hate your life, then nothing could be more appealing. Trust me.

When I was drinking heavily, that's all I wanted. *All I wanted was to feel nothing.* An end to the pain. If you had offered me heroin at that point, then I'm quite sure I would have switched from alcohol overnight.

Alright, I think it's time we headed back to Antibes and caught up with me in my cell. Poor little Bobby sitting in a cell. Not a prison cell I should point out. I've never been in prison but I have spent a few nights in cells and it's not something I'm ashamed of either. It gives me empathy for the people I want to help.

Without it they would look at me and ask, 'What do you know?'

And they would be right.

By now, I was fully sobering up and entering into my own personal hell. On the one hand, I had the knowledge of what had just happened although I didn't have any idea of the full extent yet. On the other hand, I had the expectation of what was going to happen once I got out of there. Whatever was going to happen, I knew it was not going to be easy or fun.

After a couple of hours had passed, I heard some noise down the corridor and it seemed they were letting other people out.

I stood by the gate waiting expectantly but when they got to me they laughed and said, 'Oh no, not you, you're not going anywhere because you assaulted a police officer.'

Gulp. I hadn't even been aware of that up until that point.

Some hours later I was led to another part of the station and questioned by a pair of male and female plain clothes police people. As usual, I was just totally sincere and told them everything exactly as I knew it. When I finished, they looked at each other and spoke in French for a minute. Then they said that considering the evidence they have they would like to press charges against Amber for assaulting me.

I deeply regret not taking them up on that offer. Oh my god, how I would have liked to see her serve some justice for that but unfortunately I was still in love with her and I was horrified at the idea of pressing charges against her. I told them that I didn't want to go down that path. I just wanted to get out of there and home again and to be honest all I was thinking about was what was I going to do once I got out of the station and back to the apartment.

Once the police understood what had actually happened everything changed. I wasn't taken back to the cell but instead given some lunch in their canteen while they waited for some things to be processed. I then had another interview where I was informed that I was going to be charged with violently resisting arrest.

They could not drop that charge even if they wanted to because I had actually assaulted one of them. I got a suspended sentence and in the end, was not even in France when my trial was held. I ended up with a criminal conviction for assaulting a police officer as a result. Not something I am in any way proud of.

I was mortified about what I had done and I asked if I could apologise to the officer I assaulted. They said to hang on a minute as they would need to find him. A minute later they came back and led me to another area where a bunch of the actual uniformed police were hanging out.

It was the same guys who arrested me and I was able to shake hands with them and tell them how sorry I was. They just laughed but were clearly touched and impressed by my sincerity and determination to make things right again.

As I was still wearing only a pair of board shorts, they asked if I wanted something to wear home. I was about to be released and I had to walk across town to get to my apartment. Although it was the middle of summer and I often walked around in just my boardies, it wasn't the done thing to walk through the centre of town with no shoes and no shirt.

Not even in the middle of summer. The only thing they could find for me to wear was a white shirt the kind you would wear for a fancy dinner or something. It was also much too big and I must have looked a proper sight walking back through town to my apartment.

However, I can tell you that how I looked was the least of my concerns at this point. Of much more concern to me right then was the fact that I had neither a phone, wallet nor…Keys. I knew The Dude was out of town and at that time I didn't have a single other friend in Antibes. Nor did I have a single person I could call for help.

What I had was myself and what I've always found about myself is that I am at my very best when you put me in a tight spot. At that particular moment, I was in about as tight a spot as they get. It was time to climb out or be squashed.

The street that our apartment was on was very narrow and not a road at all. No cars went up and down it but only pedestrians. At this time of year, Antibes old town is very much like a theme park. Tourists are everywhere and just wander around looking at everything as though it's, well yes, part of a theme park. I hated it. It was my home and it just felt horrible to live in a place where you were constantly being scrutinised by all these people.

Every single day of August our street would be crammed full of pedestrians from mid-morning to late evening. It's literally like a stream flowing both ways with people mostly shoulder to shoulder. This is right outside the front door. I had been hoping that the shutters would be open but I was wrong. I stood there looking up at the only window to the apartment that was behind the set of traditional French louvred shutters.

It didn't look hopeful when I first arrived but before I had got there I had formed a plan to try and climb in the window. I knew it was at least vaguely possible because I knew there was an air conditioning box just below and to the left. But until I got there I really had no idea how feasible this would be.

Standing there, looking up at the window, and the AC box, my hopes went up a little. The AC box was quite new, looked pretty solid and was close enough that I should be able to reach the window from it. Plus, there was a drain pipe running up the wall that I should be able to climb to get up there. The only question was, what would I do when I got there, as the window was still behind the closed shutters?

I knew the window would be open as we never used to close the actual glass part. So, in theory all I had to do was find a way to get the shutters open. There was only one way I was going to find out if I could open those shutters and that was to try. So, like the proverbial rat, I went up that drain pipe in a flash. I didn't care who saw me and if anyone did see me they didn't stop to remark.

There I was, sitting on the AC box about five meter above the street. It seemed prudent to pause there for a moment and consider my situation. I sat and watched as the tourists all continued walking up and down the street, oblivious to me sitting up there. The absurdity of the situation was fully apparent to me but what could I do except go with it?

Now my attention turned to getting those shutters open. I shuffled over to the edge of the AC box and reached over to see how far I could get my hand. I was able to reach the middle of the shutters and actually up to the height of the latch that held them in place. This was just a simple metal bar that lifted over and fell into place to hold the doors in.

To get it open all I would have to do was to slide my finger inside the slats of the shutters and lift it up and over. Looking at it, it just didn't seem possible and for a while, I just sat there not thinking but just trying to compose myself.

Then I went for it and reached up and tried getting my fingers in and under. It worked and I was able to find the latch and little by little I worked it up and over it fell. As the latch released my weight came onto the hinges and the shutter door swung open with me hanging from it.

For a couple of seconds, I was left hanging by my fingertips above the street. Thanks to all the rock-climbing, I was able to reach the wall with my toe and hook myself back in. I swung in, leapt through the window and was home.

Home to a scene of devastation. There was broken glass everywhere and bottles from the struggle and also all the mess from my week of drinking previously. Not at all a pretty sight and I had a grim few days ahead of me.

For the first couple of days, I was back at the apartment I still had no keys. Amber had taken them with her. My wallet and phone had been there but I was running very low on cash by now anyway.

As such I had to continue climbing in and out of the window for a couple of days until I was able to get hold of Amber and convince her that I was sober and that she could trust me with the apartment. As it was, I had paid half the deposit and rent so I had an equal right to them anyway.

Shortly after this, I needed work so I went back to do some exhibition work in Cannes. During the first day, I fell sick with chest pain and a flare-up of my old blood clot issue. I found myself in the hospital once again being checked out by a team of doctors and nurses for a possible new blood clot.

It turned out to be just stress causing the old scars to flare up again but the fact was that I found myself in hospital less than one week after I had been in jail. For two unconnected things. The medical staff had left me alone for a good long time and I had time to think about my current situation without any alcohol in my system.

The fact that I was in hospital and then jail, during the space of one week, for unconnected things told me that it was time for me to make some kind of big change in my life. This was the first resemblance of any kind of good sense on my part but unfortunately, I made the wrong choice of how to address it. I decided to quit cannabis, not alcohol.

And I did. I just stopped it dead. I was already using it less and less and it had become more of a daytime thing when I wasn't drinking hard. So, it seemed like an easy thing to stop and that it would help me get my life back into some kind of order.

I got that polar wrong. It turned out to be the worst possible thing I could have done. I spent the next five years without touching cannabis. It was only after I started using cannabis again that I was finally able to quit alcohol even after trying to quit for more than a year.

At the point when I stopped cannabis, I was living in the south of France and still had some friends and the chance to get work in that area. By the time I started again, five years later, I was back in the UK, homeless and had alienated almost everyone I knew.

Well, there you go. I told you this was going to be spicy and not fun for me. It's going to get worse yet as well. The next chapter contains two stories that tell of some of the ways in which karma was about to teach me the lessons I needed to be able to be here writing this for you. So, without further ado. Let's get into it.

19

A Pair of Double Whammies

Alright, for the purposes of telling this next series of stories I am coming out of the timeline and I'm going to jump around a little. Not literally you understand.

Part 1. La Ballon

The first of my double whammies came way back in the late noughties. This was while I was living in my apartment in Antibes. It was the second summer I spent based in Antibes and beach life was in full swing. Work came periodically but parties came almost every night.

Antibes is one of those places that always has a stream of wild, wonderful and colourful characters passing through. The longer a person stays in Antibes the more of these characters they meet and during the summer months life becomes one long party. Well, it did for me anyway.

It was during this summer that I met Amber and her friend Sonja. At this point, Amber was still with her ex and they didn't know that many people in Antibes. They found their way to the toilet bowl and had noticed our group so they were looking for a way in. They started hanging out on the beach every night and dared to play disc on our spot.

As they both looked like decent sorts it didn't take long for us to get chatting and soon after I found myself back at their apartment. It turned out Amber was renting an apartment just around the corner from my place. They had really good taste in music which was super unusual in yachting circles back then. I hardly knew anyone who was into electronic music like I was.

Don't forget I was a DJ and playing gigs quite regularly in the Blue Lady by this point. But it was still the late noughties and electronic music had yet to make the impact on the world that it has now. None of my friends were really into house or techno. They didn't mind it as such and they all liked the mixes I used to make.

However, it wasn't something they would play for themselves at home. So, when Amber put some music on and it was LTJ Bukem, I was like, 'Oh!' The three of us were to enter into a triangle that was to have long-lasting reflections and implications upon us all. Well, you've heard about some of it by now so you have some idea.

For now, we are going to focus on Amber's friend Sonja as she was the main other player in this story. Although it all started on the beach as so many of my misadventures seemed to.

As was the usual thing I had been down on the beach since late afternoon drinking beers, smoking spliffs and playing disc with around 10 other people. The group would circulate as people would come and go on various missions. There were usually at least four people playing disc and that meant at least two discs would be flying. If not more.

Things could get spicy with three discs flying around in the dark. It was accepted etiquette that if someone was not paying attention you could launch the disc at them with full intention of hitting them. We were all pretty skilled at frisbee and could pick each other out pretty accurately from a great long distance away.

As such it was hilarious to see your mate talking to someone or something and just be like, 'Right I've got you.'

Then launch the disc at them, full force, with every intention of a direct hit if possible. In general, everyone was smart to this and paid close attention to what everyone else was doing and as such it was very rare that anyone actually got hit. But it kept you super sharp, even when the beers were flowing fast and it was dark. Happy times attempting to decapitate one's friends yes, yes.

Once or twice a week it was usual for something a little more potent to turn up. Coke wasn't in any way practical on the beach but it was a perfect place to drop a pill. Playing disc on the toilet bowl with a circle of good peeps while high as a kite on MDMA ranks as one of the best things I've ever done and I'm not ashamed to admit it.

Those nights on the beach were some of the most hedonistic of my life and also accordingly the most fun. I think the best thing about it was that I wasn't on holiday and none of it was in any way planned. When I had work, I would work but when I didn't, I'd go to the beach and have the time of my life.

I was still really lonely though let's remember. By now, it had been a long time since I had split with Ariel. Earlier that summer Amber had introduced me to her friend Sonja. Sonja was very close to my idea of a perfect girlfriend at that point and I was to fall in love with her almost immediately.

Just like Amber, Sonja had seen me as a potential target the moment she laid eyes on me. Shortly after we first hooked up she successfully scammed 500 Euros out of me and convinced me not to tell anyone. What happened was this. The very first time we had sex I didn't wear a condom. My bad, yes I know. She insisted I wear one the second time, however, which was the same night, and then every time after.

Although it was only a handful more times that we actually had sex. Shortly after that, I fell seriously ill with my first blood clot. I was in the hospital in quite a serious way and I had an I.V. and various pipes connected up to me. Although I wasn't in pain as such I wasn't exactly in the best of shapes. Imagine my pleasant surprise then when Sonja said she would come and visit me in the hospital.

When she arrived, she sat down and without beating around the bush told me that she was pregnant. She said she didn't sleep around and that it could only be mine. She didn't want a baby and as such I was going to have to pay half the cost of the abortion. She continued to say that most important of all was that I didn't tell anyone about this, especially not her best friend Amber who I was now quite close with.

At this point, I was still thinking of Sonja as a potential girlfriend and so I was in no way suspicious. In fact, I had no idea that this is actually a widely used and well-known scamming routine. In fact, I didn't work it out until many years later when I was talking to a friend.

I told her the whole pattern of events and she looked at me and laughed and said, 'You got done, mate.'

It was so clear afterwards but at the time I was totally taken in. I gave her 500 Euros cash and we never said a word to anyone else about it. Well, until now that is. Names might have been changed but all I'm going to say is karma catches up with everyone. So, in fact it could be said that this first double whammy was in fact a triple whammy because of what had already happened just a month earlier.

At this point, Amber was still with her ex but he was away working on a boat. However, she still had an apartment close to mine. Sonja lived in Nice but was coming to visit Amber quite a lot. Whenever she did I would try and get in her knickers again. Never again with any success, I would add. But it didn't stop me trying that whole summer.

So, on the night this tale begins we had been down the beach since dusk doing all the usual stuff but that night we had also taken an ecstasy tablet each. As had become the norm a group of us headed back to Amber's apartment to carry on the party for a while. Sonja was in town visiting and we had been playing disc together on the beach.

Both Amber and Sonja were very capable disc players. Something that I found very attractive about them both. Although there were many girls in our circle, none of them played disc. It was very much a thing the boys did while the girls sat around and drank wine. Sorry, but that's just how it was. It wasn't something that I was happy about and as Amber and Sonja came as an exception to this and it was certainly something that caught my eye.

We had a really good time to be fair. Playing disc on E, on a beautiful beach with beautiful people, is about as fun as it gets without taking the rest of your clothes off. So back at Amber's place, the mood was great and we were enjoying music and chatting but at some point, Sonja announced that she needed to get back to her boat.

By now, she had taken a job on a small motor yacht that was berthed in Villeneuve-Loubet. A large apartment complex with a small marina that was located just 10-minute drive along the beach road. It wasn't that late and trains run until 12ish so she was planning to get the train back. However, Bobby had other ideas. I am deeply ashamed to say that I used to drink and drive a lot when I lived in France.

This is in no way intended as an excuse but the fact is that a lot of people did. All my friends and peers did. John, who I worked for, used to measure journeys by how many beers he would be able to drink during the trip and used to maintain adamantly that he was a better driver after 10 beers than any Frenchman was sober. This was my employer and in some ways my role model at this point.

So, you see then it may not come as such a surprise that I offered to drive Sonja home rather than let her take the train. Bad Bobby, stupid Bobby, very bad Bobby. Oh dear. All she had to do was walk 10 minutes and a train would drop her to within another 10-minute walk to her boat. But no.

In my infinite wisdom, I thought that if I drove her home it would help improve her mood towards me (she'd been ignoring me most of the night) and that it might help me get in her good books again.

So, when she announced that she was heading off I offered her a lift. Which to start with she refused but I insisted and eventually she accepted. Let's just remember that I had been drinking beer all evening and had also taken an ecstasy pill earlier in the evening. I wasn't really still feeling the effects but MDMA comes in waves and I was certainly still a little high.

Once you get out of Antibes town, which took just minutes from where I lived, it's a long straight road all the way down to Villeneuve-Loubet. On one side, you have the beach and on the other side, you have the train tracks. It's the SNCF mainline so there is a big wall and fence all the way along.

It must have been midnight by the time we set off and I was more interested in trying to play some music for Sonja than I was in driving. I had an iPod (remember those?) with a playlist I had made for her but I couldn't find it and was trying to look for it while driving down the road.

I think it's fair to say my driving wasn't the best and there was definitely some swerving as we made our way down the empty road. Except that it wasn't empty. There was a car following very close behind and Sonja mentioned this several times to me but I was more interested in telling her about why this music was so amazing.

It was only a short drive so pretty quickly we were arriving at the junction where the entrance to the marina was. There waiting for me was a Gendarmerie roadblock. About 10 of them were all in position to swoop down upon me the moment we arrived at the traffic lights. Fuck.

I was directed to park a short way over on the side of the road and then their team set to work checking all my documents and checking my car over for possible things they could book me for. At that time, I was driving a Peugeot 406 diesel estate called Bertha. Shout out Bertha. Man, I had some adventures in that car I can tell you but she ended up getting cubed.

I had inherited Bertha from John and the best thing about her was that she was registered in England, so UK plates, but insured locally in France as it was still possible to do that back then.

Driving an English-registered car in France had a variety of pros and cons. The disadvantage was that all the other drivers treated you like shit, but they do this to each other anyway, whereas the advantage was that the police tended to look the other way because in general, they could not fine you for anything except speeding or drinking.

I had a massive collection of unpaid parking tickets that lived in the passenger door and were never paid because there was no way to trace back the owner of the car from the UK. I bet that's changed now.

It should also be noted that the French attitude to drink driving was in general much more relaxed than in the UK and I knew of people who had been pulled over while shitfaced and still managed to talk their way out of it. So, at this point, I wasn't too worried. I had all the papers in order. I had a valid MOT and insurance in France with a local company.

There existed a kind of grey area back then where you could keep a UK-registered car in France and get away with a lot. I did for years and in fact I very nearly did on this occasion.

Basically, everything was in order. By now, the adrenaline had sobered me up and I was sitting bolt upright smiling at the Gendarmes and trying to look relaxed.

After they had gone through all the usual checks and come up with nothing, the big boss man looked pissed off and stormed around the car one last time before announcing, 'Donnez moi la Ballon.'

What he meant was breathalyse this guy. Fuck.

Now, I knew, I was in trouble as if nothing else, I had been drinking beer all evening. La ballon was duly blown into and of course, came up positive. It was like they had won the lottery and the reason was that it meant they could all go back to the station now to process me.

The party started and I said my farewell to Sonja as I was led to one of their cars. She was still pleading with them to let me go but they were having none of it and I was going to the station for some more tests to find out exactly how much alcohol I had consumed.

I still thank my guardian angels that they didn't think to either search me or test for anything else. They did neither. While driving I had in my pocket my packet of rolling tobacco with a lump of hashish and big rolling papers. All they had to do was ask me to empty my pockets and they would have had me for weed and then if they blood tested me as well?

They did none of that. They never even asked to look in my pockets. As it was I managed to empty my pockets in the back of their car on the way to the station.

When we got to the station their party continued. I joined in as I didn't really feel too bothered about what was going on and it seemed smart to be nice to these people. They had been treating me with the utmost respect and it seemed only civil to return the sentiment. Once they learnt I worked on the big yachts they wanted to know all about it and I became quite the celebrity for a while.

I was sitting on the desk telling them all stories about sailing across the Atlantic while they were testing me again and were writing out all their forms. Once finished they announced that I would have to come back first thing the next morning to sit in front of a judge and get my sentence for the drunk driving offence. Also, they added that I was under a driving suspension so could not drive anywhere that night.

However, they asked if I wanted a ride back to my car. The station they had taken me to was about a 15-minute drive down some long fast roads so it was going to be a very long walk back. I couldn't believe my luck and it just goes to show that simply being nice can get you a long way in life.

They were quite severe in telling me not to drive home though. I understood and assured them I didn't intend to drive anywhere. What I didn't tell them was that I had some more weed stashed in the back of Bertha and I wanted a joint more than anything by now.

I called Sonja who was nearby on her boat and asked if I could crash out on her boat for a while before I had to go back to the station to see the judge in the morning. She wasn't too thrilled about the idea of letting me onto the boat she was working on but there was no one else on board and she let me sleep in the spare bunk for a few hours. Not that I could sleep. I was thinking how was I going to be able to carry on working if I didn't have a car.

I was freelancing for a local company doing little bits and bobs of joinery work on villas and most of the work was miles out in the countryside. I couldn't work without Bertha. There was also the fact that I was going to have to walk back to the station as there was no public transport. Let's remember that it's the middle of the summer and I am now coming down from the effects of a pill and a night's drinking.

It hadn't been a big night (well not by my standards) so I wasn't in that bad a shape but I was far from a happy bunny in the morning as I set off to get back to the station. As it happened I had left really early because I couldn't sleep and I ended up waiting for hours in the police station waiting room. It felt like an eternity but eventually, I was called in and sat in a small room with two other Gendarmes.

One was the judge and the other was there to translate for me. My sentence was a two-month ban and a 200 Euros fine. Looking back, I can see that that was an incredibly light sentence and that I got off very easy. However, at the time it still seemed like an eternity.

Nonetheless, I took it on the chin and standing up to leave I offered the judge my hand as a mark of respect. I think I must have been the first person ever to do this because he looked at me like I was some kind of complete mentalist. Still, he shook my hand and I was free to leave.

No ride was offered this time, however, and I had the deep pleasure of a very long walk back to Bertha. Now it was mid-morning and getting hot. It must have taken a good two hours to walk back. I knew I couldn't drive Bertha home but I had some things in the back I wanted to collect before heading back to Antibes.

Imagine my face when I came around the corner to find her gone. In my befuddled state, I simply couldn't make any sense of this. I had left her right where the Gendarmes told me to on the side of the road by the main turning to the port. What I didn't know yet was that I had left her in a no-parking zone.

That morning while I was at the station receiving my sentence the traffic police had come along, who are totally separate from the Gendarmes and found poor Bertha sitting there all alone and lost. She had duly been towed to the yard. For me though at that point, I was still in a bit of a daze as to what had happened.

A mate of mine was working as skipper on one of the yachts berthed just down from Sonja's and he came over to see if he could help.

I explained the situation and he laughed at me and said, 'Mate, you've been double-whammied.'

'Eh?' I said, not following.

'You've been towed, you muppet, you left the car in a no-parking zone.'

There was a big sign saying this very clearly just down the road.

'But it was where they told me to leave it,' I whined.

'Try telling them that when you go to get it back,' he laughed.

As it happened I didn't try telling the staff at the yard. I had to pay another 80 Euros to get Bertha back a few days later although I still couldn't even drive her.

I'd like to make it clear that I'm not, in any way, proud of any of this. Driving under the effect of either alcohol or drugs is stupid, reckless and is mainly putting other people's lives at risk. That's why those good people were out on that road looking for twats like me who might have been the cause of a serious accident.

I consider myself deeply fortunate to have avoided any kind of accident or serious injury, to myself or anyone else, while I was driving under the effects. It certainly wasn't the result of my judgement or decisions I can tell you.

Part 2. A Short Stop in Puerto Rico

Okay, so the second double whammy comes a few years later but still, curiously, indirectly involves Amber. In the end, I lived in my apartment in Antibes for just over three years. But as inevitably happens with every place we call home; the time came for me to close the door for the last time and walk away never to return. At least, not yet anyway.

In the end what led me to do that was the offer of a "dream job" as ship's carpenter aboard one of the world's largest private yachts, Al Mirqab. This was a yacht like no other I ever worked on and could be the subject of many chapters all of its own. Al Mirqab was 113 m and took a full crew of 55.

As a private yacht, she was still only allowed to carry 12 guests. However, the Quatarie owners would bring a whole entourage of their own people with them, another 30 or so, and there was a whole deck just to accommodate them.

I spent the vast majority of my time as a crew member repairing minor damage on the interior. The biggest problem I encountered while performing my duties was getting lost. One of my favourite stories is about being left alone in the owner's walk-in dressing room, which was a maze of leather and mirror, floor-to-ceiling panelling.

There were no handles or doors or anything that resembled a way in or out. The chief stewardess had left me in there to repair a door hinge and when I finished I couldn't find my way out. We had UHF radios for inter-crew communication but I was always forgetting to charge mine and it was dead. I had to wait more than 30 minutes to be rescued. I got the door fixed though.

Al Mirqab was unique amongst all the boats I worked on for a bunch of reasons. One of these was that she had a strict "no alcohol on board" policy and a total ban on any form of drug taking on or off the boat. This was enforced with random testing. Another unique thing was that there was a live aboard team of ex-Gurkhas as the full-time security for the yacht.

They manned the passerelle and had a large X-ray scanning machine for checking baggage. In theory, everything that went on or off the boat had to pass through here and be scanned. Every person entering and leaving the yacht had to be patted down (yes actually patted down) upon reboarding. Any baggage would be passed through the X-ray machine.

In fact, by the time I left the boat, I had gotten really friendly with these guys and they never searched me or my bags. As such it wasn't exactly unusual for me to sneak the odd beer onboard. Oh, Bobby. I was such a naughty boy.

One night I even got them pissed. The smokers amongst the crew had a spot on the dock next to the passerelle where we would hang out and, well yes, smoke ciggies, innit. Beers were often purchased from a nearby vending machine (yes they had those in Spain back then) and sometimes a little party would spring up on the dock.

One night the Gurkhas got talked into having a couple of beers with us and it turned into a bit of a bender. When the head Gurkha guy found out what was going on, he came down and went ballistic. I kept a low profile with them after that but they were always super cool with me.

And yes the sharper of you lot will have already seen where this story is heading. Not hard to work it out is it? I had a serious love for the party. Both drink and drugs and I had taken a job on a boat where I could not drink on board or take any drugs, on or off, period.

A voice in my head is singing, 'There may be trouble ahead.'

It's a familiar tune by now, isn't it? Things didn't start that well on Al Mirqab and gradually got worse the longer I remained on board.

I joined the yacht in Palma after finally moving out of my apartment in Antibes. The first place I had ever been able to call my own home. As much as I was ready to leave, I was also really sad to leave that place as it had been my home for a good long while and I had many happy times there. Still, I was leaving on a high note, at least in one respect because I had got my dream job, at last.

But on the other hand, it was a period where I was deeply depressed because Amber had left me and gone back to her ex. At that point, she was in America with him. We were still in touch, however, and had had a night of wild sex right before she left for the States. Amber had been playing her ex and myself off against each other for that whole summer.

In fact, by now it was mid-autumn and still she couldn't make her mind up which one of us she wanted. We both wanted her. That was clear and she knew it well. So, she played with us both for the better part of a year in the end. Did I mention something about karma once or twice before? Anyway.

At the point, I took the job on Al Mirqab, Amber had again decided she didn't want her ex and left him in the States while she went to St Martin to pursue her one and only true passion in life. Cocaine.

She did have some vague excuse about getting a job but we both knew that the main reason she was there was for cheap, pure cocaine. I couldn't really avoid knowing about this because we were in touch on a daily basis and she was telling me in detail all about every line she did.

In the past, we had a lot of sex while high on coke. In fact, getting high on coke and having all-night sex sessions was our favourite thing to do together. If you've never tried it, I can tell you that, with the right partner and with some MDMA thrown in for good measure, it is undeniably one of the most pleasurable and mind-expanding things you will ever do.

All I'm going to say is moderation is key and, that which is fun on one occasion is not always fun on every occasion. Perhaps a case of stating the bleeding obvious but I'll leave it hanging, nevertheless.

So, every day that I was working on Al Mirqab I was chatting with Amber, who I knew was getting high every night and being surrounded by sexy men in a place where hedonistic behaviour is the accepted norm. Hmm. Did it play on my mind? Perhaps a little yes.

Add to this the fact that we were now crossing the Atlantic and on route to Puerto Rico where we would pick up the owners for a cruise around St Martin and St Barts. Amber and I had some vague hope that I would be able to get some time off and we would be able to see each other again. But we knew in reality this was going to be unlikely. Still, it seemed better to be closer to each other than on the other side of a big ocean.

All the way across the Atlantic all I could think about was doing coke and having sex with Amber. I did manage to do a lot of good work on the interior and by now had become quite a celebrity with the interior girls. A lot of the interior joinery was not of a very high standard although it was still getting a lot of use.

As such a lot of stuff was broken or breaking. With a little love and care, I found it could be put right with no major work. This made me a popular man. Inside. Outside I had become the hated one with the deck crew.

Technically I was part of the deck crew as well as the ship's carpenter. This meant that when the owners were on board I would slot in with the deck crew and work alongside them with the various duties they needed to perform. There were 10 deckhands, plus two senior hands and a lead hand.

Every morning, we had a team meeting before we started work and every morning I would be dismissed into the interior to go and work on my projects while the rest of them had to do stuff they thought was tedious and boring like washing the boat.

Washing the boat was, of course, exactly what they were employed to do but they seemed to think that I should have to do this with them despite the fact that I had been employed to fix the interior.

This created a tension right from the start that just grew and grew until I basically hated most of them and they mostly basically hated me. As we didn't actually have to overlap at all it didn't cause any problems, as such, but it was a bubbling cauldron that was ready to spill over at any time.

When we reached Puerto Rico, it was getting close to the time when the owners would arrive. This is usually a very tense and stressful period on any yacht. The owners pay the bills and that includes everyone's wages. If the owners turn up and they don't like what they find then they can, in theory, sack the entire crew on the spot.

Things were slowly starting to change but back in my days on yachts, there was next to zero law regarding what could and would go on during the process of a private yacht employing crew. It was not unheard of for a whole crew to be fired on the spot if the owners were not happy.

This is the same on any yacht big or small. However, what changes on a bigger yacht is that there are more crew to share all the stress. More crew means more politics and more politics means division and division means strife. So, on a yacht with 50 crew, this was off the charts. One of the reasons I'd taken a big step back from crewing was because of the politics on bigger boats.

So, you could be forgiven for wondering why I'd taken a job on a boat like this? I think it's fair to say that I was also wondering the same thing by this stage. However, I had a long list of projects to keep me busy on the interior and for the most part, I was able to stay out of the way of the other deck crew.

After arriving in Puerto Rico, we, the crew that is, had one weekend free before the owner's trip was due to start. A "night out" was organised by some of the crew and by the time Friday evening rolled around most of the deck and interior crew were going along. It won't come as any great surprise to hear that I was planning to tag along and that I had plans to do more than get drunk.

Almost all the crew had been drug tested over the course of the past few days since arriving in Puerto Rico. I had been one of those tested and of course, had come up clean. So wise old Bobby was thinking that if we had been tested just very recently the chances of getting tested again was next to nothing.

As such I figured it would be safe to sniff out a little coke during our evening out. Do you see what I did there? Sniff out? No? Oh, you get it but…Okay, I'll get on with it.

Now I'm not, in any way, attempting to make excuses here. Honestly. No really. But after listening to Amber talking about coke, nonstop, for the last month and having been at sea for two weeks, it's fair to say that I was in the mood for a party of my own. One of the worst things about me when I drink, and especially with spirits, is how much I love to shoot my mouth off.

I mean I guess you could say that this whole book is just an example of me shooting my mouth off. And I would have to agree. But I'm not drunk now and as such I have an awareness of consequence and care very much about the implications and manifestations of the things I say and do.

When I was drunk, I didn't care about anything and I suppose this is a good moment for me to share some thoughts about alcohol and in fact, on mind alteration in general.

I was once described as a *psychonaut* by a therapist who I'd been seeing for a while. *He meant it in a positive way,* I think. He came up with that after listening to me telling him about the various mind-altering effects I experienced while under the effects of the different substances I've taken during my life. The fact is that my list is actually very short and I can share it right here and now.

Legal – Alcohol, Xanax, tobacco and junk food.

Illegal – cannabis, cocaine, MDMA (ecstasy), LSD and psilocybin (magic mushrooms).

That's actually a very short list I can assure you. But I guess it's relative. Something I find curious is that out of the list of illegal things, three out of the five are now being used in a legal medical market in various places round the world.

If you break it down and look at it in its most simple form, then all alcohol really does is remove a person's sense of consequence. All of the behaviours people exhibit after consuming alcohol can be traced back to a loss of the sense of consequence.

So, let's think about that last statement, 'All alcohol does is remove a sense of consequence.'

What is a sense of consequence? It seems obvious but let's talk it through anyway. Every human develops a sense of consequence as a normal part of the process of growing up and becoming a functioning human being.

Even if you are to take a person out of normal life and put them in a situation where there are no rules or authority then they will still have to live with consequence. It's as simple as "if you bang your head against a wall then it will make your head hurt".

I think someone who might have done something important once or twice might have said something like, 'Every action has an equal and opposite reaction.'

This currently remains a fundamental truth and building block around which our understanding of the universe is based. As we navigate our way through life we learn all about these equal and opposite reactions. We learn to adjust what we say and do in order to encourage more suitable actions and reactions in the world around us.

However, this can be a tiresome process and depending on a person's life situation it can become an overwhelming challenge. Imagine then the relief if you are to give said person something that takes away all of this thought, consideration and anxiety. The more serious the concerns are the more intense the sense of relief will be.

I want you to understand the effect alcohol is having on you every time you consume it. Whether you are aware of it or not. I'm not trying to say everyone should stop drinking alcohol completely. Although I do firmly believe the world would be a much happier place without it. But people have to choose for themselves what they do and do not do. And that's where education comes in and that's what I'm trying to do now to a certain extent.

So where were we? Oh yeah. I was getting drunk…and being the wise old chap I was by this stage I decided to mouth off to one of the senior deckhands about my plans to score some coke and have a little party. He wished me good luck and a good night and we said no more.

A little later I saw a likely-looking character and shortly after had a little bag of white power in my pocket. I didn't waste time and headed straight to the toilet for my first line in months. It was good coke and I was immediately high as a kite.

For someone who's never done coke, it's going to be hard to understand how I felt right then but the effects of coke are actually almost as simple as the effects of alcohol. One stops you from caring about anything and the other gives you confidence. Because that's all coke really does, it just makes you feel super confident. Which is a really nice way to feel I can tell you.

Even for someone who has a lot of self-confidence already, the effects of coke are really very morish. It doesn't last long. One good line will have a person high for 15–30 minutes. Then if you want to keep that initial buzz you'll need another dose. The longer you want to stay high the more you need to do.

Once I got that first line down, I decided that I would bail on the rest of the group's party and go looking for my own. Now, I was in Superman mode and I also had a decent amount of cash on me so the world was my proverbial oyster. And a good party I had. I located a club nearby that was pumping out some good tunes and I got in there and just danced and drank and snorted all night.

I didn't care that I was alone and actually got chatting with some locals pretty quickly and spent the rest of the night hanging out with them. They gave me a ride back to my boat at around 04:00. Bear in mind that Al Mirqab had a full-time team of ex-Gurkhas as security.

Everybody going on and off the boat was logged and searched. As such there was a record of what time I came home and it was a long time after everyone else.

I woke up early the next afternoon with my nose stuck to the pillow. Not the best way to start the day, I can tell you. It's normal after a coke session to get a runny nose. However, I'd done a lot of coke before but never woken up with my nose actually stuck to the pillow. Coke has an effect on the sinuses that makes the nose run after. It's always easy to tell a cokehead by the sniff.

I kept a low profile for the rest of the weekend but I had this steadily rising fear that I was in deep shit. On Monday morning, I was at work organising my tools when the call came over the ship's Tannoy system that there was to be a spot drug test for a selection of the crew. A list of names was read out and for a moment I thought I was going to be spared but my name was read out last and, I might add, with some emphasis.

Looking back, I can see how I could have actually got through this. The drug test took the form of a urine test. What I should have done was prepare before the night out and have a sample of clean urine stored in a zip lock bag somewhere in my cabin. I had time after being called for the test to go to my cabin and walk around a fair bit before I had to go to the ship's medical room.

Once there, I had to go into another private booth and produce a sample of urine. So, in theory I would have had time to retrieve my clean sample, stash it in my pocket and then use that to provide the sample once I was in the private booth. Thanks to the movie American Beauty for that little gem. If I had thought a bit more quickly and been a little better prepared, I could have gotten away with it.

But I wasn't and I couldn't and…No…I did not.

Urine samples were given and about 30 minutes later the same Tannoy system announced, for the entire crew to hear, that I was required to visit the captain's cabin. Fuck.

I sat down in front of him and the first mate and he put the test result down in front of me and said, 'You've tested positive for cocaine. What have you got to say for yourself?'

What could I say? I tried a lame excuse about meeting some locals who I got chatting with and they gave me a drink they said was really special and it must have been spiked with coke.

The captain looked me straight in the eye and said, 'I don't know much about cocaine but I do know one thing and that is, you do not drink it.'

Let's face it. This guy didn't end up being the captain of a mega yacht by being taken in by chumps like me.

About one hour later, I was in a taxi on my way to the airport. While I was waiting on the dock for the taxi, a handful of the crew who I had been friends with came out to say goodbye. They were quite shocked at how blase I was and asked why I didn't seem bothered.

'Don't do the crime if you can't do the time,' was my response.

For many years, that was something of a motto for me and to a certain extent, I suppose it still is.

Before I had even walked off the boat, I had got a Xanax down me. It was the first thing I did after being fired. Well, that and inform Amber. That certainly ranked as one of those phone calls you pray you will never have to make.

'Hi honey, oh yeah by the way, I've just been fired for doing coke.'

By this stage, Amber had actually declared her love for me. Something she was only to do a handful of times in the whole five years we were together. She seemed to want me to get to St Martin just as much as I wanted to get to St Martin and it was clear that even if Al Mirqab had been going there we would not have had a chance for anything more than a quick hello at the very most.

If you combine that with the fact that I hated the situation on board Al Mirqab, then it's clear to see that I really wasn't actually that bothered at all about leaving.

When the owners arrived, I was going to have to stop being a carpenter and start being a deckhand. This had always been part of the deal. I couldn't be doing messy work around the interior while the thing was being used. Since joining the yacht, I had only spent a handful of hours working with the deck crew and since then my relations with them had become very poor.

As such the idea of having to become their most junior team member was not something that appealed to me. Nor them. I think it's fair to say that this was an outcome that suited everybody for the best. It just didn't look very good on my CV thereafter.

As it was I had been lucky to get the job at all. When considering my job application, the first mate had decided to contact Clive (captain of Adela) for a reference. Clive told him not to give me a job. I know this because the first mate told me so over the phone. He had refused to give me a written reference based on the fact that I had left the boat when I did. Regardless of my 2.5 years of hard and loyal service.

He was so bitter that he told the first mate of Al Mirqab that I was not to be trusted and shouldn't be employed. Of course, he was completely right. But at the time the first mate came to me and asked me what my response was. I said that Clive was just bitter because of the timing of my departure and that my work had always been first-class.

I was also completely right. I got the job and proved that in the end, Clive was right and that I shouldn't have been given the job. Still, I did a very good job of fixing up the interior before they fired me so it wasn't all that bad.

However, I think it was a fair assumption that a reference wasn't going to be possible and that this was going to leave a big black hole in my CV. Did I care? At that point…Yes and no. I'd have rather not been fired for doing drugs but I was certainly not sad to be leaving that yacht.

I had a flight back to France organised as I had been able to convince The Dude to give me a place to stay for a while when I got back. That was another phone call that I didn't really cherish. He was livid when I told him what I'd done. We were like brothers back then and he could see how much damage I was doing to myself.

It must have been really hard to try and be my friend through all that. Both The Dude and his wonderful girlfriend had done everything they could to convince me to leave Amber. They were nice about it as they quite liked her but they hated what she was doing to me. I ignored their advice. What a twat.

The moment I arrived at the airport in Puerto Rico the first thing I wanted was…Yes you guessed it. Beer. I sank a couple of cold ones in the bar and then made my way through check-in and boarding. I had a connecting flight to Miami before the main hop across to Nice.

Once I was in Miami it seemed the sensible thing to have another couple of beers. By now, the combo of Xanax and beer was making me quite drowsy and it had taken me all this time to realise that my satchel was feeling a little light. I used a satchel as my carry-on bag as it was perfect for carrying around my pride and joy MacBook Pro laptop.

It was a few years old and covered in stickers but still a very high-spec model and the centrepiece of my DJ setup. This was still long before I got my first iPhone and as such my laptop was my only access point to the internet.

Let's just remember that at some point in the not-distant past, browsing and everything else you might do online, was something that was only done on a computer. It seems almost inconceivable now. But anyway, I suddenly noticed my bag felt light and opening it I found it devoid of a laptop.

I knew in an instant what I'd done. When you pass through boarding checks, you have to take your laptop out and put it in a separate tray when it goes through the scanning machine. Somehow in my befuddlement, I had just taken the tray with all my other bits and walked off leaving my laptop with the airport security people.

They still had it. I found an info booth and the people there were really helpful. They were able to call directly to the Puerto Rico airport and speak to the people there who confirmed they had a laptop of my description and that I would have to organise shipping it back to me at a later date.

So, all was not lost and I decided to have another couple of beers to both celebrate and commemorate. I then boarded a transatlantic flight and spent about 12 hours passed out on a cocktail of Xanax and beer.

You might recall me mentioning that I had previously had a blood clot. At this point in my life, I had an issue with my blood meaning that it had a tendency to get too thick at times. I was supposed to be taking medication for this and had run out while I was working on Al Mirqab.

Some of you might be aware that taking a long flight and remaining seated is a high-risk situation for anyone at risk of a blood clot. As such I arrived in Nice with a new blood clot.

So, I guess you could say that this was a triple whammy just like the last one. Fired for drugs, lost laptop and a blood clot. All in the space of 24 hours. I think that ranks as a record-low spot even by my standards.

However, as was my way I took all this on the chin and soldiered on accordingly. There was nothing for me to do in France and The Dude was not loving having me staying at his. After not speaking to my parents for more than two years I had to call them up and ask if I could come back and stay for a while. I didn't say anything about why. I spoke to my dad who said he'd think about it.

He actually came back and said, 'No we don't want you here.'

That really hurt. I did my best to explain that I had really run out of options and that I was broke and had nowhere else to go. Eventually, he grudgingly accepted that I might be allowed to come and stay at home for a while.

What ended up happening was that I went to work with my dad and ended up spending the next two months doing a desk job that I hated more than any other job I've ever done. But it was a big help and a great bonding experience with my dad and I plus it gave me the money to get a flight back to St Martin (and Amber) and all the fun and games that would come with that.

Next, we have the penultimate chapter and this one is really a special and unique story. After sailing across the Atlantic five times, I was about to encounter my worst ever storm on a lake in the middle of the Swiss Alps. It could only happen to me.

20

Shipwrecked in Switzerland

It could only happen to me.

I'd like to make something clear.

When I say, 'It could only happen to me,' I don't mean this in a bad way at all.

On the contrary. I see every experience as an opportunity to grow more into a person I'd like to be. It's worth noting that the experiences that are the most painful, traumatic and stressful are also usually the lessons which teach us the most and help us to grow the most. I can give one single perfectly clear example of this.

In the summer of 2018, I spent approximately three months living in a tent. Not out of choice. There's no point in beating around the bush because the fact is that I was homeless. Initially, it was my choice to leave my last place of residence. However, I was only pre-empting the inevitable forthcoming eviction.

I went on to spend the next three months, mostly, walking the Southwest coast path, here in the UK, with my dog Patch. Towards the end of the period, I became weary of constantly moving and was blessed to be able to find a place to live without too much trouble.

I know it's all relative but compared to what most people go through who end up in similar circumstances what I experienced was more like a holiday than an ordeal. Firstly, the weather was stunning. One of the best summers I recall in my memory of British weather. It only rained a handful of times during the whole period.

I was based in an area that most people would be happy to come to for a holiday. In fact, during that time I was mostly surrounded by holiday makers. Not the worst crowd to be immersed in. I had my dog Patch for company and security. I had government benefits, every two weeks which actually gave me enough money to buy a little cannabis and to feed myself and Patch.

We both got skinny but I was able to medicate regularly, every day, for the whole period. I never had to go without for more than a few hours. I'm certain that this was the only thing that got me through this period without losing my sanity altogether. I also learnt to forage and being a splendid British summer there were blackberries everywhere which I was constantly collecting and feasting upon.

I somehow had an iPad Pro. Yes, the massive one. It was a gift from the gods that kept me sane and allowed me to focus on doing something I loved which gave me all the distraction I needed from my own personal internal hell. I kept a sketchbook and a set of pens and pencils and I was able to draw and make art whenever the battery on my iPad was low or I just wanted something different.

During this time, I learnt to make electronic music and gained a good understanding of the whole process of layering tracks to form a single piece of finished music. Even while still homeless I sent some music to a world-famous DJ who replied saying she loved the tunes and that she was going to play one of them at a big festival she was performing at. It was also during this time that I started drawing graffiti letters in my sketchbook.

So, the fact is that the whole experience of being homeless was, for me, the single most important thing that has happened in my life to date. I learnt more about myself, the world around me and how I relate to it in those three months than in the rest of my life combined. Yet it's something that I would have fought tooth and nail to have avoided. And that's something that I find hard to understand.

The thing that was the most valuable lesson of my life to date is also something I feared more than anything and would have done anything to avoid. How can I learn from that? How can I approach my life now knowing that things I fear and want to avoid might actually be the very best things for me?

Clearly, a large dose of common sense has to come into this. While following one's moral compass is always an integral tool to life's navigation. Oh, hang on, wait a minute. I'm entering Yoda mode again.

'Hmmm, if in three thousand years still behaving like the petulant boy you are, then walk the streets some more you must, yes, yes, hmmm.'

I have one more point to make on this subject before I go onto tell one of my most incredible experiences to date.

From as early an age as I can remember it seemed to me that the majority of authority was unjust. Which is something I still believe, to a certain extent. At an early age, I became something of an anarchist in spirit. I would rant and rave about how terrible our government is and that the institution needs to be torn down and blah blah blah.

I was anti-capitalist, anti-institution, anti-this, anti-that, anti-anything that didn't look like short-term gratification. As my life became more challenging I increasingly found myself depending more and more on those around me.

To start with this was my circle of friends but they gradually became thin on the ground until I had only family. In time, I wore out my welcome with them. Then I found myself with no one to turn to for help. This was before I had to start sleeping in the tent but I was still essentially homeless. I was squatting in my workshop from my previous business.

I had sold all my tools and everything I could find that was worth anything at the resale level. I had no money in any bank, no cash and no income. I ran very low on food and for about one month slowly became malnourished. I reached a point where I was so hungry that I could not think straight and things got rather weird for a time.

It's deeply ironic to me that I was actually living in a location where I was surrounded by millionaires. Literally. Galmpton is a very posh part of Devon and it was where my workshop was. Patch and I became quite sick before a good friend (shout out Terry) implored me to sign up for government benefits. I was aware that this was possible but I thought it would be really hard to get it started and was terrified of the idea of having to talk to any kind of institution.

In the end, I was able to get myself onto benefits just literally in the nick of time. The day my first payment came through I was fully prepared to commit a crime to get money to buy food because of how hungry I was. The point I'm getting to here is that in my darkest hour, it wasn't my friends who came to my rescue, nor was it my family.

Despite me being a lifelong anarchist, it was the state that saved me. Without our government and the amazing people who comprise it, I would have been in a lot of trouble very soon after.

I would strongly urge anyone who thinks of themself as "anti-establishment" to have a good long think about what I've just said. The fact is that without the establishment you wouldn't have a platform to complain from. You would be far too busy just trying to stay alive to have time to complain about anything. Alright, that's all for now. But I hope I've given you something to think about.

So how the bloody hell did I come to be shipwrecked in Switzerland? Well by now you will be quite familiar with this vortex of chaos that follows me around. I don't see it as a bad thing. Not at all. It creates equal amounts of good and bad things but then that's all a question of perception isn't it?

By the time we came to this final chapter, I had left France and returned to the UK. Alas very much with my tail between my legs. By now, I was a full-time alcoholic and at the point of this story, I had finally accepted that I had a problem and was actively seeking help.

I suppose one thing that differs significantly about this story from the last few is that this one does not involve me drinking or even actually doing anything stupid. Yes, yes, alright, I know that's hard to believe. But in fact, I behaved admirably I'm proud to say. Well right up until the end but we'll get to that.

The fact is that one never really knows how one will behave until the shit actually hits the proverbial fan. I have been racing on big boats when stuff has broken and someone has had to go up the mast to fix it and I have been shit scared. On other occasions, I manned up and did stuff no one else wanted to.

The fact is that every situation is unique and you never know how you will handle the particular set of circumstances that you find yourself in. I am by no means the bravest man but then there's not much I shy away from either.

So, I found myself living back in Torquay again after nearly two decades in the south of France. That didn't go down well with either me or Torquay. For years, all I wanted to do was leave again and I tried and tried. However, every time I made a break I always ended up right back here and now I know why.

One good thing about being back in Torquay was the opportunity to go racing on one of the fleet of cruiser racers that were part of the local yacht club. The Royal Torbay Yacht Club has a long and prestigious history. Alas currently it is in a shambolic state but it was once a powerhouse in UK yachting. With all my experience, I quickly found boats that needed crew and I had some fun races on a few different boats.

It didn't take long though before I was headhunted by the local big dog, PJ, and soon after I joined his team. I went on to spend three seasons racing with PJ, mainly aboard his performance cruiser racer X. I slowly became a central figure within the team and moved around various spots on the boat as and where I was needed.

However, my main spot and my traditional role aboard any racing yacht was always bowman. If you know anything about racing yachts and the types of people who generally crew on them, then you will be aware that I was about as close to a stereotypical bowman as you could get. Short and light but strong and quick. Also hedonistic, cocky, arrogant, aggressive and bigmouthed. Yes in fact I think that sums me up perfectly back then.

If I'm honest, I'm not really that good a bowman. I can make a damn good fist of it when I try but if I'm really honest then I'd have to admit that I'm not really that good a sailor in general. Fortunately, I was good enough, and fun enough to have onboard (remember that mouth?), that we all generally got on really well and a lot of laughs were had in the process of winning a lot of races.

Believe me that while racing on X things would get really crazy on a fairly regular basis but that's just yacht racing and a large part of what we all love about it. The unpredictability of it. The fact is that you can be as well prepared as possible but when you get out there and into it there's a million things that can and do go wrong and you just have to deal with it and make the best of it you can.

Very much like real life and that's one of the things I love about yacht racing to this day. The number of analogies that can be drawn between yacht racing and real life is really interesting. I often find myself using this as a tool for making sense of my own life and helping to interpret what's going on around me.

The topic first came up at the club bar, as so many topics do. PJ was chatting to his longtime henchman, Porky, about some upcoming yachting event and they seemed to be talking about me being involved. I would have been a few pints deep already so in good humour and generally quite agreeable. It transpired that there was to be a yacht racing competition on a lake in Switzerland later that summer.

This was to be the world championship for the six m class. The smaller sisters of the 12 m America's Cup yachts of yesteryear. Porky had a brother, Simon, who was a businessman and lived in central London. Simon was a keen yachtsman and raced regularly in the Solent. Apparently, they did this six m event every year as the World Cup moved to a different location annually.

Many of the other yachts and crews that would be there also followed the event around the world each year. On this occasion, it was to be held on Lake Lucerne next to the town of Brunnen. It transpired that all the plans were in place for this event and that the only thing missing was a bowman. All eyes turned to me. Obviously, I was thrilled to be asked and it was all agreed and finalised by late spring.

The actual event was in late July and it was always a part of the plan to get there a week early and spend at least four days practising as a crew before the event itself would start the following week. The others had all sailed together in these events a good few times before but with a new bowman, the need was felt to get a really good amount of training in before the main event.

The year before this team had narrowly missed winning the event. Both PJ and Porky are world-class sailors and would win other international events on occasion. As such they wanted to get me up to speed to ensure that I wouldn't be a weak link.

I was a bit nervous about this as I knew that doing bow on a six m was very different from the other yachts I raced on with PJ and that there was going to be a steep learning curve. As it was, I nailed it right from the get-go. It wasn't me that was the problem this time. In fact, it wasn't anyone on board.

Lake Lucerne is known for having a particularly violent storm, the Fohnstrum that can strike with little warning even when the weather is calm just a few hours before. The lake is located high in the Swiss Alps. For the first few days after we arrived, I had to keep pinching myself to check I wasn't dreaming. It was literally like something out of a fairy tale.

Vast snow-covered peaks soar straight out of the lake and while sailing you have a view all-around of stunning mountains. Mostly still covered in snow even in the middle of summer. It was a place like no other I've visited and I long to return there and to be able to take the time to actually enjoy the place. Because at that time I was there to work and I really didn't get many chances to enjoy anything.

I was taking a break from drinking and using a form of medication to stop me from being able to drink if I wanted to. This was supposed to work by making me really ill if I consumed alcohol while I was taking the medication.

The fact was that after a couple of months, I just stopped taking it a week before I wanted to drink because at some stage, no matter what I tried to do, my need to get drunk (and to be able to forget about all my emotional pain) would become more important than anything else and I simply had to find an escape for a short while at least.

It is very much like getting an itch that you know will go away after you scratch it. But then comes back much worse. Itch, scratch, short-term relief...worse itch, scratch again...Cycle continues. I can't think of a better analogy.

Don't forget that I had stopped using cannabis or any other form of recreational drugs years before. This meant that when I was not drinking I was completely sober all the time. At that point in my life, that was not something that suited me in any way, shape or form. Its most apparent outcome was to leave me utterly miserable as by this time alcohol had become the one and only thing that I really enjoyed.

For the time being, however, I was totally focused on doing well in this competition. For the first few days, the training went really well. I picked up the new skills I needed quickly which was a relief to everyone. We all relaxed and started to enjoy ourselves. The final practice day was the Friday before the event was due to begin on the following Monday.

Up until that morning, we had been blessed with mostly blue skies and searing heat as it was the middle of summer. Lake Lucerne is famous for having a wind that is the result of the thermals created by the particular shape of the mountains in that area. On a typical summer day, this wind would start to blow early to mid-afternoon and carry on till sundown. It would always blow straight down the lake in the same direction making it perfect for yacht racing.

Lake Lucerne is a big L shape and the wind typically blows from the top of the L down the leg but not really along the foot. All the racing would happen up and down the leg of the L.

Although the marina complex where all the yachts were based was around the middle of the foot.

Six m yachts are not blessed with an engine. In reality, they are a kind of large dinghy as they have an open cockpit and no interior. Still, at over 30 ft, this is the size of a yacht and it took five of us to race her. On this day though we were only actually four.

PJ had more important things to do with his time than practice with the rest of us. He wasn't due to arrive until later that same day. This hadn't really been a problem because PJ trimmed the mainsail normally but for the sake of practice, Porky could handle it.

Getting in and out of the marina wasn't exactly a simple thing in a 30-foot yacht with no engine. One thing that helped was that there was generally very little wind in the morning when we wanted to leave. Also, the marina was in a sheltered spot tucked away down on the foot of the L. The usual approach was for me to sit on the bow with a canoe paddle and basically be the engine.

Surprisingly this worked just fine and we never had any issues getting out of the port. In fact, we never had any issues getting back in either. Or at least not before or after this day. This day was a day unlike any other I have experienced, either in the mountains or at sea. By this time, I had spent quite a bit of time in both.

Our exit from the port that day had been smooth and normal. We'd been out practising for about an hour and basically just going up and downwind practising gybes, hoists and drops. At some point, I noticed some very ominous-looking clouds building up behind the taller mountain peaks nearby. I've spent more than enough time, both at sea and in the mountains, to know that this means trouble.

I made an observation to the rest of the crew that I did not like the look of those clouds one little bit. It's worth noting that even on the most well-drilled and slickly crewed racing yachts you would find it a rare event for everyone on board to agree about something. Sailors tend to be quite an opinionated bunch and this crew was no exception.

Therefore, it was actually a little worrying when we all said, 'Let's get back to that marina, ASAP.'

Of course, this was the moment the wind decided to drop. And the same moment that we noticed the warning lights had come on.

Since we arrived in Brunnen there had been talk about this storm that could come rolling through the place and tear it right up. It was known to happen more often in the summer months and as such the lake was equipped with a series of "early warning" lights located up and down the shore of the lake.

We'd been aware of the location of these lights but up until now hadn't had any reason to pay attention to them. Now they were flashing red. We figured that was probably bad.

By now, my first observation had been 30 minutes or so before and we had only made it to around the bottom of the leg of the L. We could see the marina at least but now the wind had started swirling around and coming from all different directions. This makes it almost impossible to make progress in any one direction and we had started actually going around in circles. All the while above us the storm clouds gathered.

We were far from the only traffic out on the lake that day. Around eight other six m had also been out practising and had also been caught just like us. In an attempt to avert the looming disaster, the marina staff had sent out a fleet of RIBs to try and tow us back to the relative safety of the marina. In fact, getting a tow was the usual way we would get home at the end of the racing but not usually under these conditions.

Any sign of blue sky had long since disappeared by now and it had begun to rain. The wind was still swirling around although not at all strong yet. We had managed to get to about halfway across the foot of the L and were now just outside the entrance to the marina. It was at this point I saw something that scared the life out of me and I can still recall it now with exact detail.

I turned to look the other way and coming up the valley was a wall of black clouds. Like a wall of impenetrable blackness and it was steadily moving up the valley. It honestly looked like something out of "Lord of the Rings" or "Game of Thrones".

We still had the full mainsail up and the number one genoa headsail. It seemed pretty clear that there was going to be some serious weather in those clouds and that it was going to be on us in a matter of minutes. Porky called for me to get the headsail down and I ran up and got it lashed down in super quick time. Then we had the mainsail to get down and all four of us worked together to get it on the deck before the wall of blackness engulfed us.

Obviously, I can't be precise but I believe we learnt later that the winds had been up to 60 mph at the worst point. When the wall hit the yacht, it turned its side or beam onto the wind. Surprisingly this is the natural motion of any similar vessel that is without its own power and is being driven before a storm. It just goes side-on and leans over. Now also came the waves with the wind and the driving rain.

We had retreated into the cockpit where we watched helplessly as we drifted away from the marina and were driven before the wind and waves. The worst of the wind only lasted a few minutes but it kept coming hard for a good 10 or so after and we were steadily being driven towards the shore of the lake. But here coming to our rescue was a RIB.

The wind and rain had eased a fair bit by now but were still coming hard as were the waves. This made it very hard for the RIB to get into position to pass us a line. Added to the complications was the fact that the two guys in the RIB appeared to be quite elderly and didn't seem to have a clue how to either drive the RIB or tie a knot.

For the next few minutes, we huddled in the cockpit and watched, utterly helpless as these two guys fumbled and bumbled every attempt to get a line to us. Finally, they managed and I was able to grab the line and make it fast to the base of our mast. Unfortunately, there were two problems coming up.

First, the guy with the rope didn't know how to tie any kind of knot and just tried to tie a lot. Which as any sailor will know, does not work. Second problem was that the guy driving saw that his mate had got it tied, or so he thought and went into full throttle. Faceplant moment.

Now, I don't want to sound like I'm moaning about these two brave men. They were not in any way trained or equipped to be in such a situation and were in fact really afraid but doing their best to help us. So please don't think I'm blaming them in any way. It's not that.

But it was a catalogue of errors. The force of the rope coming tight so fast meant that it both broke and came off the cleat at their end. This exact same process happened another two times. Each time they got the rope and just wrapped it around the wrong way then tried to speed off. The third time one of the guys hurt his hand and they left.

By now, we could see the shore of the lake and the waves were driving us towards it quickly. Just to our side was a large metal post sticking out of the water that had some lights and navigation stuff on it. I knew I could swim the distance to this post and screamed at Porky to let me take a rope and swim it.

The lake water was not that cold and it had been my job to get in and clean the hull every morning before racing.

So, I had been swimming already that day and felt really confident that I could make it. Porky saw it differently and told me no way. I didn't much like Porky and told him I was going anyway but the others both screamed at me to shut the fuck up as I wasn't going anywhere. My natural respect for authority afloat kicked in and I resigned myself to our inevitable fate.

Just at that moment, we felt the first bump as the keel touched the bottom for the first time. Just like their bigger sisters, the 12 m, 6 m yachts have some very open rules about what you can do with the keel. Ours had long wings sticking out either side of the back of the bottom of the keel. They worked like foils to give the yacht more lift and power.

Any sailor will tell you that having something like that on the bottom of a yacht is an accident waiting to happen. Any number of kinds of debris and sea life can be hit causing damage to wings like these. As such they are only used on the most radical racing yachts as these are generally stored out of the water when not being raced.

The fact of the matter is that we were very lucky that day. Through the process of trying to get back to the marina and the timing of when the storm actually hit us we had ended up being driven onto the only part of the entire lake that had a soft sandy shoreline. All around the rest of the lake, the shoreline was hard rock but here there was a sort of beach and marshy area.

That's where we ended up and as each wave bounced us off the bottom it began to not look good for the wings. By now, quite a few other boats had come to try and help but nothing could be done to prevent us being shipwrecked on that beach. The poor yacht was sitting right over on her Starboard side and we were perched along the port rail looking a little bedraggled, I'd say.

Some kind people were able to rescue us with a RIB now that the wind had died and the rain had slowed to a drizzle. It was cold now though. The day before the temperature had been in the high 20s and now we could see our breath.

We weren't dressed for that and as such we were fading rapidly. The RIB whisked us back to the marina while a team of locals remained and started work on salvaging the stricken yacht.

Back at the base, there was a lot of activity but it seemed as though we were the only ones to have not made it back in. Still, a storm like that can wreak havoc even in the relative safety of an enclosed port area like this one. By the time we had got a couple of hot drinks down and warmed up a bit, they had our yacht back at the marina and were getting ready to lift her out to assess the damage.

In fact, we had got off very lightly considering. Everything was fine with the hull, the rudder and all the important stuff. There were some scratches and gouges around the base of the keel and…Well, yeah. As expected the wings were gone.

We wouldn't be able to be competitive without the wings. The boat would sail fine and be watertight and everything else would work like normal. Unfortunately, we would be noticeably slower than the rest of the fleet and by the first mark would be left behind. So, there would be absolutely no point in even starting.

It was Friday, early afternoon. The World Cup was due to start on Monday and we had a wingless keel. Yep. it was another *FUCK* moment. Although this time it wasn't in any way due to my own stupidity. Fancy that. What happened over the next 48 hours has always amazed me.

Within hours of being shipwrecked, the owner of one of the other six m had got chatting with our owner, Simon. I haven't really mentioned him so far because he didn't really have that much of a role to play in anything. Except for paying for everything obviously.

One thing I will share with you is that shortly after meeting Simon we were in the airport and I had lost his younger brother, Porky, who was not only the youngest of a brood of five boys but was also much smaller and generally less successful than his older brothers.

I believe some might call this the runt of the litter. So, when I saw Simon I said to him, 'Oh I've lost your brother.'

He gave me a big grin, laughed and said, 'Well done, I've been trying to do that for years.'

So, Simon got chatting with this other owner and it transpired he had a spare set of wings that would fit our keel with some work and small alterations. At that moment said wings were in a workshop in Geneva but by the next morning, we had them unpacked and laid out next to our stricken yacht. Which was now located well away from the marina in a large warehouse in another part of town.

We were given access to any kind of tools we needed and the marina chandlery was equipped with all the materials that we would need for such an operation. The only problem was that, despite having done a fair amount of boat-building by now, I had absolutely no idea how we were going to attach the bronze foils to the gnarled stump of the lead keel.

And that's where PJ came in. He had arrived that afternoon and was none too impressed to learn that we had been shipwrecked earlier that same day. Nonetheless, he took a positive attitude to the possibility of a repair and we set to work cleaning up the keel and preparing the new foil for fitting.

Now I have to give full credit to PJ here as it was he and he alone who thought this whole project through. He came up with this plan to pass two sections of stud bar through the keel. Using this stud bar the two wings would locate onto each other and be able to wound down tightly together fixing them, like aeroplane wings to each side of the keel. I know that's not very clear but believe me, it wasn't at the time either.

This involved the most awkward of drilling operations where we had to get right down low on the floor and really push hard together to get these large drill bits through the lead keel. Lead is quite soft and as such it's not that hard to drill big holes in it and we managed to bore out two channels for the stud bar and get one side fixed in by the end of Saturday.

By Sunday afternoon, the repair was completed and all that was left to do was make it all smooth and pretty again. This was my speciality and I was left to get on with it into the late hours of Sunday night.

Monday morning rolled around, as it inevitably does, and we had a fully functional six m ready to go out and race with the fleet of 15 others. Our ship wreaking and successful repair had turned us into local celebrities and we had a good following rooting for us to do well in the competition.

It was a four-day event and going into the final day we were in third place with a good chance of catching first if we did well in the last two races. Unfortunately, we didn't have a good day and ended up fifth but still, we were all very happy considering the previous events.

I had managed to stay sober through all of this. Despite the fact that the others were all downing beers at every opportunity. However, I'd been planning a session at the end of the week and had stopped taking my medication accordingly. After everything that had happened on the trip so far, I hit the beers hard and had a very messy night.

The next day Porky was expecting me to help him pack the yacht away. This was his job and not something that anyone else had told me I had to do. By now, I had come to really dislike Porky and in my hungover state, I wasn't in the mood to take shit from him. We had a blazing row on the dock and I told him to go fuck himself.

I went off into town and spent the rest of the day getting drunk. We all met up for dinner at the end of the day and I had another blazing row with Porky in the middle of a restaurant. Unfortunately, I was due to be travelling home with him the next day as our flights were the same and he lived in Torquay as well as me. Needless to say, we kept our distance during that journey home.

I continued sailing with PJ for a few more years after that. Porky and I would see each other in the bar and around town and sort of say hello and be civil but it was pretty clear what we thought of each other. Still, all's well that ends well and one hell of a jolly good story was had. I hope you enjoyed it.

Epilogue
How I Quit Alcohol

I'm not sure at what point I finally accepted that it was going to happen. I think the fact is that it was a long, slow, agonising process. I fought it tooth and nail in my mind for years as I simply could not accept the idea that I was one of them. One of the failures. Like my auntie W.

Every time I thought about someone who is an alcoholic I got the image of her, leering at me, on the last occasion I saw her. Every time I thought about it the memory would send a shiver down my spine. I just could not get my head around the idea that I was going to end up like her.

Long before I stopped drinking, Auntie W was dead from a disease directly connected to her consumption of alcohol. She'd been ill for years and had been told over and over by the doctors that if she did not stop drinking she would die. She did not stop drinking and she died. So, I suppose doctors are right occasionally.

With hindsight, I can see that having that in the back of my mind was quite an aid to my own battle with alcohol. In a number of ways really. Firstly, I knew I was not alone in suffering this affliction and that it was really not my fault nor the consequence of any decision I might have made.

Regardless of what some of my family might think. Secondly, it was a constant reminder that if I did not stop there was a very strong chance that I would end up with the sort of medical issues that had been her demise.

Auntie W had died a few years before I moved back to the UK. By then, I was already a raging alcoholic but still in firm denial. I've come to understand that there are a number of stages in the process of an addict coming to terms with their condition. Clearly, it's essential for the patient themselves to be fully aware of their own condition before they can attempt to treat it. Well, it seems clear to me at least but perhaps I should explain a little more what I mean.

When a patient is suffering from a physical condition, either accident, illness or disease, in the majority of cases it's not in any way necessary for the patient to understand the problem or to be involved in any way in the treatment. In general, the patients themselves remain passive and the medical staff and medication do the work. Clearly, there are exceptions to this but overall, I'd say this holds true.

For example, a patient may have to take pills but they are only responsible for consuming the medication. Not actually carrying out the action of treatment. That is done by the medication without any involvement by the patient. They take the medicine and it works or not as the case may be. But in either event, the patient is passive.

For a patient who is suffering from mental health issues the approach of the NHS is much the same as it is for any physical condition and that is to treat them with medication. What's become increasingly clear over the last few decades is that this does not work for the most part. Certainly, some people suffer from conditions that are so severe that some form of medication is necessary, at times, just to keep them manageable.

However, for people suffering from mild to moderate mental health issues, the only solution lies in therapy and the person's own will to help themselves. A combination of both works best.

Unfortunately, therapy is of very little interest to the NHS because there is no way to make a profit out of it. Therapy is a service provided by a person and as such is an expense that does not facilitate profit for a third party. Medication on the other hand is produced by a private company in a factory and must be purchased by the NHS.

The purchase of the product creates both profit for the supplier and the demand for more. Simple economics. Obviously, both things cost the NHS relative amounts. However, one thing provides an income for a private individual and the other creates profit for a large pharmaceutical company.

Personally, I've had nothing but fantastic treatment by the NHS and the amazing people who comprise the organisation, however, it's clear to me that the principal reason we have the NHS, and not private systems like the rest of the world, is so that the government can control exactly who gets the pharmaceutical contracts.

Let's just remember that the pharmaceutical industry is the UK's second largest after weapons. If I need to explain this any further, then I'm probably talking to the wrong person but if you're still reading then I hope I've given you something to think about at least.

There simply is no magic pill that can fix the vast majority of mental health disorders. Certainly, there are things which can help ease the symptoms but these should in no way be mistaken for fixing the problem or being a solution. Cannabis, for example, has massive potential to help people suffering from a great number of mental health issues including addiction. However, it should in no way be considered a cure to anything.

In reality, there isn't any such thing as a "cure" for the majority of these problems. It's really a fundamental flaw in our society and our way of thinking that leads us to think that there should be any such a thing as a "cure".

What I'm trying to establish here is that in order for a person to attempt to treat a condition they are suffering from they must first accept the fact that it is they who are going to have to do the majority of the hard work. No one is going to wave a wand.

For the lucky few who can afford to pay for private healthcare, there are any number of highly talented professionals out there who can help in a variety of ways. As a general rule where there is money, there are solutions. But even the lucky few still have to actually do the hard work themselves.

All the same truths apply. They just have a silk-gloved hand to hold as they walk the path. For the rest of us, for the most part, there is very little help available through the NHS.

During my battle with alcohol, I was lucky enough to be referred to a special clinic here in my hometown where a team of NHS doctors specialised in treating people suffering from mental health issues. I received a series of counselling sessions with a very nice man who I was able to connect with and learnt to trust. He held my hand for about six months and during that time I was able to make a lot of progress towards coming to terms with my own problems.

However, I made very little actual progress in stopping drinking alcohol. At the end of the six months, my time was up and I wasn't able to continue getting any help. I more or less went back to square one and continued periodic bingeing.

In the last chapter of "The Stoner's Guide", I am fairly well advanced in my decline and internal war. By decline, I mean that little by little, my life was falling apart and spiralling out of control. By internal war, I mean that I was fighting with myself about the need for alcohol to have a place in my life.

By that stage, a large part of me was sick to death of the whole drinking thing. I hated everything about alcohol and being drunk and hated myself for going back to it over and over. Yet when I was drunk it was the only time I felt any kind of relief or fun and I couldn't stop myself wanting it.

Each time I would binge I would buy a large quantity of alcohol and just guzzle until I passed out. When I woke, I would do the same thing until I either passed out again or ran out of supplies. At the point when I would run out of supplies was when I would often drive to get more.

This became the thing that I hated about myself the most. The fact that I would put other people's lives at risk just to get more alcohol when all I needed was to pay for a taxi. Sometimes I would get a taxi, sometimes I would walk, often I'd drive and in the end, it was my undoing.

I mentioned earlier that there are a number of stages that a patient must pass through before they can in any way attempt to address the condition they suffer from. Up until I returned to the UK and for a good while after, I was convinced that I didn't have a problem with alcohol and that I just liked a drink a little too much. I was sure that at some stage I would be able to get control of it and moderate my drinking so that I could carry on where and when I saw fit.

This is a perfect example of the power of denial. One of my favourite quotes, from the movie "American Beauty" is 'Never underestimate the power of denial.'

I don't believe this was a reference to kayaking. Take a lesson from this and give yourself a long hard look in the mirror. I was a full-time raging alcoholic who had been bingeing for years already at this point. Five-day binges and I was still telling myself I didn't have a problem and actually believing it.

Before I even left France, I had been going to an AA group for a while. I met a number of characters in that group and one of them was a very nice man who was actually very kind and helpful to me. After I had decided not to continue going to the group, we met up for a coffee and were sitting in a cafe by Cannes market. While chatting he said that he didn't think I really wanted to quit drinking.

It was shortly after one of my binges and the horror of that recent episode was still with me so I was feeling very much like I really wanted to stop for good. The problem was that the feeling never lasted more than a few days. My friend knew this and he said that when he was trying to stop drinking, if you had told him that running around the whole marketplace naked would have fixed him then he would have done it.

I was shocked. I couldn't conceive of doing such a thing or wanting something badly enough to make me do such a thing. Thus, his point was proved.

For me, it was possible to continue thinking that I wanted to quit right up until the point where the craving would start again. Once the craving starts the only way to beat it is with distraction. Which can work completely but requires either outside assistance or a lot of willpower by the person.

The problem is that, typically, once a person gets their craving and wants to engage with their addiction then any thoughts of helping themself or fighting it just go out the window. Or at least it did for me.

My friends and family would all say, 'If you feel down or like drinking then just call me.'

If only it was that easy. Once I felt down and wanted to drink then the last thing I wanted to do was talk to anyone or to put something in the way of that drink.

It was almost as if there was a breaking or tipping point. On the one side, you had my will to stop drinking and to fight the addiction. On the other hand, you had my desire for relief from the pain in my head. That was literally all I wanted by that stage. The whole time I was sober I was riddled with anxiety and depression about every single aspect of my life. Nothing made me happy. I had no one and nothing to turn to for help.

Except my dad who stood by me for a long while but in the end, even he had to step back for a while. A big part of the problem was that it was all a result of me alienating myself from those around me and failing to recognise the sources of help that were actually available. I just couldn't cope and could feel myself slowly falling apart.

Imagine a nightmare where you are walking around and parts of your body just start melting and falling off very slowly. Almost in slow motion. Like you can see it happening and watch it but nothing you do stops it. More and more of you start to fall off. All over your body. More and more until you are walking around just trying to stop yourself falling apart and the more you try the more parts of you fall away.

That's very much how I felt the whole time I was awake and the only thing that pulled me back together again, for a short while, was alcohol. Of course, the net result of consuming alcohol was to accelerate the disintegration. But as it was the only thing that seemed to help in the short term it was the only thing on my mind most of the time.

I would even dream about drinking when I was going through sober phases. I would reach a point where I was walking around thinking about nothing else for days on end. It was always at this point that I would stop taking the anti-alcohol medication and start planning my next binge.

Chapter 20 of "The Stoners Guide" takes place in the summer of 2017 at which point I was already on the medication but periodically bingeing. Each binge would last a few days and would then render me incapable of anything constructive for the next few days. While attempting to run a thriving business this was not the path to success. It's fair to say.

The pattern continued until my birthday. My 40th birthday on 30th April, the following year. I was living at my parent's house and as they had gone away for the weekend I planned to get drunk on Friday. My birthday was actually on Sunday and my parents were due back later on Saturday afternoon so we had a plan to all go out for a nice lunch together on Sunday.

It was always the way that I would only plan to drink for one night. I would always swear blind that no matter what happened later I would not drive. However, what always happened was the pattern I described before. But here it is again.

I would hit the booze hard right away. As soon as the coast was clear I would be off to the shop to stock up. Once back home I would start trying to get it in me as fast as possible. By this stage, that meant drinking rum with a selection of mixers but the measures would be very big and I could easily finish a large bottle of rum in one night.

This would usually be enough to knock me out for a good while but then I would wake up feeling like death and knowing that all I needed was another drink and I would feel great again. If there was more alcohol available at home, I would tuck into that and if there was not I would go and get more one way or another. I would then drink again until passing out and repeat until I would usually start throwing up or just gagging once my stomach was empty.

I believe that the only reason I survived my early alcoholic binges in France is because of my body's built-in defence against this excessive abuse. At some stage, it just says no more and try as I might, I can't get more alcohol into me. The moment I drink it I just throw it back up again.

Every time I would eventually reach this stage and it was the only thing that saved me from alcohol poisoning and death I'm sure. It still amazes me that I didn't get any worse side effects considering the quantities I was consuming.

So, on that Friday afternoon before my birthday, I waited until my parents had left and got myself settled in for a good one. As it was my birthday I had decided to treat myself to some coke and made enquiries with a mate as I didn't know any dealers myself.

I'd not had confirmation though and was still waiting eagerly for news from my mate. The usual thing happened and I passed out quite early surrounded by empty bottles and crisp packets. I woke up like a snap at around midnight and saw on my phone a message from my mate saying the eagle had landed.

He'd only just sent the text so I replied saying I was on my way. There was just one problem. He was on the other side of town and I was still well under the effects of the alcohol from earlier. It had been maybe four hours since I drank anything but anyone can tell you that's not enough for alcohol to pass out of your system.

Although I felt relatively sober, I was in fact very far from that. In the past, it hadn't always been a foregone conclusion that I would drive in such a situation. I'd often taken taxis when I needed to resupply in the past but this time I didn't even stop to think about it and jumped in my VW transporter.

This was my work van and also my camper on the weekends and was valued at around 20 grand. We didn't own it exactly but had it on finance at great expense. None of this crossed my mind as the only thing I cared about at that point was getting my hands and nose on that coke.

What became my undoing was the fact that I didn't actually know where my mate was and got kind of lost looking for him. Oh, that and the fact that I forgot to put my lights on. I think that's what is called a schoolboy error.

I was driving very sensibly and had made it to the other side of town without a problem but I couldn't work out exactly where my mate was. I'd pulled over to the side of a quiet residential street and was looking at the maps on my phone when a police car pulled up alongside me. Fuck. In that very second, I knew I was fucked and that another big part of me had just started peeling off.

They asked if I knew I didn't have my lights on. Faceplant moment. I'd just driven all the way across town without my lights on. I wonder how many people have been busted by that little slip-up. I replied that it had slipped my attention but that I would be sure to keep them on from there on. They asked where I was going. I said to see a mate.

They asked if I had been drinking. I said yes a little bit a while ago. They said I had better blow into the box. I blew and duly tested positive. Right there and then I knew my business was fucked and that I was now going from a very bad situation to a much worse one.

Down at the station, all I could think about was getting hold of that coke once I got out again. So the moment I got out I walked home from the police station and called my mate to see if he still had the coke. He did and I still had quite a bit of alcohol at home so I tucked in again without thinking.

The mate appeared with the coke and I tucked right into that as well. It was late Saturday morning by now and I was expecting my parents' home later that day. Yet the only thing on my mind was snorting coke and downing rum. So that's what I did for the rest of the day.

When they arrived, I decided not to even go out and say hello but just pretended to be busy doing a music project. I sent a text saying I'd see them the next morning for a chat before lunch. This told them right away that I was drinking again but they didn't decide to challenge me about it at that point. So, I finished the coke and kept drinking all night until I passed out again.

I slept a little here and there but by Sunday morning, I was feeling very twisted. The come down effect of the coke was in full swing and drinking more wasn't helping me feel any better. My mood was getting worse and I could only drink more to try and moderate it.

By late morning, I knew I could not possibly go to lunch with my parents as I was in a really bad state. I sent my dad a text explaining that I was not feeling very well and wouldn't be able to go to lunch with them.

But my mum read the text and came bursting into my room accusing me of drinking again. I reacted quite aggressively and she ran off crying. Dad said or did nothing. I stayed in my room for the rest of Sunday and finished what alcohol I had left.

By Monday morning, I was planning my next trip to the shop to resupply. This time I got a taxi but when I got back home again Dad had locked the door and wouldn't let me in. He sent me a text saying that he wouldn't allow me to continue drinking in the house.

Unfortunately, we have a semi-detached house and I was able to simply walk down the side of the house and go into the cellar instead. There was a mattress in there and I just laid on it taking gulps of rum from the fresh bottle.

Then the emotions hit so hard that I could not do anything but scream. I lay there and just screamed and screamed as loudly as I could. All I wanted was for someone to come to me and make it all stop. To take me in their arms and say it will be okay. You'll be okay. I've got you, it's okay. But there was nothing but cold emptiness for me in that cellar and I screamed until my throat became sore.

For some reason, I became aware that my phone was getting low on charge and I decided I wanted access to my stuff that was in the house. I went to the back door which was also locked so I started banging on it and kicking it. Now Dad got mad and came out the door and shoved me hard back down the steps. I came back at him up the steps and again he was able to fend me off.

The third time I dodged his fend and tackled him to the ground. We fought on the floor for a short moment until I was grabbed from behind by one of the neighbours. He had heard me screaming first and then Mum screaming for help as I had been fighting with Dad. Another neighbour appeared and as they were both big men I was subdued and just sat down sobbing.

They told me the police were on the way and I should just stay put until they arrived. I started crying out for more alcohol. I begged them to let me go to the cellar and drink more. I told them it was dangerous to let an alcoholic stop drinking but they didn't care. The police arrived shortly after and then I was arrested and taken back to the station.

Things got weird in that cell. By this time, I had been heavily drunk for around three days. A lot of that time I had been drinking spirits. As a general rule, I had worked out that if I only drank beer or wine then things never got too messy. The moment I hit the hard stuff all bets were off.

I was awake the whole time I was in the cell but my memory only goes in and out at times. At one point, the door opened and the officer in charge had a stern talk with me as I had been observed on camera drinking from the toilet and standing up having a long and animated discussion with myself. I was unaware of any of this.

He was just concerned and I would like to take this moment to give a massive shout out to all the policemen and women who dealt with me during this period. Without exception, they behaved admirably and performed their duties without fault in my view. I made a point of saying this to them and thanking them for being so nice to me before I was released.

The senior policewoman who was on duty gave me a funny look to start with. This was clearly not something that she was used to. But I made my point and she was very appreciative. Several times later this was something that was to come back in my favour.

What happened next could be considered the most important single moment of my life so far and I remember it as vividly as if it were yesterday. Sitting there in that cell I had to accept and realise what had just happened. After some time contemplating, I said this sentence to myself and I'd like to make it clear that it was these very words:

Alcohol has taken away from me everything I hold dear. If I ever drink alcohol again, I would have to be the biggest dickhead in the world. Now I may be a dickhead BUT I AM NOT THE BIGGEST DICKHEAD IN THE WORLD.

I'm not quite sure why I chose the word dickhead as it's not slang I'm normally fond of. Regardless, at that moment it seemed fully appropriate. Somehow I think it still does.

And that was it. Just like that it was done. I knew there and then that it was over. I didn't know how exactly as there was no way I possibly could just then. But I knew I had to quit for good and that was just that. After a while, I was interviewed by two plainclothes officers. They explained everything that had happened and said that I would be charged with assaulting my father.

After everything else that had happened that just broke me and I felt a deep sense of remorse at what I'd done. I'm sure this was evident as the discussion didn't last long and I was taken back to my cell.

They seemed to think it would help if they kept me in until I had sobered up but the fact was that all I wanted to do was get drunk again as soon as I got out. There was a new problem though. I didn't have anywhere to live. One of the conditions of my release was an order not to go to my parent's house or attempt to contact them in any way.

Not for the two weeks until my court case. As I had been living there this created something of a problem. However, I had access to money and had to book myself into a Travel Lodge hotel which was located about halfway between my parent's house and the police station.

As soon as I got myself booked in there I was back out to the shops to get alcohol and then hard on it again. I must have finished the first bottle of rum within hours and woke up to find the room an awful mess. It looked like I'd missed the toilet while trying to shit and then walked it around the floor. It was also on the bedding.

I just ignored this and went to the restaurant to eat. I knew I couldn't afford to stay for long in the travel lodge so I went looking for cheap B&Bs as an alternative. However, despite my best efforts to appear sober, I must have been in a real mess by then. Funnily enough, I couldn't find a room anywhere else.

That night things got weird again. My memory snaps back while I'm standing naked in the hotel corridor. It's the middle of the night and the night porter is asking me what I'm doing. I didn't know. Back in my room and a panic sets in. Something flips in my head and I'm off through the night to my parent's house. I need to get in. I need to get home. I need to feel safe. Please, please, let me in, let me in, let me in.

Then a flashing blue light in the corner of my eye and arms took me carefully but firmly. I struggle. Fighting them but it's pathetic and they calmly escort me to the car. Back at the station and it's the same policewoman who I had been so nice to a few days before.

She gives me a big smile and says, with genuine warmth and concern, 'Now, what are you doing back here again?'

Because I had broken my bail at the weekend I had to go to court in Plymouth for them to decide what to do with me. This meant a journey in the meat wagon. Out of everything that I went through during this time I think that hour or so I spent in that vehicle was the worst. I'm not sure why but somehow the combination of sobering up and being in a mobile cell was a solid low point.

In the Plymouth courthouse, I had to sit in a tiny cell while I was waiting for my case to be heard. Out of all the cells I've been in, this was by far the smallest and most uncomfortable. After some time, I was interviewed by the public defence lawyer who would represent me in the court. She was an amazing woman and we spent an hour or so chatting.

It was a massive help for me to vocalise a lot of the stuff that was going on in my head but the main thing I needed to tell her was that I still could not stop thinking about drinking. It was all I could think about. I was also quite concerned about my personal possessions as I didn't know where any of my stuff was. But mainly all I could think about was getting drunk again.

But actually, now I didn't want to be drunk. I wanted to drink but I didn't want to be drunk. Still, right now I knew I needed that familiar sensation of cold liquid washing down my throat. But something had changed. For one thing, I knew that if I drank spirits again I would end up right back in jail.

I knew it without a shadow of a doubt. I simply had no control over myself when I was on spirits. But I knew I needed to get at least a small quantity of alcohol in me to give me the head space to think about what to do next.

In the court, I was given a stern warning that if I broke my bail again it would have much more serious consequences. I took it seriously and once again my sincerity worked wonders for me. I was released and relieved to get my wallet back which had cash and cards but no phone or anything else. Still, I knew I still had the room at the Travel Lodge and most likely my phone and all my stuff would be there.

Once back out on the streets of Plymouth, the first thing I did was head to a Wetherspoons and have a pint. It was Saturday, around midday by now and the place was quite full. I sat at a table with my pint looking at everyone else drinking and thought if only they knew. I didn't feel any kind of jealousy or sense of loss. I drank about half my pint and headed to the train station.

On the train, I worked out a plan. I could get off at Totnes and get a taxi to my workshop where it was nice and quiet and I could have some space and peace to find my way out of this mess.

I couldn't face going back to the Travel Lodge at that moment because I knew there was going to be a big mess and I thought the staff might have a big cleaning bill for me. The taxi stopped at a shop allowing me to get some supplies which were mostly healthy food but also one six-pack of small Heineken cans.

Back at the workshop, I was able to relax enough to phone the travel lodge who told me that the room wasn't as bad as I thought and there was no major problem. Also, they had seen my phone and other personal stuff on the floor and it was all fine. This was a massive relief. One of the guys who had a workshop nearby was a friend and he drove me over to Torquay to get my stuff and check out of the hotel.

That night I made myself a good meal and slowly sipped my way through three of the cans. I was now feeling relatively relaxed. I had just enough alcohol in me to let me relax but not to start thinking anything stupid. After the third beer, I went to bed. I got up in the morning after a reasonable night's sleep and poured the other three down the drain and to this day I have not touched another drop.

The next few days were hard. I'd taken on a job restoring the bottom of a speedboat and it involved a lot of laborious work in really uncomfortable positions. Combined with having all the dust and debris falling into my face and all over me and the weather decided it was a good time to get hot. In a way though that job saved me. That and the SMART group.

I had been told about the SMART groups while previously receiving the therapy. The problem was that I was such an arrogant twat back then that I considered myself far too superior to lower myself into group meetings with a bunch of addicts. Funnily enough, this now seemed like a good time to give it a try and I went along to one of the local meetings two days after that last drink.

So far, I had not had any cravings and had been focused solely on getting this job finished as I had a good cash payout due at the end. But it was very early days and I already knew it was only a matter of time.

SMART is an acronym for self-management addiction recovery training. The whole philosophy revolves around the concept that if we have free will to choose to drink we can also choose not to drink. Somehow this made a lot of sense to me and I was able to take this concept onboard. At this first meeting, the session was led by a chap I never saw before or after. I never got his name either.

He gave me two really important bits of advice that were to go on to save me in the near future. The first was that if you are having cravings and you want to fight them then the first thing you can do is write down *I will not drink, I will not drink, I will not drink,* over and over until the cravings stop.

Second, he said, 'If that is not working then you can say it out loud instead.' He said, 'By getting the message out of your head and onto paper or into the air it makes it more real and easy to follow.'

The next day I worked hard to finish the project. It was grim and by lunchtime, I was thinking about drinking. I've not mentioned him yet but as he's sitting here next to me so it's about time I should. In all of these events, my dog Patch had been staying with my parents. My dad had always been close with Patch and had taken him into his care when I was drunk a few times before.

Since the events resulting in my bail, I had not been able to see Patch and this was starting to really bother me. He was my dog and as such my father really had no right to keep him from me. However, as long as Patch was at my parent's house there was nothing I could do to get him back. By the end of my third day without a drink, this was starting to become a big problem for me.

I wanted my dog back and simply could not accept the injustice that I could not even see him. This was all the ammunition my mind needed to start the cravings up with a real venom. Now I wanted to drink and wanted it badly.

At that time, I still had my driving licence as I hadn't had the court case yet. My van was sitting right outside my workshop and there was a local shop just a few minutes away. Little by little I felt a similar process happening in my mind. The resignation to it. The acceptance of it. It was the only thing to do. To drink again.

'I had to. I had to go to get booze now. Come on, let's go. Let's go. Get in the van and drive, you cunt. Fucking go, go, go, go. Only drinking will help. You neeeeed it, you neeed it give it toooo meeeee.'

I was going into a meltdown but there was something on my mind. I was sitting there looking at the speedboat I was working on. It only needed about two hours more work to be finished and ready to deliver back. At which point I would receive a fat wedge of cash. But the voice said you'll be fine. Just drink tonight. Don't drink too much. Just keep it sensible. You know you can do that.

You'll still be able to work tomorrow and get paid. It will be fine, trust me…Trust you? I looked at that boat and knew that if one drop of alcohol passed my lips there was no way in the world that I was going to do anything except keep drinking the next day and again after that. I think we all know where that was going. I also desperately wanted Patch back and could already see that the only way to get him was to stay sober.

For the first time ever, I was ready for the fight and I had two weapons. The SMART group came back to me and I remembered the message about writing and saying. I immediately started doing both simultaneously and it worked. All I can say is that it worked. The combination of good sense, the desire for both money, a companion and the SMART tools got me through.

I simply went for a long walk instead. I was blessed to be in one of the most beautiful parts of Devon, the Dart Valley, and I was able to take a walk in gorgeous woods next to a stunning river and even amidst the chaos and carnage I was able to find some kind of solace.

I returned to the workshop and got a good night's sleep. Don't ask me how but I did. The next day I got up and finished the boat. The wedge of cash was handed over and I went to north Devon to spend my last weekend with a driving licence at some of the places I had enjoyed the most over the last few years.

My court case was the following Wednesday. My sentence was the lightest they could give me for the crimes I had committed. However, what was done was done and I was found guilty of both driving under the influence and assault.

And this is where I am going to cut it off, I'm afraid. The fact is that I've just told you how I quit drinking. But at this point, I was still only one week sober. You will recall that I had managed to stay sober, up to three weeks, quite a few times before in the past few years.

As such, I was still very much in the heart of the danger zone. How I stayed sober is going to be the title of another chapter or perhaps even book; and for that, my friends, you are going to have to wait a little. Or just find me and ask me yourself. Don't worry, I don't bite. Well, not hard unless you want me to.